Community Organizing
for Stronger Schools

Community Organizing for Stronger Schools

Strategies and Successes

KAVITHA MEDIRATTA
SEEMA SHAH
SARA MCALISTER

HARVARD EDUCATION PRESS
CAMBRIDGE, MASSACHUSETTS

Library of Congress Control Number 2009927817

Paperback ISBN 978-1-934742-34-1
Library Edition ISBN 978-1-934742-35-8

Published by Harvard Education Press,
an imprint of the Harvard Education Publishing Group

Harvard Education Press
8 Story Street
Cambridge, MA 02138

Cover Design: Schwadesign, Inc.

The typefaces used in this book are Sabon for text and Gill Sans for display.

Contents

Why Community Organizing?

In 2000, a group of community organizers and public school parents involved with Oakland Community Organizations (OCO) undertook a simple, yet profound, task. They sketched a map of their city. First, they charted elementary schools located in the wealthy hills section of Oakland. Then they mapped schools in the low-lying flatlands of the city. For each school they noted the number of students attending and its ranking on the state Academic Performance Index (API). The map revealed dramatic disparities between smaller, higher-performing schools in the hills and overcrowded, low-performing schools in the flatlands. Schools in the hills ranged in size from 240 to 370 students, compared with student populations of up to 1,400 in the flatlands. While hills schools boasted API rankings at the top end of the performance scale, flatland schools were almost universally ranked at the bottom. In bold letters, the map's headline asked, "Is This Fair?"

Oakland Community Organizations' question crystallizes an obvious but often neglected truth: the world is pretty much in agreement on what educational experiences children need and deserve. Educators, municipal leaders, parents, and even children have an intuitive sense of the schooling environment and opportunities that foster children's academic, social, civic, and physical development. Anyone who doubts this point need only visit schools in our nation's wealthier communities to observe the high-quality schooling that supports children's success.

This is not to say that all children learn the same way, or that inner-city schools should replicate the strategies of their affluent or suburban counterparts. The enduring question that decades of school reform have failed to solve is how, as a nation, we can ensure that inner-city schools—what writer and researcher Norm Fruchter calls "the basements of opportunity in American schooling"—provide the kind of educational experiences students need to flourish.[1] Put simply, how do urban schools develop the capacity to deliver educational opportunity to the students who need it most?

THE PROBLEM OF POWER

Why are low-performing urban public schools the way they are? Groups like Oakland Community Organizations believe that the poor conditions and outcomes of urban public schools stem not from a lack of technical know-how, but from the differential distribution of power in society by class, race, gender, and the like. Poor communities, like those in the flatlands of Oakland, have overcrowded schools with dismal levels of academic achievement because local residents lack the political power to force systems to invest the necessary resources and capacity in these schools.

The premise that community conditions are shaped by political power, and that improving undesirable conditions requires building the power of neighborhood constituencies, draws on a long tradition of social justice organizing in the United States. The civil rights, women's liberation, immigrant rights, and labor movements all used organizing strategies and imparted methods, tactics, values, and norms that shape community organizing today.

Though school reform organizing builds on this history, it is also grounded in theories of social capital in economic and educational attainment. First conceptualized by French sociologist Pierre Bourdieu, *social capital* refers to the benefits gained by individuals through the social context of community life.[2] Trust, shared values, and a sense of obligation and connectedness between community members provide the basis for social networks through which community members can gain benefits from their relationships with those around them and, in return, facilitate benefits for others. Social networks are not static but they can be reinforcing—that is, social cohesion is shaped by the degree to which members perceive gains as having material or social value and are willing to invest in maintaining them. To the extent that individuals in the network have access to economic resources and cultural capital, such social networks can open up new possibilities for community members; for example, these networks can help youth find summer employment opportunities, or help parents identify good schools for their children.

Within the field of public education, social capital theory has helped to elaborate the positive and negative effects of social context on educational outcomes. Instrumental studies in the 1970s and '80s explored the influence of racial isolation on the opportunities available to youth of color, and the ways in which familial cultural capital shapes children's educational opportunities, capacities, and outcomes.[3]

But the concept of social capital captured national attention when Harvard political scientist Robert Putnam applied social capital theory to the relationship between levels of civic engagement in public life and the economic well-being of communities and nations. Drawing on a study of civic life in Italy, Putnam observed that functional communities have high levels of social capital and generate new social capital for members through their participation in voluntary associations. Applying this finding to American life, Putnam noted a decline of participation in traditional forms of associational activity (like bowling leagues and the PTA) that, he argued, threatened to have grave consequences for the economic strength and social vitality of the United States.[4]

Putnam's theoretical and empirical assertions regarding social capital have been the subject of some debate, particularly for their failure to address the "complex set of power-laden relationships—both internally, within communities, and externally, between actors in the communities and the rest of the world," that profoundly influence the outcomes of social capital for community members.[5] Nonetheless, social capital's rising prominence in democratic political theory during the 1990s brought new legitimacy to community organizing, which had been previously associated with radical activism. Along with a host of community building and community development projects, community organizing gained support among scholars and funders for its potential to build new social capital by increasing public engagement in civic life and, in doing so, increasing economic opportunity and reducing social isolation for racially and economically marginalized communities.[6]

Although the principles of community organizing are consistent with social capital theory, organizing for public school reform brings two core propositions to the fore:

- First, building new social capital, while necessary, does not mean that communities will possess the *political* capital needed to rectify inequity and ensure educational opportunity for its members. How political capital flows, and to whom it flows, determines who reaps the benefits of the wealth of economic resources in the United States—and who does not. From a community organizing perspective, the central problem is not the lack of social capital in poor communities and communities of color, but rather the lack of democratic control over how economic and cultural resources (which enrich the benefits communities gain from social capital) are distributed and deployed.

- Second, because what happens in schools is so deeply intertwined with the social and economic conditions of communities, organizing groups conceive of and pursue school improvement in the context of community improvement. Organizing groups thus embed education reform activities within a larger frame of strategic political action to assert stronger accountability over existing resources in their communities and gain access to new forms of capital. Creating the kind of educational opportunities comparable to those found in affluent communities begins outside of schools, not in the form of services or advocacy for families, but through community-based efforts to build power.

What Is Community Organizing?

In community organizing, power is defined as the ability to act. A key source of power in low-income communities is the capacity to mobilize large numbers of community members to challenge political priorities that keep things the way they are. Developing an organized constituency is labor-intensive, ongoing, and iterative. The process begins with the strategic development of relationships between people who are directly affected by low-performing schools. Whether through neighborhood outreach, in which organizers knock on doors of residents, or through institution-based strategies, in which organizers identify and meet people through informal networks in churches or schools, organizers aim to engage people to actively confront and change unjust conditions.

In school reform organizing, parents, students, community members, and sometimes educators are invited into a group process in which they discuss concerns and analyze causes of problems in their schools. Often this process involves research activities, such as conducting surveys, examining school data, consulting academic research and experts, and meeting with decision makers to explore issues and the feasibility of various reform proposals or "demands." A crucial component of the organizing process is the *power analysis*—that is, an assessment of who has the institutional authority to make decisions concerning organizing demands, and which allies might be mobilized in support of the organizing group's campaign.

Organizing groups use the power of numbers to gain the attention of decision makers. But their persuasive sway stems not only from the ability to mobilize large numbers of people directly affected by poor schooling quality, but also from members' knowledge of schooling issues, the strength of their proposed solutions, their relationships with influential allies, and the legitimacy of their demands for justice for poor and disenfranchised communities. Each "win" draws in new members, strengthening their development as organizational leaders, and building cohesion within the group. The growing base of supporters and sense of shared purpose expands the organization's power and enables it to take on more complex issues and ambitious campaigns.

This book explores the potential of the community organizing as a strategy for public education reform. Does the effort to equalize power relationships contribute to improved educational outcomes for low income urban students of color? If so, in what ways is community organizing transforming public schools, and under what circumstances?

Drawing on a six-year, mixed-methods, national study of community organizing, we discuss how community organizing is influencing the capacity of schools to educate students successfully. What lessons can be drawn about promising strategies for successful organizing in different contexts? What are the implications for alliance building with educators? In Part One, we examine the field of education organizing nationally and offer evidence from our study on the impact of organizing on districts, schools, and student educational outcomes. Part Two explores how groups are organizing to improve schools, with a focus on delineating the strategic choices and organizational characteristics that foster successful initiatives. In Part Three, we consider the implications of school reform organizing for increased civic engagement in communities and stronger school-community alliances for sustained and lasting reform. We close with a discussion of challenges facing this burgeoning field as it enters a new era of American politics.

RESEARCH DESIGN

To date, research on community organizing for school reform has been mostly qualitative, and includes numerous reports, as well as excellent and detailed book-length analyses of organizing efforts.[7] But few research studies have assessed the effect of community organizing on local schools and communities. Our research offers the largest and most comprehensive longitudinal analysis to date of the relationship between community organizing and student educational outcomes.

Beginning in 2003, our research team collected and analyzed a wide range of qualitative and quantitative data on the school reform organizing of eight groups nationally. All are mature groups with at least five years of education organizing experience prior to the start of the study. These groups, listed in table I.1, were also selected for their variation across different organizing models, the diversity of their core constituencies, and their geographic location.

Researchers reviewed documentary information on organizing campaigns and "wins" and interviewed a wide range of stakeholders in each site, including educators who were targeted by organizing groups' campaigns (see table I.2). The voices of the organizers, educators, parents, and youth we interviewed during the course of our research are interspersed throughout this book. We also surveyed organizing group members and teachers, and examined publicly available administrative data on the schools involved in each group's campaigns. These data were analyzed to understand perceptions of the impact of organizing across multiple stakeholders, and to guide our analysis of student educational outcomes.[8]

Like most community change efforts, community organizing for school reform is multidimensional in scope, involving a diverse set of actors in a range of tactics to promote reform. Our mixed-method multisite case study design responds to three challenges inherent to such complex initiatives:

Causality:
Research designs typically used to establish causal inferences between actions and outcomes are not particularly useful in assessing the impact of community organizing for school reform, given the dynamic nature of organizing and schooling change. Randomized field trials that assign schools to "treatment" and "nontreatment" assume a level of control over context that is not generally the case in organizing initiatives. Organizing groups make decisions based on the real-time priorities of community members

TABLE 1.1   Study sites

Study site	Youth organizing	National network
Northwest Bronx Community and Clergy Coalition (NWBCCC)	Sistas and Brothas United (SBU)	
Oakland Community Organizations		PICO National Network
Chicago ACORN *		Association of Communities Organized for Reform Now (ACORN)
Austin Interfaith		Industrial Areas Foundation (IAF)
Milwaukee Inner-city Congregations Allied for Hope (MICAH)		Gamaliel Foundation
People Acting for Community Together (PACT) (Miami)		Direct Action and Research Training Center (DART)
Community Coalition (Los Angeles)	South Central Youth Empowered thru Action (SCYEA)	
Eastern Pennsylvania Organizing Project (EPOP)**	Youth United for Change (YUC)	PICO National Network

*Note: The work described in this book was carried out by Chicago ACORN until January 2008, when the director, staff, and board left ACORN to start a new group called Action Now; they are continuing the education and other organizing campaigns they initiated while affiliated with ACORN.
**Note: In 2009, EPOP separated from the PICO National Network.

and the urgency of problems in their local schools. Intervention strategies are constantly in flux, as are the set of schools targeted for reform.

Even if a true experimental design were possible, asserting organizing as the "cause" of schooling changes is inherently suspect, given the many contextual factors also in play and the difficulties in controlling for these factors through statistical methods. High turnover of superintendents,

TABLE 1.2   Data sources

Data sources	Scope of data
Archival documents	Review of materials produced by the organizations, including grant reports, training materials, and brochures, to understand organizational practices
Adult member survey	241 respondents from the core leadership of seven groups: • Measured level of involvement in organizing and impact of involvement on civic and school engagement
Youth survey	124 youth members from the core leadership of three groups: • Measured level of involvement in organizing and impact of involvement on political and community engagement and school motivation
Observations	75 observations of leadership development sessions, public actions, and negotiations with policymakers
Interviews	321 interviews of parents, youth, organizers, school- and district-level educators, and other education stakeholders to understand: • Organizational theory of change and trajectory of organizing campaigns • Impacts of organizing on adult and youth leaders • Impacts of organizing on district- and school-level policies and practices
Teacher survey	509 teachers in Oakland, Miami, and Austin (sites where intensive school-based organizing had occurred) using a matched comparison design: • Measured teacher perceptions of school climate, professional culture, and instructional culture • Analyses of teacher characteristics found no significant differences in demographics or years of teaching experience between teachers in target and comparison schools.
Public administrative data	Analysis of district-level data such as graduation rates, dropout rates, and demographic data to assess school district context and measure student outcomes
Media coverage	1,700 articles of local media coverage on education to understand shifts in policy contexts

principals, teachers, and students; the presence of other reforms at the school; and the ebbs and flows of organizing itself that occur over time potentially confound the results of statistical analyses.[9] In our study, inferences in support of our research hypotheses are based on the consistency of evidence across multiple data sources and analyses, rather than the establishment of a causal link between the actions of organizing groups and the outcomes they promote.

- *Context:* Whether focused at the school, district, state, or federal level, education organizing demands and strategies are influenced by the historical moment in which groups emerged, their organizational capacity at any given time, and the opportunities for successfully moving an agenda in their political environment. All of these factors shape how organizing groups operate and the reform interventions they define. In our study we reviewed a wide range of organizational documentation and media coverage to understand how leadership transitions, new reforms, policy initiatives, and other factors in groups' contexts influenced organizing campaigns. Though we draw insights about the potential of organizing across the eight study sites, we caution the reader to bear in mind the intrinsically context-specific nature of organizing work.

- *Construct validity: Construct validity* refers to the extent to which research measures are appropriate to the phenomenon under study. Clarifying the phenomenon can be difficult in an organizing context, where strategy and interventions are rarely fixed. Our research draws extensively on the literature on community organizing and education reform. We also engaged in a collaborative research process with our sites to test the legitimacy of our research questions, design, findings, and conclusions. Such dialogue was necessary to ensure that groups' intimate knowledge of their work and the local school, district, and community contexts informed our methods, data collection instruments, and understanding and interpretation of the data.

Mapping Organizing Theory to School Change

With the above methodological caveats in mind, our research asserts a theory of action for how community organizing groups work to reach their school reform goals. This theory of action, shown in figure I.1, proceeds

FIGURE 1.1   Theory of action

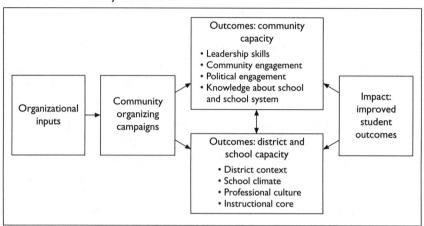

as follows: In the initial phases, organizing groups recruit and convene community residents, parents, and young people impacted by low-quality schools to develop relationships with each other and discuss and define problems and solutions. Engagement in organizing campaigns deepens the skills and leadership of community members involved in the effort. Parents, youth, and community residents develop an awareness of their power to create change through collective action. They develop the confidence and skills to articulate their self-interest and speak on behalf of their community. And they expand their understanding of how to address schooling problems.

Through cycles of campaigns, organizing groups build their organizational power to influence district priorities and operating procedures. To the extent that organizing demands focus on increasing equity, quality and accountability in public schools, greater organizational influence can generate new policy and resource allocations that expand the possibilities for reform in schools serving low-income neighborhoods and communities of color. Successive campaign victories combined with increased parent, youth, and community engagement in schools can also help generate improvement in the capacity of schools to support successful student learning.

Community capacity and school system capacity are dynamically related. Greater knowledge of schools among parents or youth, for example, increases their ability to propose strategies for improvement in schools. Similarly, greater awareness among school leaders of the community organization's mobilization power and political influence increases the likelihood that they will acknowledge community proposals for change. Communities and schools with these expanded capacities interact to generate improved student educational outcomes.

Our theory of action offers a simple and linear conceptualization of the path to educational improvement, although, as we will discuss, the organizing path to change is far from simple or linear. The organizing process is often quite circuitous, and is interspersed with inspiring gains and frustrating setbacks as groups search for ways to transform schools into the enriching environments their communities deserve.

PLAN OF THE BOOK

Part One examines the emerging field of community organizing for school reform through the experiences of the eight organizations in our study. In chapter 1, we discuss historical influences on how groups work, elaborating on the ways in which Saul Alinsky's work, together with the traditions of farm-worker organizing and the civil rights and women's movements, shape organizing methodology today. We then examine why organizations began organizing for school reform and trace the arc of the developing field across the past two decades. Community organizing groups' entrée to education issues often came through problems at the nexus of neighborhood revitalization and school improvement, such as drug-free school zones and school safety, or through members' concerns about the poor quality of their children's schools. Over time, education organizing shifted from a focus on local school problems, such as overcrowded or crumbling school facilities and the lack of crossing guards, to pursue district- and statewide campaigns for larger-scale systemic reform.

In chapter 2, we examine the evidence of the impact of community organizing on districts, schools, and student educational outcomes. Our research found that organizing campaigns increased the responsiveness of district leaders to the concerns of low-income parents and community members; secured substantial new resources and ensured their equitable distribution; and introduced new policy to improve curriculum, school organization, teacher recruitment and preparation, and parent engagement. At the school level, organizing groups' involvement led to improvements in school climate, professional culture among educators, and schools' instructional core (resources and strategies). In three sites where school-based organizing was sustained over a number of years, we found evidence of improved student achievement as measured by standardized tests and graduation rates.

Part Two delves into the strategies that organizing groups have developed to move complex reform campaigns. Chapter 3 discusses how organizing groups have balanced district and school-level strategies. Drawing on the work of three sites—Austin Interfaith, Oakland Community Organizations, and People Acting for Community Together in Miami, we argue that pressure and engagement at both the school and system levels is essential to achieve reform. In chapter 4, we turn to the role of coalitions in moving equity demands at the system level, highlighting campaigns led by Youth United for Change in Philadelphia, the Northwest Bronx Community and Clergy Coalition in New York City, the Community Coalition in Los Angeles, and Chicago ACORN. We discuss how and why organizing groups have convened broad-based civic coalitions as part of district- and state-level campaigns, and examine how organizing groups' participation in civic coalitions influences reform priorities and coalition dynamics. In chapter 5, we examine the challenges of scaling up reform, exploring the competing pressures of "going deep" to change the normative beliefs of educators, district leaders, and local stakeholder organizations about the capacity of communities they serve, while also "reaching wide" to develop the political relationships necessary to initiate, expand, and sustain reform.

In Part Three, we discuss the implications of education organizing for longer-term community capacity and alliances with educators. Chapter 6 examines how organizing groups, through the careful development of grassroots leadership, build new community capacity in the form of social and political capital to demand justice. In addition to the skills of campaign planning, parents, youth, and community members of organizing groups develop new knowledge about schools and the political system, new aspirations for themselves and their families, and, crucially, a deep sense of their own capacity to create change through collective community action. In chapter 7, we explore the relationships that organizing groups have built with teachers, principals, and district officials and identify the conditions that facilitate or hinder collaboration between organizing groups and educators. When educators and organizing groups share reform priorities and understand each other's cultures and methodologies, we argue, they can forge sophisticated, mutually accountable collaborations that provide a powerful platform for reform.

PART ONE

THE EMERGENCE OF A FIELD

CHAPTER ONE

A National View

Ever since the U.S. Supreme Court's ruling on *Brown v. Board of Education* in 1954, our nation has struggled with the question of how best to deliver on the promise of educational opportunity for all children. Each decade has brought new reforms and players who take their respective roles on the national stage with demands for more resources, accountability, and innovation through a wide array of strategies.

Federal, state, and local policies reflect the push and pull of competing viewpoints. Great Society and school desegregation initiatives, for example, prioritized resources to encourage public school systems to respond to the needs of poor children of color. School-improvement strategies of the 1980s and early 1990s called, alternately, for decentralizing school-site management to improve schools through greater educator autonomy and parental influence, and for centralizing governance and standardizing how and what teachers teach.[1] Whole school reforms of the mid-1990s proposed greater coherence in school organizational and instructional strategies, while privatization and vouchers initiatives aimed to dispense with public schooling altogether.[2] The high-stakes accountability of this decade has sought to pressure schools toward higher performance and penalize those that fail to improve.[3]

Despite all this reform, vast inequities persist in the quality and outcomes of public schooling, defined as they have been historically by the confluence of race and class in America.[4] Indeed, as noted in the *Washington Post*: "Nationwide, white students averaged 1579 on the SAT in 2007; blacks averaged 1287. The gap, 292 points, has scarcely changed in the past 10 years: It has increased by two points each on the reading and math sections, which were joined last year by a new writing assessment. The disparity has endured for decades and is perhaps the classic example of the racial achievement gap in public education."[5]

Community organizing for school reform emerged as a distinct field of work during the late 1980s and early 1990s. Working in low-income neighborhoods, far removed from the debates of national education policy makers, community-based organizations built campaigns that were pragmatic and action-oriented. Organizers, parents, and local community residents mobilized to confront appalling local school conditions—rampant overcrowding, dirty bathrooms, truancy—and low levels of student achievement. Eschewing traditional forms of parent and student involvement (through parent-teacher associations and student governments, for example), these organizing efforts aimed to expose and change conditions and dynamics in schools, rather than to promote fundraising and volunteerism in support of the status quo.

In a relatively short period of time, community groups had established organizing as a force for change in urban school systems. By the late 1990s, community organizing had attracted national attention as a means of influencing the priorities of local school boards, superintendents and principals; increasing parent and community involvement; and winning wide-ranging school-level improvements such as school facilities repairs and construction, after-school programs, teacher professional development opportunities, class-size reduction, new textbooks, and much-needed classroom supplies.[6] Survey research and other studies had begun to define the contours of this new field, documenting a dramatic growth in the number of education organizing groups across the country and defining emergent strategies and cross-cutting challenges for organizing.[7]

This chapter looks at the field of community organizing for school reform through the experiences of the eight groups in our study (see table 3.1). We begin with a discussion of how organizing groups work, examining the historical traditions and methodological distinctions that shape how organizing groups recruit and build leadership among community members and how they conceptualize the role of campaigns in developing organizational power. Turning to education organizing, we review how and why organizing groups became involved in public education reform, and discuss the ways in which organizing groups situate their demands for educational equity within a larger vision of expanding democratic participation in their communities.

TABLE 1.1   The evolution of education organizing in eight sites

Study site	**Austin Interfaith (AI)**
Membership type	Institutional—congregations, unions, schools
Affiliation	Industrial Areas Foundation (IAF)
Origins	Initiated in 1985 by the Catholic Bishop in Austin and a group of local African American ministers familiar with the IAF's work.
Impetus for education organizing	Became involved in education issues through its support of a local bond package in 1990. Adopted the IAF "Alliance Schools" model in 1992 and organized parents, teachers and principals in sixteen elementary schools and five middle and high schools.
Study site	**Chicago ACORN***
Membership type	Direct
Affiliation	Association of Communities Organized for Reform Now (ACORN)
Origins	Founding organizer Madeline Talbott, who had worked with ACORN organizations in Arkansas and Detroit, initiated Chicago ACORN in 1983 to organize low- and moderate-income families for economic justice.
Impetus for education organizing	Began organizing following the passage of the 1988 Chicago School Governance Reform Act, which created new parent majority councils and leveraged private foundation funding for parent leadership training. Helped parents get elected to local school councils. Campaigns focused on winning facilities improvements, opposing school closings, training parents, and improving teacher quality in low-income neighborhoods.
Study site	**Oakland Community Organizations (OCO)**
Membership type	Institutional—congregations, community organizations, schools
Affiliation	PICO National Network
Origins	Founded in 1977 as a neighborhood-based organizing project by John Baumann, SJ and Jerry Helfrich, SJ, who went on to establish the PICO national network. OCO later transitioned to an institution-based model with PICO's help.
Impetus for education organizing	Began organizing in 1989 to address school safety concerns raised in church-based local organizing committees. Early campaigns focused on school level issues, such as drug-free school zones, as well as district-wide policy to expand school-to-work and class size reduction programs, and replacing low-performing schools with new, autonomous, small schools.

(continued)

TABLE 1.1 (continued)

Study site	**Milwaukee Inner-city Congregations Allied for Hope (MICAH)**
Membership type	Institutional: congregations
Affiliation	Gamaliel Foundation
Origins	Founded as the third Gamaliel Foundation affiliate and the first outside of Chicago in 1988 by founding organizer Sheryl Spivey Perry. MICAH was initiated as a multiracial, interfaith organization after a two-year process of individual and group meetings with inner-city clergy.
Impetus for education organizing	Began organizing in 1992 in response to congregational members' concerns. First campaign focused on improving district-level recruitment of minority teachers. Other major campaigns include maintaining statewide funding for early grade class size reduction, school finance equity, increasing the number of school nurses, and reducing mobility.
Study site	**Eastern Pennsylvania Organizing Project (EPOP) and Youth United for Change (YUC), Philadelphia**
Membership type	EPOP: institutional—congregations, parent groups, community organizations YUC: direct—high school students
Affiliation	PICO National Network (EPOP)
Origins	Founding organizer Steve Honeyman, who had worked with the National Training and Information Center and other PICO groups, initiated EPOP in 1993 after conversations with local clergy and parents, to "give voice to the voiceless." YUC began as a youth leadership and media project in 1993 and later shifted to an organizing strategy. YUC is a dues-paying member of EPOP.
Impetus for education organizing	EPOP began organizing in schools in 1993 in order to reach neighborhood residents, and formed school-based parent committees when leaders' focus turned to education issues. Early campaigns focused on school-level improvements in safety, facilities, access to full-day kindergarten, and improved reading instruction. Other major campaigns include opposing school privatization, a district-wide "Right to Know" campaign to improve communication with parents, and blocking the redistribution of Title I funding to less-needy schools. YUC began school-based organizing in 1993 in response to issues raised by leaders. Early campaigns focused on school facilities, library resources, and safety. Major campaigns include: college access curricula, school facilities improvements, and restructuring high schools to create new small schools.

(continued)

TABLE 1.1 (continued)

Study site	**Northwest Bronx Community and Clergy Coalition (NWBCCC) and Sistas and Brothas United (SBU)**
Membership type	NWBCCC: mixed—congregations, neighborhood associations, individuals SBU: direct—middle and high school students
Affiliation	unaffiliated
Origins	Founding organizers Roger Hays and Pat Dillon joined a group of clergy and neighborhood residents in 1974 to form the NWBCCC to fight the arson and disinvestment that were sweeping through the South Bronx. SBU began in 1999 as a youth project of one of NWBCCC's neighborhood associations and became a member organization of the NWBCCC.
Impetus for education organizing	Formally initiated an education committee in 1995 in response to severe school overcrowding. Initial campaigns combined school- and district-level organizing to alleviate overcrowding through facilities improvements and the creation of new schools. SBU began organizing in schools in 1999 in response to leaders' complaints about facilities, safety and inadequate resources.
Study site	**People Acting for Community Together (PACT), Miami**
Membership type	Institutional—congregations, schools
Affiliation	Direct Action and Research Training Center (DART)
Origins	Founding organizer Holly Holcombe worked with local congregation leaders, in particular Monsignor Gerard LaCerra of the Miami Archdiocese, to create PACT to build community power and overcome systemic injustice for low- and moderate-income communities.
Impetus for education organizing	Leaders identified education as a priority for organizing in 1995. Initial campaign focused on improving reading instruction, which led to a ten-year campaign to allow low-performing schools to adopt the Direct Instruction reading program. Other state-level campaigns addressed expanding access to prekindergarten and afterschool programs, and improving teacher quality.

(continued)

TABLE 1.1 (continued)

Study site	**Community Coalition, Los Angeles**
Membership type	Direct—Black and Brown residents of South Central LA
Affiliation	unaffiliated
Origins	The Community Coalition was founded by Karen Bass, who had worked with crack addicts in emergency rooms, in response to the crack cocaine epidemic in South LA and resulting police harassment of youth in the late 1980s. The organization was established to address the conditions supporting poverty, crime and addiction in South LA. A youth organizing project, South Central Youth Empowered thru Action (SCYEA), was established in 1993.
Impetus for education organizing	Initial education organizing focused on mobilizing local support for a statewide school facilities bond referendum. In 1997, SCYEA began organizing high school youth into school-based chapters to improve neighborhood high schools. Initial campaigns focused on facilities improvements and college access tracking.

Note: The work described in this book was carried out by Chicago ACORN until January 2008, when the director, staff, and board left ACORN to start a new group called Action Now; they are continuing the education and other organizing campaigns they initiated while affiliated with ACORN.

HOW DO GROUPS ORGANIZE?

Community organizing as an approach to social change is often traced to the 1930s and the work of Saul Alinsky. Drawing on his experiences in the labor movement, Alinsky asserted that poor people could be organized into powerful neighborhood organizations on the basis of their self-interest in better economic and social conditions. With support from a professional organizer, neighborhood constituents could win concessions from municipal and business leaders if community members were willing to use collective action and confrontational tactics.[8] Working in the white, working-class Back of the Yards neighborhood on Chicago's Southside, Alinsky built an "organization of organizations" that united the leadership of existing local institutions, including Catholic clergy, area merchants, neighborhood residents, and leaders of a union local of stockyard workers. Within a scant few years, Alinsky's Back of the Yards Neighborhood Council had won a wide variety of services, including an infant welfare station, hot lunch and milk programs in local schools, new employment opportunities, and resources for neighborhood development programs.[9]

Alinsky's work in Chicago, and later in Rochester, New York, began to define a model of organization building for power in low-income communities. This work evolved a set of operating principles about self-interest-based campaign development, confrontational direct-action tactics, and the role of the "professional" organizer that continues to influence community organizing methods today. There were other antecedents to modern organizing, notably organizing of small farmers in the 1890s to gain control over local economic conditions from local merchants, banks, and railroad companies, and the settlement house activism and labor organizing efforts of the early part of the twentieth century.[10] But Saul Alinsky's methods and philosophy of "populist pragmatism" launched much of what we now associate with community organizing.

Community organizing methods have evolved considerably since Alinsky's early work, though, as organizers responded to challenges and opportunities in their local contexts. For example, organizing in immigrant communities in California by Fred Ross defined a door-to-door model of canvassing and "house meetings" to bring neighborhood residents into local organizations—as individuals rather than as representatives of existing institutions. Ross's model, which became the basis of the Community Service Organization, also introduced the structure of statewide organizations as a platform for advancing local neighborhood demands.[11] Other major influences include organizers' experiences of consciousness-raising in the women's movement, which elevated consensus-based, nonstratified norms of decision making as an alternative to hierarchical, male-dominated decision making by clergy and other institutional leaders. Civil rights–era activism of the Congress of Racial Equality (CORE) and the Student Nonviolent Coordinating Committee (SNCC) demonstrated the power of student and youth organizing and of going beyond "interest group" politics framed on short-term economic self-interest to define a larger vision of social justice as the basis for organizing demands. Along with the black power movement, these groups brought issues of structural racism to the fore, and fought not only to change existing institutions, but also to create new institutions that prioritized the leadership, needs, and experiences of people of color. Influenced by the lessons of the civil rights movement and the women's movement, immigrant groups, and organizations led by young people of color have crafted models of organizing that emphasize intensive political education and foster a critical consciousness about social and economic inequalities. Organizing demands and strategy evolve out of this analysis of structural oppression.

Within the field of community organizing today, groups are often differentiated on the basis of their organizational membership structure. Two organizational models are dominant: *institutional membership* organizations that recruit local institutions as members; and *direct membership* groups that recruit individual community residents to become members of the organization. We use the categories of institutional and direct membership to distinguish broad differences in how organizing groups operate.

Five of the groups in our study—Austin Interfaith, Eastern Pennsylvania Organizing Project (EPOP), Milwaukee Inner-city Congregations Allied for Hope (MICAH), Oakland Community Organizations (OCO), and People Acting for Change Together (PACT)—use an institutional membership model, with congregations of various faiths making up the bulk of their membership. Chicago ACORN, a member of the national Association of Community Organizations for Reform Now, and the Community Coalition in Los Angeles use a direct membership model, recruiting local residents directly as dues-paying members. The Northwest Bronx Community and Clergy Coalition uses a mixed model of institutional and direct membership. The three youth organizing efforts in our study recruit young people directly as members.

Institutional Membership Organizing

Institutional membership groups draw on the existing relationships and leadership of churches, community groups, and other institutions to build organizations capable of mobilizing large numbers of people. The major national networks—the Industrial Areas Foundation (IAF, founded by Saul Alinsky), PICO National Network, Direct Action and Research Training Center (DART), and the Gamaliel Foundation—employ a community organizing model that draws on the religious traditions of member institutions as the basis for a collective response to societal injustice.

The early institutional membership model relied on the existing leadership structures of powerful neighborhood institutions. Over time, institution-based organizing shifted to emphasize the development of indigenous, grassroots leadership, reflecting the influence of the Industrial Areas Foundation. During the 1970s in Texas, and later across the southwest, IAF organizer Ernesto Cortes began to focus on the development of relational networks between members of church congregations and other local institutions. Cortes held individual meetings with members to identify potential leaders, and brought these people together in house meetings, as scholar Mark Warren observes, to "talk among themselves to identify their concerns and find a basis for cooperative action."[12] These conversations helped to build a sense of mutual responsibility and obligation among leaders that became the basis for mobilizing people to action. Expanding the emphasis on pragmatic self-interest, Cortes brought Judeo-Christian values of social justice into the IAF's vision of grassroots participation.[13] He also refined the principle of unilateral power to incorporate the concept of relational power, defined as "the power to act collectively."[14] These innovations influenced the institutionally based organizing approaches developed by the DART, Gamaliel Foundation, and PICO networks.

In all institutional membership groups, the organizer's goal is to develop "leaders" within member institutions who understand power and are willing to work for social justice. As we will explore in chapter 6, leadership development begins with an individual meeting (known as a one-on-one or one-to-one) between an organizer and a congregation member who is actively involved in the institution. In these meetings, organizers probe these members' life experiences to identify what they feel passionate about, what makes them angry, and what drives their participation in congregation and community life. As leaders' skills and knowledge develop, they are encouraged to take on increasing responsibility, joining their congregation or institution's core team as well as cross-institution issue committees. They are also expected to identify and develop other potential leaders from their congregations who can be mobilized for actions or other organizational events.

Not surprisingly, religious leaders play a particularly important role in the institutionally based community organizing approach because of the historical predominance of religious institutions at the neighborhood level. Three of the institutional membership groups we studied were initiated by local clergy who worked with organizers from national organizing networks to establish new organizations. In 1986, a group of African American ministers familiar with the work of the IAF in Texas joined with the leadership of the Catholic Diocese in Austin to establish Austin Interfaith. Similarly, organizer Sheryl Spivey of the Chicago-based Gamaliel Foundation led a two-year process of developing relationships with clergy in Milwaukee as the basis for establishing MICAH in 1988. In that same year, DART organizer Holly Holcombe and Monsignor Gerard LaCerra established PACT in Miami, with support from a group of local clergy.

OCO was initiated by John Baumann and Jerry Helfrich, two Jesuit priests trained in the Alinsky tradition. In 1972, Baumann and Helfrich began organizing in the low-income Fruitvale and East Oakland neighborhoods. They initially used a neighborhood-based model of organizing and later transitioned to a congregation-based model as a strategy for building organizational power and sustainability. OCO organizers conducted individual meetings with congregation members of a local church to build an organizing committee and initiate a campaign. The outpouring of community members at the committee's first public action convinced OCO organizers of the mobilization potential of the institutionally based organizing model.

In Philadelphia, EPOP's founding organizer Steve Honeyman brought experience with both direct and institutional membership organizing groups in Rochester, New York, and Camden, New Jersey. As with OCO, Honeyman's assessment of the difficulty in sustaining direct member organizing led him to build EPOP as an institution-based organization. EPOP's model included schools, community-based organizations, and other institutions in addition to churches because of the dwindling number of religious organizations in Philadelphia's urban core.

Direct Membership Organizing

Direct membership organizing to demand rights for poor communities grew during the 1960s and 1970s, drawing on the work of Fred Ross as well as the experiences of organizations like the Students for a Democratic Society (SDS) and the National Welfare Rights Organization. Rather than relying on the relationships that exist within neighborhood institutions, direct membership groups emphasize the recruitment of local residents into tenant, block, neighborhood, or issue-focused groups that take action to resolve shared concerns. Organizers or leaders find community members through canvassing the neighborhood and knocking on doors, distributing flyers outside schools, or through house meetings. The organizer's goal is to build, maintain, and continually enlarge the group's membership by bringing in new people and helping to develop their leadership capacities.

Like Fred Ross in the Community Service Organization, direct member organizing responds to the social context of local communities. "You work with what you've got," explains Madeline Talbott, formerly lead organizer of Chicago ACORN and now with Action Now. "If there are churches, you work with them. It would be silly not to. But in a lot of neighborhoods, you have to build those institutions."[15]

Direct membership groups view the development of issue campaigns as the basis of building powerful organizations. Groups attract new community residents by appealing to their concerns about local neighborhood conditions and foster a sense of common purpose and vision within the group through issue campaigns. Clay Smith, former staff director with the Northwest Bronx Community and Clergy Coalition, observes: "The job of the organizer and of the core leadership is to go out into that neighborhood and organize tenant associations, block associations, and neighborhood campaigns—to go out and knock on people's doors and say, 'What are your concerns? Do other people have the same problems? Are you interested in starting a tenants' association to build some power to fix the problem?'"

"What we do is help people understand that as individuals, they don't have any power," Smith says. "The landlord won't listen to them, and the city probably won't listen to them. But as a group, they have power to put pressure on the landlord or on the city or on the bank that has the mortgage on the building and they can get their building fixed. So, we start teaching them the power of collective action through tenant organizing."

Direct membership organizations believe that practical self-interest initially draws people into the local group and motivates them to action. Actions that produce victories create a sense of group power and increased investment in the organization's long-term struggle for justice. "Every new member believes that what's possible is what's on their block. We're constantly moving them through an understanding of what is a legitimate issue to target. People who brought up the crossing guard issue five years ago are now leading the effort around teacher quality," Madeline Talbott explains. In the same way that leaders in institutional membership groups move into positions of increasing responsibility on core teams, issue committees, and boards, leaders of direct membership organizations are drawn into longer-term campaigns beyond their immediate self-interest. These campaigns provide the platform for leadership development of their members.

Two of the three direct membership groups in our study were initiated by organizers who were trained by national organizing networks. Madeline Talbott established Chicago ACORN in 1983, after working for ACORN organizations in Pine Bluff (Arkansas), Houston, and Detroit for seven years. The largest direct membership organizing network in the country, the ACORN national network was initiated by Wade Rathke in Arkansas in 1970. ACORN's organizing model emphasizes door-knocking to recruit new members into neighborhood-based chapters that work on issue campaigns. Drawing on Rathke's and George Wiley's work in the National Welfare Rights Organization, ACORN's model developed with an explicit focus on building a "political majority" of low- and moderate-income families on the basis of their shared economic and social disenfranchisement.[16]

The Northwest Bronx Community and Clergy Coalition combines direct membership and institutional membership approaches. NWBCCC grew out of the efforts of two groups—local clergy and neighborhood residents—to shore up the Northwest Bronx against the arson and disinvestment that swept through south Bronx neighborhoods during the 1970s. Founding organizers Roger Hays and Sister Pat Dillon were trained in the Alinsky tradition. Hays and Dillon developed a hybrid organizational structure in which local residents were organized into neighborhood associations along-side religious institutions. Clergy of the large local Catholic parishes were particularly active in the organization's leadership in its early years. Today, the NWBCCC's complex organizational structure weaves together nine neighborhood-based associations—comprising residents who participate in tenant associations, block associations, church-based social action commit-tees, and school-level parent committees—with organization-wide youth and clergy organizing committees.

In contrast with ACORN and the NWBCCC, the Community Coali-tion's direct-membership approach emphasizes political education and crit-ical analysis, rather than issue campaigns, as the basis for recruiting and developing leaders. The Coalition was initiated in response to the crack cocaine epidemic of the early 1990s by Karen Bass, a social worker who had previously worked with drug addicts in hospital emergency rooms. In creating the Community Coalition, Bass hoped to catalyze a mass social movement to fight economic and social inequities that fostered high rates of addiction and crime in south Los Angeles communities. From its inception, the Coalition has emphasized the development of "black and brown" unity among African American and Latino residents who have often been pitted against each other in city politics. The organization developed an extensive political education training sequence to cultivate a shared vision of social and economic justice among members and introduce them to the organiza-tion's movement-building analysis and strategy.

The distinctions of institution-based and direct membership offer insight into the larger set of principles from which groups operate. These principles inform not only the broader organizational goals groups are trying to achieve through their work, but also their reasons for becoming involved in educa-tion organizing. Responding to members' concerns about local school condi-tions was a primary reason for initiating education campaigns. But organizing groups also approached schools as neighborhood institutions, and thus as places in which to engage more members and to pursue broad equity goals.

ENTERING THE PUBLIC SCHOOL ARENA

The transition into education organizing for most organizations followed an extended period of organizing to address other neighborhood issues, such as the lack of affordable housing, high rates of crime, and environmentally hazardous conditions. Issues at the intersection of neighborhood and school—drug use and violence in neighborhoods surrounding schools, as well as insufficient access to health care, jobs, and youth recreational activities in poor neighborhoods—catalyzed initial campaigns and served to build the organizational power to take on issues of district leadership accountability and school performance. Several groups' education work began by tackling overcrowded and deteriorating facilities and outdated textbooks that made teaching and learning difficult. Other groups used schools as places to find and develop leaders.

In Oakland, for example, education organizing was a response to community members' concerns about school and neighborhood safety. OCO's initial campaigns in 1989 demanded the creation of drug-free school zones. OCO subsequently organized to expand school-to-work programs, reduce class sizes, open charter schools, and ultimately usher in a districtwide strategy of small-school creation in the Oakland Unified School District. In 1992, MICAH began organizing to increase the number of teachers of color in the Milwaukee Public Schools through a campaign focused on districtwide recruitment; the organization later pursued state funding for class-size reduction in early elementary school grades and built campaigns to improve student mobility and student access to health services.

Though organizing was a pragmatic response to local school problems, organizations made use of openings in the broader educational landscape. For example, Chicago ACORN's entry into education organizing followed the 1988 Chicago School Reform Act, which created parent-majority Local School Councils with authority over school budgets and principal hiring. In the initial years of the reform, Chicago ACORN helped eighty-seven of its members to win seats and provided training to councils on school-reform issues and organizing skills. Early school-improvement campaigns focused on facilities repairs, school closings, and the creation of new small schools. The organization later became deeply involved in a statewide effort to improve teacher quality in low-income neighborhoods.

In Texas, a combination of statewide accountability pressure and weak union protections created an opportunity for school-based alliance building between organizers and educators. Dennis Shirley and Mark Warren have documented how the IAF initiated what became a statewide network of "Alliance Schools" committed to implementing parent leadership development and participatory problem-solving through school improvement campaigns.[17] In Austin, organizers conducted intensive training on community organizing for principals, teachers, parents, and community residents as a strategy for changing how these core constituencies related to each other. As one parent involved in Austin Interfaith explains, "When you begin to have those conversations and the teachers feel safe about talking to parents because they both know what their objectives are, it builds accountability on the [educators'] part. Knowing that the parents are there, being active, being proactive, advocating for their children, willing to work and listen, teachers become more open, [and] principals become more open and willing."

Though IAF groups were among the first nationally to focus on transforming school cultures through organizing, organizations affiliated with the PICO national organizing network were similarly focused on building new and more effective relationships between educators, parents, and community members. PICO member organizations utilized a strategy of home visits to introduce educators to their students' communities and develop a sense of connection and mutual accountability for improving student learning. These ideas became foundational concepts in OCO's ten-year effort to restructure Oakland's failing schools into small autonomous ones. In the new small schools, organizer Liz Sullivan explains, organizers "come in and ask questions to people that help them think about things in a different way . . . [to] sit down and listen to one another and be intentional in building relationships . . . So instead of thinking bureaucratically—I'll call a meeting, I'll send home flyers, I'll do this or that—the principal thinks, Who do I need to have a conversation with?"

As multi-issue organizations, many organizing groups link their school-reform organizing with community revitalization efforts both practically and conceptually. In 1993 the Eastern Pennsylvania Organizing Project (part of the PICO network until 2009) began organizing in north Philadelphia schools as sites from which to tackle neighborhood blight and safety. Parents' concerns led EPOP to press for school facilities repairs, new after-school programs, additional library resources, and a host of other issues. As an institutional membership group, EPOP used a relational approach of organizing that emphasized leadership development and relationship building among leaders. But unlike the IAF groups, EPOP viewed parents as its primary constituency in schools. Campaigns began with intensive training sessions for parents on EPOP's model of organizing, and organizers deliberately worked to engage parent-teacher associations in an effort to draw on the energies of existing parent leadership in the school.

In the Bronx, the Northwest Bronx Community and Clergy Coalition's education organizing responded to concerns that the poor quality of local schools was an impediment to neighborhood stability. Founded in 1975, the NWBCCC worked for twenty years on a number of issues that impacted neighborhood quality and were driving away residents—poor housing conditions, crime, and economic disinvestment. But in 1995, mounting complaints from parents about overcrowded school buildings pushed the NWBCCC to initiate its first education campaign. Transferring the model it had used in housing campaigns, NWBCCC organizers ran school meetings "the same way we do tenant meetings," an organizer explains. "We see what issues people are concerned with and we try to prioritize [these concerns] to see what we can do." NWBCCC campaigns focused on persuading city and state officials to provide resources for facilities improvements and new-school construction to alleviate school congestion.

Similarly, in Miami, the education organizing of People Acting for Community Together (PACT) responded to concerns expressed within member congregations, particularly by immigrant parents, about poor reading skills in schools, and the school system's practice of passing children along despite their inability to read. Gloria Whilby, formerly an education consultant with PACT recalls that, "With all the [economic and cultural challenges] that these families faced, to have their children leaving school and not be able to read was too much." PACT created an organization-wide education committee of clergy and congregation members (including parents and teachers) that conducted intensive research on reading interventions for low-income schools, laying the foundation for a ten-year effort to bring the Direct Instruction literacy program to twenty-seven low-performing Miami-Dade County schools.

Education organizing strategies are influenced by the distinctive histories and methodologies of groups. Direct and institutional membership organizations may conceptualize education campaigns differently, but in practice how they work with and in schools is shaped by specific organizational histories and by the opportunities available for action in neighborhood, municipal, and state contexts. Organizers are also learning from the experiences of other organizing groups about what works in education reform.

Youth-led School Reform Organizing

During the 1990s, community organizing by high school students emerged as a distinct form of school-reform activity. The organizational base of youth organizing efforts varies widely. Some groups, like Youth United for Change in Philadelphia, began as independent youth organizations and developed alliances with adult organizations. Other groups were initiated as components of an adult organization. In Los Angeles, South Central Youth Empowered thru Action (SCYEA, pronounced *say-yeah*) emerged from the leadership development and mobilization activities of the Community Coalition. And in the Bronx, New York, Sistas and Brothas United (SBU) coalesced out of a youth project of the NWBCCC.

Like parent and community organizing, youth organizing responded to deplorable conditions and outcomes in local high schools. But it did so with an eye toward building the power of young people as a distinct constituency. Rebecca Rathje recalls the impetus for YUC's evolution from youth development to youth organizing:

> We planned for months to address the school board and demand that they have a young person on the school board . . . Our students were lined up to speak, and the school board president gets up and leaves. So rather than say her speech, this one girl says, 'What I want to know is when the students of this district get up here, why does the [school board president] get up and walk away?' [And when the school board president came back, he said], 'I heard that I was reprimanded for getting up and leaving. Well, if I have to get up, I have been here since six o'clock in the morning. I don't get paid to do this, and if I have to get up for a minute . . . that's none of your business. And as for your request, I've got 215,000 students in my district, why should I listen to a handful of you?

That experience prompted YUC to "really think about what little power we had—15 students speaking versus getting a roomful of students. It made us go back and figure out how to build power," Rathje explains. Under Rathje's leadership, YUC worked with EPOP to develop the idea of organizing students in schools "where you find large concentrations of young people with the most potential to come together on common goals and values and visions." YUC's organizing initially focused on school-level campaigns, winning commitments from district officials to improve facilities and bring in new resources for libraries and instructional programs. The organization later expanded its focus to include district-level campaigns, and in 2005 succeeded in restructuring two large failing high schools into campuses of small schools. Similarly, in New York City, SBU led local campaigns to improve facilities conditions and school safety, and in 2005 worked in partnership with the New York City Department of Education to open a new small school based on a design that young people generated. SCYEA also led campaigns to improve facilities conditions in the late 1990s, and subsequently shifted its attention to college preparation and access.

FROM SMALL WINS TO SYSTEMIC REFORM

Over the past decade, organizing strategies have evolved to reflect organizers' and leaders' deeper understanding of the institutional context of the schools they are trying to change, and which strategies are most effective in their particular communities. Issues like safety, facilities repairs, and overcrowding are concrete and immediate impediments to student learning that serve as useful entry points for organizing parents and students. Yet groups working at the school level have quickly learned that school-level leaders lack the institutional authority to change overarching issues such as how much money schools receive from the district or state budgets, or how teachers are trained and schools are structured. And, as one former organizing director points out, "The strategy also depends on the issue we're working on . . . As you get into instructional issues, the work becomes more dependent on buy-in from administrators."

"Rarely is the individual principal the real source of the problem," explains Aaron Dorfman, formerly executive director of PACT. "Most principals, as with most teachers, want the schools to succeed, want the schools to do well, want the same things that parents want; and so we've generally taken the attitude that local school folks are allies and that the district is the system that we're trying to change." Consequently, as Madeline Talbott observes, "We've learned to target the central board of education and use the tension inherent in the relationships with the principals to move them."

Ongoing superintendent transitions, shifting district priorities, and principal and staff turnover also make schools an unstable base from which to work for change. In this context, observes Andi Perez of Youth United for Change, a strategy of successive school-level campaigns is often not powerful enough to substantially improve student outcomes. "There's the warm, fuzzy belief that if kids have heat, they'll go to school . . . And we can justify that. Did we get textbooks distributed? Yes. Did we get a certified librarian? Do all those things add up to a higher quality education? Yes. But they're not enough. There's still a 70 percent drop-out rate in the Latino community in Kensington, [Philadelphia]."

The limited impact of school-based struggles propelled groups to begin organizing on a larger stage—expanding from a focus on a cluster of schools to districtwide and state-level efforts. Reflecting on the evolution in strategy, former EPOP organizer Gordon Whitman recalls:

> "The question was, How do you move from local work? You do local problem solving for seven or eight years, and you kind of hit these walls where you can only hold the police captain and the principal and the sanitation department accountable for so long. You realize that there's policy stuff, but from just one neighborhood you can't really play in the policy world, it's much harder. So if you want to be able to be proactive, you have to think about how you build broader power . . . EPOP needed to be able to influence policy, and we couldn't do that unless we had a citywide base."

Increased access to research, data, and policy expertise helped groups to utilize political opportunities in the local, state, and national context to develop proposals for systemic change. In Chicago, Los Angeles, New York, and Philadelphia, organizing groups formed deep and sustained relationships with research allies. For example, EPOP joined with Temple University's Center for Public Policy to create a joint research institution called Research for Democracy (RFD), designed to help community leaders use research to influence public policy. The alliance led to "A Right to Know," a report that leveraged the No Child Left Behind Act's reporting mandates to demand greater parental access to data about student performance and teacher qualifications in their schools. Similarly, the Community Coalition in Los Angeles collaborated with the Education Trust-West and UCLA's Institute for Democracy, Education, and Access to produce reports on college access that were instrumental in the organization's campaigns.

Funding also played a crucial role in the expansion and increasing sophistication of education organizing. Organizing groups generally will not accept public funds in order to maintain their independence in demanding government accountability. Instead, they rely on a mix of membership dues and philanthropic foundation grants. Organizing efforts gained prominence during the 1990s in a context of economic growth nationally, and this expanded visibility increased foundation interest in the work. Funding from national foundations, including the Charles Stewart Mott, Edward W. Hazen, Ford and Surdna Foundations, among others, encouraged community organizations to expand their education organizing efforts and provided crucial opportunities for these groups to learn from the work of organizations in other school districts.

Today, youth- and adult-led community groups are organizing for system-level equity-oriented policy and resource reforms. Many campaigns blend strategic pressure for improvement through large-scale public meetings or events with research-based proposals for program innovations that draw on community knowledge and expertise. Chicago ACORN, for example, released a series of research reports and conducted teacher recruitment fairs and home visits to stop the exodus of new teachers from local schools. Through these efforts, organizers and parents came to understand that conventional approaches to improving teacher quality would not work. The challenge their schools faced was not finding teachers to come into their schools, but finding teachers with a deep knowledge and a sense of personal commitment to the neighborhoods served by the school. Working with a broad coalition of higher education institutions, community organizations, and advocacy groups, Chicago ACORN built statewide support for a new teacher pipeline program. This program—known as Grow Your Own—prepares community residents and teacher paraprofessionals to become certified to teach in schools in their neighborhoods, where they have established the relationships and cultural knowledge to succeed.

Like Chicago ACORN, the Los Angeles-based Community Coalition and its youth component SCYEA played a pivotal role in bringing together diverse stakeholders in a citywide organizing effort to increase rigor in the high school curriculum. With roughly 20 percent of public high school students in South Los Angeles meeting the basic entry requirements for the state's public universities, young people and their adult allies argued that access to a college preparatory curriculum was necessary to increase educational equity and ensure a prosperous economic future for their city. In June 2005, following an intensive organizing campaign by the Community Coalition and allied organizations that integrated data and policy analyses, community mobilizations, and media outreach, the Los Angeles Unified School District (LAUSD) school board passed a resolution mandating a college preparatory curriculum for all students in the district. Billed as "bold" and "historic" in one local newspaper, the policy was described by then-board president José Huizar as "one of the most significant reforms this district is embarking on in the last twenty years."[18]

DEMANDING EQUITY, EXPANDING DEMOCRACY

Within the national landscape of public education reform, community organizing groups have consistently framed demands for equity. OCO's query, "Is this fair?" about disparities in the Oakland school district echoes in the demands of high school students in Philadelphia who challenged the prioritization of schools in gentrifying center city neighborhoods over those in poor, racially isolated communities, and in the voices of parents in Miami whose children were passed on from grade to grade even though they could not read. In every case, the problems organizing groups addressed were not new, nor were they hidden from public view. Education officials and city leaders knew about desperately overcrowded school conditions in the Bronx, for example, and about the revolving-door job pattern of young inexperienced teachers in low-income Chicago neighborhoods. Through a variety of tactics, organizing groups worked to frame the status quo as an egregious injustice that could no longer be tolerated.

Theorists in the fields of sociology, media studies, and psychology assert that how organizations and leaders frame social issues determines what is viewed as important in a particular context and what actions should be taken.[19] The concept is also popular with management consulting firms as a way to help senior executives shape effective organizational cultures. One such firm offers a helpful definition of the role of frames: "Contrary to the central concept of rational choice theory (people always strive to make the most rational choices possible), framing theory suggests that how something is presented (the 'frame') influences the choices people make. Frames are abstract notions that serve to organize or structure social meanings. Frames influence the perception of the news of the audience; this form of agenda-setting not only tells *what* to think about an issue (agenda-setting theory), but also *how* to think about that issue."[20]

Framing theory suggests that, to the extent that organizing groups are successful in shaping the public perception of an issue, they will be more likely to build political will among district leaders to take action to redress inequities, particularly when those actions involve a redistribution of a limited pool of resources or run counter to traditional views of who deserves what in America.

The history of public education in the United States traces the struggles of competing frames to define the obligations of public schools. Education scholars Jeannie Oakes and John Rogers observe that reform strategies have long been dominated by the frames of merit, deficits and scarcity—indeed, these frames shape what teachers, parents, district leaders and public officials have thought possible to achieve through public school reform. Oakes and Rogers write:

> Powerful cultural narratives or "logics" frame these social struggles and give shape to how people make sense of schooling: the logic of merit, the logic of deficits, and the logic of scarcity. The first assumes that young people compete for schooling advantages with their talents and effort in a context of equal opportunity. The second presumes that low-income children, children of color, and their families are limited by cultural, situational, and individual deficits that schools cannot affect. That they systematically get fewer education and social advantages is a result of these deficits and not of structural problems in the educational system. The combined effect of these narratives is compounded today by a logic of scarcity—the belief that our society can afford only limited investment in public life and public education. Hence the supply of "quality" schooling is shrinking at the same time that good jobs (and middle-class lives) demand more and better education. Together, these narratives, or logics, make it difficult for Americans to see that inequality is the result of flawed policies and structures that undermine democracy."[21]

Educational inequities are preserved, then, by frames that justify the exclusion of large segments of our national population on the basis of inherent inadequacies, resulting from race, class, gender, and immigration status. Immigrant families in Miami don't work hard enough, youth in Philadelphia are not smart enough, and urban districts in general lack the resources to provide schools in the Bronx or south Los Angeles the level of support they need—or so the logic goes.

In contrast, education organizing proposes an alternative frame about equity and its role in a strong democracy. Organizing demands for educational improvement assert the "logic" of the *institutional failure* of school systems to educate poor children and children of color. This logic grounds accountability pressure for systemic reform and participatory strategies to help school-level educators work in new ways with students, parents, and community members. In the next chapter, we examine the results of this frame and the demands that flow from it. We present evidence of how organizing is beginning to influence district decisions and examine how involvement in schools is helping to shape more powerful and effective learning environments for students.

In chapter 6 we will return to the role of organizing in promoting strong democracy, and consider the impact of organizing demands for equity on the lives of the people who make them. Here it suffices to note that, for organizing groups, expanding equity in public education and strengthening democracy are deeply linked. Insisting on the right of children from poor communities and communities of color to be educated to their fullest potential brings new constituencies into the political process and increases transparency in public decision-making, thus expanding the possibility of greater democratic control over America's wealth of resources. The end goal, explains lead organizer Christopher Boston of MICAH, "is to create a just democracy that works for all people, not just for the upper and middle class."

CHAPTER TWO

Evidence of Success

In light of the increasingly ambitious goals of community organizing, what evidence do we have that organizing actually strengthens public education? Findings from our study reveal that community organizing strategies can indeed make major contributions to improving student learning in the schools and communities most in need. Across the sites in our study, we found strong and consistent evidence that effective community organizing efforts are helping to increase equity within school districts, build new forms of capacity in schools, and improve student educational outcomes. In this chapter, we review the evidence of community organizing success.

DISTRICT GAINS

An analysis of thirty-eight interviews with superintendents, school board members, and senior district staff found three main effects of organizing at the district level. First, organizing increased the responsiveness of district officials to the needs of low-income parents or youth of color. Responsiveness was demonstrated through regular meetings between education officials and organizing groups, as well as educators' participation in organizing events and public acknowledgement of organizing efforts. At several sites, organizing groups and educators reported meeting on a monthly or quarterly basis to discuss community concerns and the status of reform implementation. District officials routinely participated in organizing group trainings in Austin and as speakers in large-scale organizing events in Miami and Oakland. Officials in these districts, as well as in Chicago, Los Angeles, Philadelphia, and New York, attended joint press events to announce reforms that responded to organizing proposals, in addition to maintaining ongoing collaboration in joint reforms.

Second, district resource allocations reflected organizing groups' demands to preserve or expand equity. Education officials across the sites asserted that organizing groups helped to protect existing resources for low-performing, high-poverty schools, such as preserving the allocation formula for federal Title I funds for high-poverty schools in Philadelphia and maintaining the district's commitment to provide free school busing for poor children in Milwaukee. Organizing campaigns generated new state resources and additional local tax revenues through extensive voter education work. Examples of public investments include $153 million in bond monies for school facilities repairs in South Los Angeles, $50 million in additional state funding for parent training and teacher professional development in Texas, $11 million in state funds for the Grow Your Own teacher pipeline program in Illinois, and roughly $8 million for the Direct Instruction literacy program in Florida. Organizing efforts also secured substantial municipal investments in new school facilities development, as in the northwest Bronx, where, in response to parents' demands, city officials created fourteen thousand new seats to relieve overcrowding in elementary and middle schools. Organizing groups' involvement helped districts and reform partners to attract philanthropic grants to support community-initiated school reform efforts. In 2000, for example, the Bill & Melinda Gates Foundation provided $20 million to OCO's reform partner in support of the Oakland small-schools reform. Similar (although smaller) philanthropic commitments were reported in Austin, Los Angeles, and Philadelphia.

Third, new policy initiatives reflected priorities and values consistent with community groups' reform proposals. These efforts included the ten-year district strategy of small-school creation in Oakland and a similar, more recent effort in Philadelphia; new teacher and principal professional development to increase parent engagement in Austin and Oakland; college-preparatory curriculum policy in Los Angeles; statewide legislation for the Grow Your Own teacher recruitment and preparation strategy in Illinois; the introduction of the Direct Instruction literacy curriculum in Miami; and amendments to the districtwide testing policies in Philadelphia and student promotion policy in New York City. In several cases, new initiatives specified explicit roles for community organizing groups.

The extent of groups' influence varies widely across districts and is shaped by organizing strategy, campaign demands, and organizational strength as well as opportunities in the local and state context. These factors will be explored in later chapters. Here we emphasize our finding that across urban districts, superintendents, school board members, and other education officials assert that organizing groups enhance their ability to address the needs of underserved low-income, African American, Latino, and immigrant communities in their districts.

Although school-reform organizing can be confrontational, we argue that the demands made by organizing groups provide essential political space for school system leaders to act for equity in their districts. Indeed, as Paul Vallas, former chief executive officer of the School District of Philadelphia, observes: parent- and youth-led groups are valued partners because of their focus on "making sure that all schools have the same resources and that those schools that are struggling, those schools that are more racially and economically isolated, have access to the additional resources they need."

SCHOOL-LEVEL IMPACTS

A long history of educational research suggests that achieving school transformation requires an extended period of time. Schools can make modest changes around the periphery in a year or two, but substantive change in the core of the organization demands a persistent focus across at least five years or more.[1] Moreover, as decades of failed reform make clear, not all changes improve the quality of schools.

All the sites in our study won commitments in campaigns to address school-level problems such as fixing school escalators, increasing access to college counselors, and improving course scheduling. Community organizing theory suggests that these kinds of campaigns are important to the development of leadership and a sense of collective efficacy in parents and youth. They help coalesce a group around a sense of its own potency as a force for change, and encourage other parents and students to join the reform effort. Yet as community groups are quick to note, sporadic and disconnected improvements are rarely powerful enough to stimulate broad improvement in the capacity of schools to support student learning.

Andi Perez of Youth United for Change observes, "Fighting for an in-school suspensions policy is really nice, but it's not going to improve the quality of education at Mastbaum High School. Is it a worthy cause? Absolutely. Is it a good first campaign in a school? Yes, it is. But now what? How can we really have a long-term effect on education reform in the schools that we're at?"

When organizing groups have pursued structural reforms, they have struggled against the constant churning of staff and leadership in schools. Long-standing research suggests that "one of the most powerful factors known to take its toll on continuation [of reform] is staff and administrative turnover."[2] Such transitions disrupt reform implementation, and make it unlikely that an incremental strategy of "small wins" will last long enough to reshape schools. Indeed, this is one feature that distinguishes education organizing from other types of issue work (like housing, for example, where serial victories can substantively improve housing conditions). In education organizing, Andi Perez notes, the role of school-level campaigns is to build "increments of power in a community, and enough credibility and recognition that when the political conditions exist we can go after some really big reform."

In several sites, after years of localized campaigns, organizing groups built campaigns to win systemic reform. The resulting curriculum policy (Los Angeles), small schools (Philadelphia), and new teacher pipeline program (Illinois), all won in 2005, require time to become lodged deeply enough at the school level to produce gains in capacity and learning. Studies suggest that these strategies *should* produce substantial gains in schools given the focus of reform, but the initiatives have not been in place long enough to assess effects.

In three sites where intensive and sustained school-level organizing was carried out for at least five years, we found evidence of improved capacity in the climate, professional culture, and instructional core of schools. We discuss the findings from these three sites next.

Assessing School Capacity

Our analysis of school-level impact examines the extent to which organizing activities helped to stimulate gains in *school capacity*, which we define as the ability of schools to support successful student learning. In this analysis, we draw primarily on our survey of 509 teachers in Oakland, Miami, and Austin to assess perceptions of their schools' climate, professional culture, and instructional core. This survey used a comparison group design in which teacher responses in schools involved in organizing were compared with responses from teachers in schools where the group was either not involved or minimally involved.

Successful schools are characterized by safe and trust-based school climates, collegial and collaborative professional cultures, and coherent and ambitious instruction. These core elements, or domains, are represented conceptually in figure 2.1 as building blocks of high-functioning schools. We define each of the building blocks of school capacity in more detail and share survey findings of the impact of organizing in the remaining sections of this chapter. As our focus in this chapter is to provide a broad overview of impact, our discussion is cursory in nature. We will turn to reform strategies in part II and elaborate there how each group's education organizing contributed to the school capacity gains reported by teachers in these sites.

Our school-capacity framework draws on a decade of research by the Consortium on Chicago School Research (CCSR) to define core aspects of school structure and functioning that make a difference to educational quality. CCSR's research identifies five "essential learning supports" (leadership, parent-community ties, professional capacity, student-centered learning climate, and ambitious instruction) that are associated with better student outcomes. While ambitious instruction was the single most direct factor influencing student learning, CCSR found that improved student learning was more likely to occur when reforms also focused on improvements in the other four supports. Schools strong in most of the essential supports were at least ten times more likely than schools weak in most of the supports to show extensive gains in both reading and math.[3]

FIGURE 2.1   Core indicators of school capacity

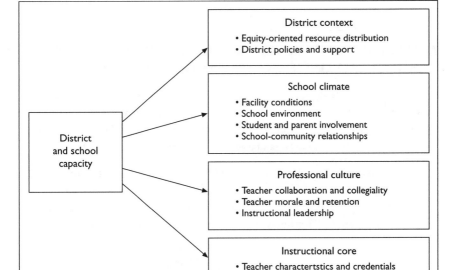

In addition, our framework also draws on Anthony Bryk and Barbara Schneider's work on trust in schools, Richard Elmore's writings on teaching practice, the National Center for Education Statistics' articulation of school quality indicators, and research on indicators of education organizing conducted by Eva Gold and Elaine Simon at Research for Action and Chris Brown at the Cross City Campaign for Urban School Reform.[4]

In three school districts where intensive and sustained school-level organizing was carried out for at least five years, teacher surveys show broad improvement in school capacity across clusters of schools (see "Assessing the Effect of School-Level Organizing on School Capacity Across Clusters of Schools in Three Districts"). With few exceptions, schools involved in organizing by Austin Interfaith, PACT, and OCO exhibited significantly higher levels of capacity across the climate, professional culture, and instructional core of schools. (See tables 2.1 and 2.2 for a summary of teacher survey findings across sites). On school-capacity dimensions where statistically detectible effects were not evident, in most cases, we found negligible differences between the averages of schools where organizing was taking place and those where organizing groups were not involved. In very few instances did we find an effect in favor of the comparison group. Such a strong, consistent trend across three different sites underscores the potential of intensive school-based organizing strategies to help improve school capacity.

ASSESSING THE EFFECT OF SCHOOL-LEVEL ORGANIZING ON SCHOOL CAPACITY ACROSS CLUSTERS OF SCHOOLS IN THREE DISTRICTS

Different comparison designs were developed for teacher surveys in Austin, Miami, and Oakland to account for differences in the reform strategy and effects. There were no significant differences in teacher demographics, years of experience, and professional credentials between target and comparison schools.

- In Miami, we compared teacher perceptions of school capacity at schools where PACT had been involved versus teacher perceptions of school capacity at schools where PACT had not been involved. The survey response rate was 57 percent in ten PACT schools and 64 percent in three comparison schools.

- In Austin, Austin Interfaith's organizing influenced a majority of low-performing elementary schools in the district, making it difficult to define a comparison group of demographically similar noninvolved schools. Our survey compared schools highly involved with Austin Interfaith against those with lower levels of involvement, arguably creating a higher bar for differences to become evident. The survey response rate was 69 in four high-involvement Alliance Schools, and 59 percent in two low-involvement schools.

- Similarly, all of the new small schools in Oakland were the result of OCO's districtwide organizing efforts, and practices at the new schools were influenced by OCO's participation in district-wide training sessions for new principals and teachers. The survey compared new small schools with existing large schools, even though the district's remaining large schools enrolled fewer Latino students, ELL students, and students receiving free or reduced-cost lunch than their small school counterparts.[a] The survey response rate was 48 percent in nine OCO small schools and 34 percent in four comparison schools.

[a] *An Evaluation of the Oakland New Small School Initiative: A Report for the Oakland Unified School District* (Oakland, CA: Strategic Measurement and Evaluation, Inc., 2007).

The depth and range of school-level effects depends on the particular school-based organizing strategy groups implemented. For example, PACT helped monitor the implementation of its Direct Instruction literacy intervention through supportive visits and conversations with classroom teachers, while Austin Interfaith worked closely with principals in Alliance Schools to build school-based organizing committees and develop school-improvement campaigns. Still, the evidence from Austin, Miami, and Oakland suggests that the impacts of organizing efforts are strongest in the school climate domain, with strong to moderate effects evident on a range of professional culture indicators. Teachers in these schools credited organizing groups with a high degree of influence on school climate and professional culture improvements (see tables 2.1 and 2.2).

School Climate

School climate refers not only to the physical environment of a school, but also to the sense of community and safety within the school, the sense of trust between teachers and parents, and parent involvement in school.[5] Our teacher surveys show effects across these indicators, with the strongest effects in Austin and Oakland schools. Statistically significant positive effects were found in at least two of the three sites on measures of the sense of community and safety in schools, teacher outreach to parents, and parental influence in shared decision making. Small positive effects were also evident on measures of an achievement-oriented culture and knowledge of student cultures.

TABLE 2.1   Teacher perceptions of school capacity

Domain	Teacher survey measures	Miami (n = 232; comparison n = 64)	Oakland (n = 29; comparison n = 70)	Austin (n = 95; comparison n = 49)
School climate	Sense of community and safety	+	+	+
	Knowledge of student cultures	(•)	•	•
	Achievement-oriented culture	•	•	+
	Parent involvement in school			+
	Teacher outreach to parents		+	+
	Teacher-parent trust			+
	Parent influence in student learning		•	
	Parent influence in shared decision-making (elementary school and middle school)		+	+
	Student influence in shared decision making (high school)		•	
Professional culture	Peer collaboration	+	+	+
	Collective responsibility		+	+
	Teacher-teacher trust	•	•	+
	School commitment	+	+	+
	Teacher influence in SDM		+	+
	Joint problem-solving		+	+
	Teacher-principal trust			•
	Principal instructional leadership		•	
Instructional core	Teacher influence in classroom		+	+
	Educational practices/beliefs	•		
	Coherent curriculum and instruction	•	(•)	•
	Instructional focus			
	Classroom resources			•

Key: + = Statistically significant; • = Not statistically significant, but small effect size in favor of the schools influenced by organizing; (•) = Small effect in favor of comparison schools

TABLE 2.2   Teacher perceptions of the influence of organizing on school capacity

Domain	Teacher survey measures	Miami (*n* = 60)	Oakland (*n* = 16)	Austin (*n* = 46)
School climate	Sense of community and trust in school	+	+	+
	School's relations with the community	+	+	+
	Safety and discipline in the school	+	•	•
	How students get along with each other	+		•
	School's relations with parents	+	+	+
	Parent involvement in school	+	+	+
	How teachers get along with parents	+	•	+
	Shared SDM between students, parents, teachers, and administrators	+	+	+
	Physical condition of the school building	+	+	•
	Changes in school overcrowding	•	+	•
Professional culture	How teachers get along with each other	+		•
	Commitment to the school	+		•
	Quality of principal leadership	+	•	+
	Professional development opportunities	+		•
Instructional core	Teacher expectations for student achievement	+		•
	Quality of curriculum and instruction	+		•
	Teaching effectiveness	+		•
	Classroom resources	+	•	•
Student learning	Student academic performance	+		•

Key: + = 2.0–3.0 on a 3-point scale, indicated high influence; • = 1.5–1.9 on a 3-point scale, indicated some influence

These aspects of school climate are closely linked to Anthony Bryk and Barbara Schneider's notion of *relational trust*.[6] Drawing on a decade-long study of more than four hundred Chicago elementary schools, Bryk and Schneider argue that the nature of "social exchanges" within schools between teachers, teachers and students, teachers and parents, teachers and administrators, and administrators and parents condition a school's capacity to improve. Importantly, Bryk and Schneider assert that the relationship between trust and improvement is not causal—improving trust does not automatically generate improved student outcomes. But improvement is highly unlikely to occur in schools that lack trust. They write:

> We view the need to develop relational trust as an essential component both to governance efforts that focus on bringing incentives to bear on improving practice and to instructional reforms that seek to deepen the technical capacities of school professionals. Absent more supportive social relations between all adults who share responsibility for student development and who remain mutually dependent on each other to achieve success, new policy initiatives are unlikely to produce desired outcomes. Similarly, new technical resources, no matter how sophisticated in design or well supported in implementation, are not likely to be used well, if at all.[7]

Effective social relationships are thus an important resource in schools that produce gains in student learning.

School-based organizing efforts by Austin Interfaith, OCO, and PACT specifically targeted social exchanges by increasing parent engagement and fostering new accountability relationships between school staff and parents and community members. OCO and Austin Interfaith, in particular, describe their organizing as an effort to build a "relational culture" within schools by coordinating teacher and principal home visits, creating and staffing school-based organizing committees, and coaching teachers and parents on effective community engagement practices.

School climate effects were less pronounced in Miami schools, likely due to PACT's focus on supporting the implementation of Direct Instruction, rather than broad-based school climate interventions. PACT's community engagement strategy combined weekly visits from parents trained in the methods of Direct Instruction, community events to celebrate school achievements, and continued advocacy with district officials on behalf of schools. In a small number of schools, PACT worked intensively to build parent committees that planned and carried out school-improvement campaigns. Interviews with educators in these schools suggest a positive impact on educator-parent relationships.

Professional culture

Key elements of professional culture include collaborative and collegial relationships between teachers, strong instructional leadership, high teacher morale and retention, as well as ample opportunities for relevant and high quality professional development.[8]

Why does improvement on indicators of professional culture matter? Put simply, schools that have stronger *professional cultures* have a higher capacity to implement strategies for improvement. Variously referred to as *professional capacity* and *collaborative professional community*, professional culture is a foundational capacity for successful schools.[9] Researcher and educator Michael Fullan observes, "The quality of working relationships among teachers is strongly related to implementation [of reform]. Collegiality, open communication, trust, support and help, learning on the job, getting results, and job satisfaction and morale are closely interrelated."[10] Indeed, as Richard Elmore argues, school reforms often fail to improve student achievement precisely because they fail to engage the deep structure of faculty relationships and norms in schools.[10] A shared understanding among school faculty of their responsibility for improving student learning and of the standards for high-quality student work is crucial, as is a practice of collaboration within schools in which faculty work together to assess and refine curriculum and pedagogy in relation to student progress.

Schools involved in organizing efforts show particularly strong effects on measures of professional culture, consistent with the focus of each group's organizing strategy. Strong to moderate effects were evident in at least two sites on measures of peer collaboration, sense of school commitment, collective responsibility, joint problem solving, and teacher influence in school decision making.

Austin Interfaith and OCO's organizing generated new opportunities for collaboration among faculty by encouraging honest dialogue about school problems, and providing a variety of leadership development opportunities that helped educators to build deeper relationships with each other. In Miami schools, PACT's advocacy produced resources for "reading super-coaches" at the district and quarterly professional development for teachers using Direct Instruction. Consistent with these strategies, teachers in Austin and Miami reported that the groups had strongly influenced various aspects of their schools' professional culture. As professional development supports to the new small schools in Oakland were provided by the Bay Area Coalition of Essential Schools (BayCES), teachers were less likely to credit OCO with influencing gains in this area.

In addition to teacher collegiality, morale and professional development, professional culture also refers to instructional leadership. There is substantial literature on the important role of principals in school improvement, and on the difficulties of making reform happen when principal leadership is weak.[12] Yet while instructional leadership is typically associated with principals, it also can be exhibited through teacher roles in school decision-making. As a number of studies assert, developing norms of distributed leadership in schools can help build shared ownership for instructional improvement across school faculty members.[13]

Though significant effects on teacher influence in decision-making were evident in two sites, there were no significant differences in the area of instructional leadership between schools targeted by groups and the comparison schools. However, teachers reported that PACT and Austin Interfaith's involvement in their schools had a high level of influence on their principals' leadership capacity, with teachers in Oakland reporting a lower level of influence. In Miami, the instructional supports provided by Direct Instruction, combined with PACT's visible support for principals, likely influenced teacher perceptions of principal effectiveness. Austin Interfaith and OCO both worked closely with principals to help shape their vision for schools and encouraged principals to integrate collaborative and relational practices among teachers. Teacher perceptions in Oakland may be influenced by BayCES's presence and its role in providing professional expertise to the small school reforms.

Instructional core

Elements of *instructional core* refers to what happens in the classroom, including teachers' educational practices and beliefs regarding student abilities, a clear instructional focus and coherent curriculum of instruction, instructional materials and resources, and student engagement.[14] Because classroom practices have been historically distal from the targeted work of organizing groups, as well as a more difficult arena to penetrate, it is natural that fewer significant results and less pronounced effects are found in this domain. Teacher surveys show a moderate-small effect on teacher influence in the classroom in Austin and Oakland. Not surprisingly, teachers attributed high influence to PACT in this area, given the focus of its advocacy—a literacy intervention.

Though teacher surveys identified few statistically significant effects on the instructional core of schools, our interview data suggest that the reforms organizing groups have introduced are changing classroom expectations. Alison McDonald, high school principal of Life Academy, a new small school in Oakland, observes the emergence of a "culture in the school that we have to academically challenge students." Principals in Austin and Miami reported similar effects.

IMPROVED STUDENT EDUCATIONAL OUTCOMES

Arguably, understanding the extent to which organizing (or any intervention) ultimately improves student outcomes is the most crucial test of impact. Test scores are the most commonly used barometers of student achievement, yet there are well-documented problems with test-score data.[15] Changes in tests over time make it difficult to assess real improvement versus artificial gains, and the exclusion of special populations, such as English language learners, may skew the assessment of overall student performance. Perhaps most importantly, questions persist about what standardized tests actually measure and the extent to which test scores are a relevant indicator of achievement.

Nonetheless, improved test scores were evident across a critical mass of schools in Austin, Miami and Oakland with sustained school-level organizing. In Philadelphia, there is descriptive, early evidence of positive trends in student engagement on a large high school campus in the form of higher student attendance rates and college aspirations.

In Oakland, new small schools developed with support from OCO received significantly higher ratings on the California Academic Performance Index (API) than the large schools from which they emerged, at all three levels—elementary, middle, and high school. New small high schools also show early signs of lower dropout rates and higher percentages of graduates who have completed the college-preparatory curriculum required for entry into the state college and university system than the large schools from which they emerged. These findings are consistent with the results of a 2007 analysis of student-level data conducted by Strategic Measurement and Evaluation, Inc. for the Oakland Unified School District.[16]

In Miami, the percentage of students meeting standards in reading on the Florida Comprehensive Assessment Test (FCAT) jumped from 27

percent to 49 percent between 2001 and 2005 in elementary schools implementing the Direct Instruction literacy program combined with intensive
community engagement support from PACT. Figure 2.2 shows that schools
targeted by PACT's organizing made larger gains than the district, and out-
paced a demographically similar comparison group of schools in the third
and fourth grades.

During the same time period, schools with Direct Instruction reduced
the percentage of students scoring at the lowest achievement level on FCAT
from 58 percent to 32 percent. Figure 2.3 shows that the 2001 cohort of
schools implementing Direct Instruction began with larger percentages of
fourth-grade students scoring at the lowest level on the FCAT, and out-
paced the district and comparison group schools in moving students out of
level 1.

FIGURE 2.2   Percent gain in mean scale scores on the Florida
Comprehensive Assessment Test (FCAT)

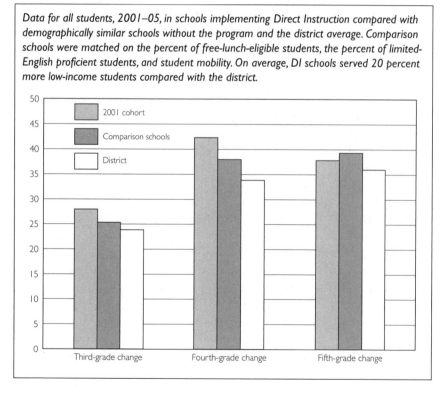

Data for all students, 2001–05, in schools implementing Direct Instruction compared with demographically similar schools without the program and the district average. Comparison schools were matched on the percent of free-lunch-eligible students, the percent of limited-English proficient students, and student mobility. On average, DI schools served 20 percent more low-income students compared with the district.

FIGURE 2.3   Percent of fourth-grade students scoring at level I on the FCAT, 2001–05

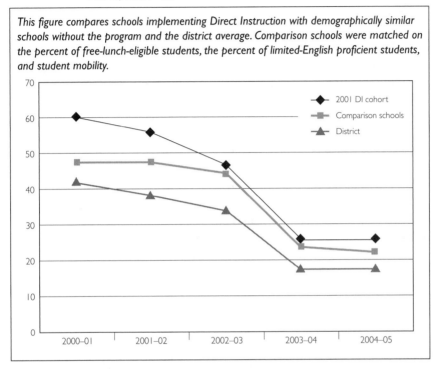

This figure compares schools implementing Direct Instruction with demographically similar schools without the program and the district average. Comparison schools were matched on the percent of free-lunch-eligible students, the percent of limited-English proficient students, and student mobility.

These findings are consistent with the theory of action behind PACT's dual strategy of Direct Instruction combined with community engagement support. They are also consistent with findings from a federally funded review of reading interventions by the Comprehensive School Reform Quality Center (CSRQC), which suggests that Direct Instruction is an effective program in fostering reading skills in low-income children of color.[17] Though there is scant literature on the effects of community engagement strategies on schooling improvement, the literature on educational change suggests that efforts to recognize educators' improvement efforts can help to sustain and deepen reform.[18]

In Austin, analyses of school administrative data show a significant positive relationship between the level of a school's involvement in Alliance School activities and student performance on standardized tests. Because the Alliance School model consists of a number of core activities, we were able to assess implementation on the basis of school involvement in these core activities. Our regression model tested the relationship between each Alliance School's "intensity" of involvement in organizing (specifically, the extent of implementation of core Alliance School activities) and the percent of students meeting minimum expectations on the state-mandated tests (see table 2.3). The analysis controlled for the percentage of students participating in the federal free or reduced-cost lunch program, the percentage designated Limited English Proficient, and student test scores in the baseline year. In other words, we looked at how variation in the level (or "intensity") of a school's involvement with Austin Interfaith influenced gains on student test scores above and beyond the effects of known predictors—poverty, language proficiency, and previous performance on tests. Our analyses found that the greater the intensity of Austin Interfaith's organizing in schools, the more likely the school was to experience gains in student test scores.

Again, these findings are consistent with the theory of action guiding Austin Interfaith's reform strategy—namely, that building a culture of participation and mutual accountability in schools can help to improve student learning. Interestingly, the length of time of involvement in Alliance School activities was not a statistically significant predictor of improved student performance independent of intensity. Continued low involvement was not equivalent to high involvement for a shorter period of time.

Lastly, in Philadelphia, new small high schools on the Kensington high school educational campus developed with support from Youth United for Change show 10 percent gains in student attendance and 25 percent gains in the percent of graduates planning to attend college between 2003–04 and 2005–06. Though these are preliminary trends, district administrators noted the improvements as evidence of the impact of YUC's advocacy and participation in schools. Former Philadelphia School District CEO Paul Vallas observes, "YUC has been largely responsible for the shape that those schools are taking."

HOW IS COMMUNITY ORGANIZING IMPROVING SCHOOLS?

What is the import of these findings? The evidence suggests that organizing efforts are helping increase equity, capacity, and outcomes in urban school districts. The high degree of convergence across our data—teacher surveys, district and school administrator interviews, and school-level administrative records—is remarkable, pointing toward a positive relationship between education organizing and educational change. Yet these gains

TABLE 2.3   Austin Interfaith hierarchical regression

Summary of hierarchical regression analysis for intensity[†] of Austin Interfaith organizing predicting the percent of all students (grades 3, 4, and 5) meeting minimum expectations in all subjects on the Texas Assessment of Academic Skills, 1994–2002.

Variable	B	SE B	Beta
Step 1			
(Constant)	47.62	20.87	—
% of all students that met minimum expectations at baseline	0.48	0.20	0.58**
% of LEP students, 2001–2002	0.33	0.16	0.48*
% of economically disadvantaged students, 2001–02	−0.02	0.20	−0.02
Step 2			
(Constant)	33.55	18.09	—
% of all students that met minimum expectations at baseline	0.43	0.16	0.52**
% of LEP students, 2001–02	0.16	0.15	0.24
% of economically disadvantaged students, 2001–02	0.11	0.17	0.14
A.I. intensity averages (until 2002)	3.82	1.58	0.50**

Notes:
N = 14
R Square = .518 for Step 1 (p = .055*)
R Square Change = .190 for Step 2 (p = .039*)
*p < .10, **p < 0.05 (Due to the small sample size, we use a p-value of .10 to test for statistical significance.)

In a multiple regression analysis, the b-coefficient indicates the size of the effect that the independent variable (in this case, the intensity of Austin Interfaith's organizing) has on the dependent variable (test scores), controlling for the influence of the other variables in the model. The sign of the coefficient indicates the direction of the effect, whether it is positive or negative. In this table, the b-coefficient indicates that the percent of students who met minimum standards on the TAAS can be expected to increase by 3.82 points for every unit of increase in the intensity of Austin Interfaith's organizing. Thus, the model predicted gains in the range of 15–19 percentage points for high-involvement schools.

"SE B" refers to the standard error of the B coefficient, or the amount that the b-coefficient varies across cases. "Beta" is a standardized form of the B coefficient that facilitates comparison across multiple analyses. The p-value indicates the probability that the effect of the independent variable on the dependent variable is due to chance. "R Square" indicates the percentage variance in students meeting the minimum standard on TAAS that is explained by the variable. "R square change" indicates the additional variance explained by adding a new variable to the model in Step 2. In this table, an R Square Change of .190 at Step 2 indicates that 19% of the variance in the percent of students meeting the minimum standard on TAAS was accounted for when the Austin Intensity score was added to the regression model.

[†]*Intensity* refers to a school's level of participation in core Alliance School activities. Each school was assigned an intensity score from 1 (low) to 5 (high) for each year of its involvement in Austin Interfaith organizing between 1994 and 2002.

are tenuous—improvements were not consistently evident across sites, nor consistently sustained across schools within sites.

In the tumultuous context of urban school systems, organizing groups face the challenge of sustaining reform while deepening the gains in school capacity and student learning. Though this challenge exists for all reform efforts, it is particularly significant for organizing groups because their work aims to disrupt the priorities, assumptions, and practices that have sanctioned poor school performance for so long.

Michelle Renée and her colleagues, Jeannie Oakes and Kevin Welner, have observed that the kinds of reform organizing groups propose engage what she calls *third-order change*—that is, change not only in the basic operations of schools, but in "educators' and community members' core beliefs about such matters as race, class, intelligence and educability."[19] Clearly, reformers must attend to the technical aspects of schooling, such as improving instructional rigor or the quality of teacher professional development in low performing urban schools. Each of the sites in our study proposed technical strategies for improving a wide range of schooling conditions and educator competencies. But, as organizing groups are well aware, a reliance on technical policies and practices "neglects the reality that normative and political forces, as well as inertial forces, would likely keep this reform from going forward."[20] Because third-order changes confront prevailing relationships between race, class, and educational opportunity, they are likely to engender resistance, even outright hostility, during implementation so as to protect and maintain the status quo. As Renée et al. note—and the superintendents we interviewed concur—continued and persistent outside force helps to root new technical strategies and foster a political and normative climate conducive to equity-oriented reform.[21]

How and why groups succeed in changing schools is discussed in detail in the next section of this book. Each chapter highlights examples of organizing campaigns to demonstrate the strategic choices organizing groups make as they grapple with the technical, political, and normative aspects of reform. As we will show, the promise of organizing lies not solely in the specific interventions that groups introduce in schools, although in some cases, these interventions have proven to be innovative, widely embraced, and effective in improving schools. Rather, the promise of organizing stems from its central premise that school reform must be conceptualized and pursued within a larger framework of community action and power. Educator and researcher Seymour Sarason reminds us, "No complicated, traditional social institution can be changed only from within. There has to be some support for change from within, but there also has to be strong external, powerful pressures for change, powerful in terms of numbers, influence, and legislative legal policymaking responsibilities. Absent those external pressures, the institution will continue the adage . . . the more things change, the more they remain the same."[22]

PART TWO

STRATEGIES THAT WORK

CHAPTER THREE

Transforming Schools

In 1998, Jefferson Elementary School in Oakland, California was a disheartening place. A steady stream of school-age children into the neighborhood had pushed student enrollment to eleven hundred, roughly four hundred students above the school's official space limit. In response, the school's administration instituted a year-round schedule and assigned students to one of four tracks that cycled through the school year. The track schedule forced teachers to relocate entire classrooms of supplies on a monthly basis, irritated parents, and did little to slow the downward trajectory of students' academic progress. Scores on the Academic Performance Index (API) hovered at a dismal 450, far below the state's proficiency target of 800. There were too many students, and too few resources to meet their needs.

The larger environs of the school echoed its occupants' fatigue and discouragement. The playground was overrun with portable trailers, parked by the school district to provide extra classroom space. In the words of one observer, "The campus—which sprawled across two unbroken city blocks—resembled an odd little city, with narrow, isolated alleys between the yellowish-tan trailers. The gaps between adjoining portables were covered by plywood, which eventually decayed, opening holes big enough to admit rats, or in some cases, children."[1]

By 2007, children in Oakland's Fruitvale neighborhood could choose from three small schools and one charter school, all of which were initiated directly or indirectly through the organizing efforts of Oakland Community Organizations. All four schools have student enrollments of 350 students or less, enabling teachers to develop close relationships with the students and their families. Two schools that have been open for at least three years have posted API scores of 675 and 723, substantially higher than those at the old Jefferson school.

The sea change in Oakland's flatland schools was stimulated by a potent combination of system- and school-level organizing. Across a ten-year period, OCO organized parents, clergy, and congregation members to develop and fight for a vision of radical reform, and then built long-term partnerships with educators in the district and the school-reform community to make this vision a reality.

In this chapter we examine three distinct and successful campaigns that contributed to positive school- and student-level effects. Each of these efforts developed deliberate and interconnected strategies to promote top-down and bottom-up reform, shown in figure 3.1. The entry point for each group's organizing campaign varied, as did the specific issues groups addressed, and the level of the system where they targeted their initial efforts. Organizing campaigns responded to local school conditions, district opportunities, and organizational factors. Yet all three organizations—Oakland Community Organizations, Austin Interfaith, and People Acting for Community Together—worked to build a favorable district context characterized by supportive policy, new resources, and increased attention to low-performing schools by district and municipal leaders. At the same time, each group carried out school-level work that built new forms of parent and community engagement, new relationships between families and educators, and a shared focus on learning in schools.

FIGURE 3.1   Cycle of change

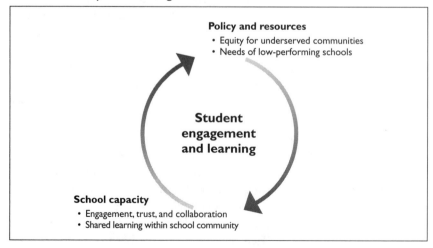

A STRATEGY OF STRUCTURAL REFORM

Oakland's small-school story begins in churches, where parents met to discuss their concerns and imagine new possibilities for their children's educational futures. As a congregation-based group, OCO relied on a structure of local organizing committees to build campaigns for change. Initial school-related campaigns established drug-free school zones to improve the safety of students walking to and from school. In 1997, congregation members at St. Elizabeth's Parish—many of whom had children attending Jefferson and Hawthorne elementary schools—turned their attention to the persistent and worsening problem of school overcrowding.

Emma Paulino became involved in OCO through those meetings. A mother of two, Paulino had struggled to help her son, who had been passed along into third grade even though he could barely spell his own name. His teachers assured her "he was fine," Paulino recalls, but he was so far behind she knew things were not okay. When Paulino saw OCO's analysis of school size and student achievement, the district's stark inequities became clear. "The system wasn't working," she says.[2]

The idea of replacing Oakland's large failing schools with small schools emerged from a book that an OCO organizer, Matt Hammer, came across as he was researching alternatives to Oakland's large failing schools. Written by Deborah Meier, *The Power of Their Ideas* introduced Hammer and the parents to two small schools in Harlem that had succeeded in creating a personalized and academically engaging learning environment in a struggling district.[3] The book captured parents' imaginations: "What if we were able to start our own school, like Debbie Meier did?" That year, while their children attended weekly Saturday morning catechism classes, the parents met with Hammer to develop their vision for a new small school.

In 1998, the OCO local organizing committee at St. Elizabeth's Parish presented Jefferson school officials with a proposal to open a small-school pilot within Jefferson Year-Round Elementary School. A small group of teachers there had worked with parents to develop the plan and strongly supported the effort. But the majority of school faculty, including the teachers' union representative and the principal, feared that creating a new small school would make conditions worse for those left behind. By drawing staff away from the larger school, the small school would exacerbate the monthly cycle of packing, moving, and unpacking for the teachers who remained.

Yet a vision of small schools had taken hold in Oakland. OCO leaders at St. Elizabeth's would not give up on the idea, and OCO leaders from other congregation organizing committees soon joined the effort. Within months, what had been the project of a single organizing committee had expanded into a core issue for the broader organization. Frustrated by the failed effort at Jefferson, OCO began exploring the feasibility of charter schools. OCO also arranged a two-day visit to New York City to see small schools in action.

Education organizer Elizabeth Sullivan traces her work with OCO to the visit to New York City. In 1998, Sullivan was a leader in a nearby OCO church and a teacher in a neighboring district. "Until that point, I had been a cynic," she says. "When I went to New York City, I was just amazed. Going to those schools and seeing kids of color—kids that looked just like our kids, black and brown kids, and seeing the quality of education that they were getting. It was like realizing that you've been blind and all of a sudden you can see or something. I realized that in California we had just settled for such mediocrity." She continues: "In California as a whole, the teaching force is white, middle-class, and doesn't tend to live in the inner cities. They don't live in the communities that they serve. And there are a lot of internalized low expectations. The teachers don't realize it. If you were to say, 'Well, you're racist,' they would be completely offended and hurt. But yet, they don't realize that what they're expecting for kids is much, much less than what the kids can actually do. And that really hit me when we were in New York."

OCO's charter school explorations led to a joint effort with an education management organization to develop proposals for five new small schools. Based on its experiences at Jefferson, OCO expected that the Oakland teachers' union would strongly oppose the charter schools as an "attempt to whittle away contract protections," Sullivan says, although that was not OCO's intent. OCO leaders held meetings with school board members and then-mayor Jerry Brown to seek their support, and in April 1999, the school board unanimously approved the charter school plan.

Two new charter schools opened the following school year, and one of these charters, Dolores Huerta Academy, served students in Jefferson's catchment area. The new small schools gave parents and teachers an opportunity to shape small, intimate communities.[4] But challenges in finding building space, hiring principals and teachers, and building a functional and effective school culture—all within a three month planning period—taught OCO important lessons that were to shape its future small schools work.

First, creating successful learning environments required a framework of support to help schools clear the logistical hurdles involved in start-up, build a shared vision of educational quality, and access necessary professional expertise (coaching, professional development) for new and often less-experienced staff.

Second, and equally important, creating a handful of small schools would not stem the crisis of poor educational outcomes for African American and Latino students in flatland schools. A districtwide strategy was needed.

In 1999, OCO launched its fight for larger-scale district reform. The visit to New York had generated a new—and ultimately pivotal—relationship with a local education reform group, the Bay Area Coalition of Equitable Schools (BayCES), that specialized in teacher professional development and embraced many of the core principles of Deborah Meier's schools. BayCES and OCO knew from research on small schools that size in itself would not lead to better outcomes.[5] Thus local autonomy, along with an emphasis on parent and community engagement, became the core of their vision for Oakland's small schools. In these new schools, parents and educators wrote, every child would be known by name, safe, and challenged to do their best by "dedicated, well-prepared teachers. They need to be surrounded by a supportive community of caring adults. Parents, teachers and students are all essential partners."[6]

Consistent with this vision, OCO organizer Liz Sullivan conducted individual meetings with hundreds of teachers. "After our experience at Jefferson, we realized that we were going to need to organize teachers, we couldn't do it without teachers," Sullivan says. "It was unlikely that the teachers' union was going to help us do this, and so we just started organizing teachers ourselves."

OCO and BayCES partnered to draft a proposal for a new district policy of small-school creation and met with school board members, district officials, and educators to build political support for the reform strategy. OCO also mobilized thousands of congregation members, public school parents, and community supporters to a public action to present the small schools proposal to elected officials. The public event, combined with behind-the-scenes meetings with district and municipal leaders and BayCES' educational expertise succeeded in winning district support. "OCO [could] get five thousand people out to a meeting," observes then–school board member Greg Hodge. In the face of OCO's pressure, district leadership "didn't have a lot of choice." Though the teachers' union did not endorse the effort, it did not actively oppose it either.

In 2000, the district passed a new policy to create ten small schools. The new policy mandated the creation of design teams consisting of parents and educators to shape the vision and practices of each new small school. The school district strategically targeted communities for new-school creation where organizing was taking place.

Former district superintendent Dennis Chaconas aimed to use OCO's political strength to move reform. "The system is so dysfunctional that if you don't have advocates pushing your agenda all over the city, you're not going to be able to move to transform it," he explains. "OCO had already demonstrated over the years that it was consistently able to turn out large numbers of people to beat up on politicians and agency heads who weren't producing what they wanted. I wanted to harness their organizing energy to help push my improvement agenda."

The new small-schools policy solidified a working partnership between the district's office of school reform, OCO, and BayCES. Together they created rubrics guiding principal selection, provided training to school staff on parent and community engagement strategies, and secured resources from private foundations to incubate the new school design teams.

As the first cohort of small schools opened, the work set off a cascade reaction within the district. Parents were involved and enthusiastic, teachers felt invested in the work. The energy behind the reforms prompted the question of how far the reforms could go, recalls OCO executive director Ron Snyder. Might the small schools form the core of a new district strategy to replace *all* of the district's large failing schools? "We began to think that we could actually get to a place where this whole district would look different. That this [was] not about ten small schools as a policy; this [was] a tipping-point strategy that moves to change the district," Snyder says.

In 2003, Dennis Chaconas was ousted in a state takeover prompted by a financial crisis. OCO held a two-thousand-person action prior to the appointment of the new state administrator and secured the support of influential state political leaders to carry the message of not abandoning the reform. These actions helped to persuade the incoming administrator, Randolph Ward, to adopt the small school reforms as the cornerstone of his reform efforts, and later to expand the district's Office of School Reform into the New School Development Group to support the expansion in new school creation. Throughout this period, OCO's involvement in the reform moved between system and school level activities. The organization maintained a constant presence in the city's political landscape, creating events that would keep "organized parents and teachers in front of these folks" to advocate for the reforms, notes Snyder.

Locally, OCO parent leaders and organizers actively participated in twenty-three school-design teams, often with prospective principals and teachers with whom OCO had already developed relationships. These local meetings, Snyder observes, gave teachers a space to dream about what kind of school they would like, and to dream "along with parents about what is possible."

In roughly a third of the new schools, OCO organizers also built school organizing committees, modeled on the organizing committees at OCO member congregations, to provide leadership training and help staff, as organizer Liz Sullivan puts it, "use the organizing model to look at relationships in the school and beyond." OCO worked closely with the initial cohort of small schools, conducting individual meetings with leaders, providing training opportunities, and problem solving to help build cohesive and effective school organizing committees. The support was crucial to avoid the internal power struggles and conflicts that can cause schools to "just fall apart," says Sullivan. OCO supported teacher-parent relationships in the schools through consistent leadership development training, and assisted school committees in conducting teacher-parent home visits for teachers to "get to know families, and the assets and hopes that they bring to the education system." Organizers recruited parent leaders to communicate with families about student data and "what parents ought to be looking for to make sure that their kids are getting good instruction," explains Ron Snyder.

Since passage of the small schools policy in 2000, the district has weathered bankruptcy, a state takeover, and three state-appointed superintendents. Throughout this tumultuous period, OCO fought to maintain the reform as fundamentally an effort of "parents and [education] professionals to generate equitable outcomes for kids." In doing so, OCO drew extensively on the resources and statewide reach of the PICO network, particularly in mobilizing other PICO network affiliates in California to advocate for the small school reform with state-level officials.

By all accounts, the Oakland story is a work in progress—twenty-two failing schools have closed, and by the 2007–2008 academic year, a total of forty-eight new small schools had arisen in their place. The new schools surpass their predecessors on key indicators of progress. Gains are evident in school climate and culture, with teachers in the small schools reporting greater parent and community engagement, higher levels of trust and collaboration among educators and between school faculty and community members, and a stronger focus on student learning. API scores of the small schools are on average 75 to 100 points higher than in the schools they replaced. Though API scores in flatland schools are still below the state's benchmark of 800, the higher scores coming from these small schools are a hopeful sign of the district's progress toward educational equity.

In 2009, as the district approaches yet another leadership transition, OCO has turned its focus to what organizers call the "second stage" of reform, making sure that the new small schools go beyond personalized and family-friendly environments to provide a rigorous high-quality instructional program for students. "We've protected the small schools through five superintendents and a state takeover," says OCO parent leader Lillian Lopez. "Parents must stay organized to ensure that the small schools . . . continue to improve and thrive."[7]

A CULTURAL TRANSFORMATION IN LOW-PERFORMING SCHOOLS

Austin Interfaith's school-based organizing emerged from a state-level strategy. In 1992, the Texas Industrial Areas Foundation (IAF) won a commitment from the Texas Education Agency to direct new funds to low-performing schools through the new Texas Investment Capital Fund (ICF). This fund made grants available to low-performing schools to pay for teacher professional development, parent leadership training, and after-school enrichment activities.

With ICF funds, the IAF hoped to create an incentive for schools to join what IAF called the "Alliance School" network. IAF organizer Sister Christine Stephens, one of the founders of the IAF's work in Texas, recalls thinking "We've figured out how to work with congregations, but we don't know how to work with schools. Let's see whether some principals and teachers will want to work with us—who see the value in this, want to do something different, and want an organization that can give them some political cover to do it."

The Alliance School network proceeded from a simple yet powerful vision: to bring parents and community members into partnership with principals and teachers to confront problems from a position of shared self-interest in school improvement and a sense of collective self-efficacy. Using this vision, the IAF aimed to revitalize schools as centers of democracy. Sister Christine says, "The original impetus for public schools was to take immigrant children and other children, and teach them the skills that they needed to be in a free democracy. It's good for democracy, but it's also good for education. Being educated in an atmosphere where they see adults coming together and learning and practicing is good for kids."

Local organizers implemented in schools the same organizing methods they used in churches. Organizers conducted individual meetings with parents, teachers and the principal to agitate people around their story, imagination, and anger. Drawing on these one-on-one meetings, organizers convened small-group or house meetings to "try to understand what needs to be changed," recalls congregation leader Regina Rogoff.

Rogoff explains: "What are the problems that people face in their lives? How do we break those problems into issues that can be tackled? We don't work on hunger per se, but we may hear an example like our kids are unsupervised after school. We start studying that problem and the issue around after school care. We develop an action team, we start teaching people how to address an issue politically, and we develop a strategy."

In Austin, the first school to enter into an Alliance School partnership was Zavala Elementary School. During the previous year, principal Al Melton had tried to initiate a public conversation within the school community about the school's dismal performance on statewide standardized tests. Distrust among parents and teachers in the school sank the effort, with each side blaming the other for the school's poor performance. Almost half of the school's thirty-eight teachers left that year, and many parents pulled their children from the school.[8]

As conflicts within the school deepened, Melton reached out to Austin Interfaith for help. With coaching from organizer Joe Higgs, Melton started the conversation all over again. This time, following the IAF model, Melton focused on building relationships through one-on-one meetings and house meetings. The first activity the school undertook was a "neighborhood walk," in which pairs of school faculty and parents went to visit students' homes to talk with families about how things were going in the school and what needed to change.

From the walk, Melton and Higgs identified a group of parents, teachers, and community members interested in working as a core team to improve the school. With Higgs' guidance and training, the core team began to analyze the causes of Zavala's chronically poor performance. The team led a successful campaign to win city resources for student immunizations and a new school-based health clinic. The team subsequently led efforts to institute new language arts and mathematics curricula, a new policy to mainstream special education students into general education classrooms, joint instructional planning time for teachers, an after-school enrichment program, and an accelerated science program. Within two years, Zavala rose from its place among the bottom half of district elementary schools to being ranked first in student attendance. By the 1994–95 school year, the school surpassed the citywide average in reading and mathematics on the state-mandated Texas Assessment of Academic Skills.[9]

The Zavala experience taught the IAF that "we finally had a model of what was really successful," Sister Christine recalls. "It turned out to be something that very closely paralleled our congregational development. We began to understand that the principal and a group of teachers and parents have got to learn [the organizing process], and then they've got to be willing to teach it. The work can't be organizer-driven. There's got to be a lot of willingness on educators' part to change the culture of the school."

Word of Zavala's successes spread through the district. When Austin Interfaith began education organizing in the early 1990s, 48 percent of the district's 69,827 students qualified for the federal free and reduced-cost lunch program; 37 percent of students were Latino, 19 percent African American and 42 percent were white.[10] Districtwide, only 58 percent of the district's African American students and 62 percent of Latino students met the minimum state standards.[11] Though the Austin Independent School District (AISD) has a larger percentage of white middle-class students than many urban districts, these students live in wealthier enclaves on the west side of the district. The city's low-income population—predominantly Latino immigrants and African American families—live largely in the former industrial core of the city. Stories of rising parent involvement, student attendance, and teacher morale at Zavala attracted other high-poverty schools to the Alliance Schools effort.

Participation in the Alliance Schools network during the 1990s grew to involve roughly a quarter of the district's elementary schools and approximately half the district's high poverty schools. These schools drew attention not only for their successes, but also for *how* they achieved them. The idea of building a new *relational* culture in failing schools, based on the principles of trust, participation, and mutual accountability, stood in contrast to traditional forms of bureaucratic accountability. In a system of bureaucratic accountability, lines of authority and input operate vertically, encouraging principals and teachers to prioritize demands from the chain of command over the concerns of parents and community members.[12] In contrast, parents, teachers, and administrators in Alliance Schools learned about each other's motivations and how to problem solve as part of a core team that represented the school's constituencies.

Principal Joaquin Gloria recalls seeking out an administrative position at Ridgetop Elementary School because he wanted to be a relational leader, rather than a bureaucratic leader. "When I came here I thought I was relational. But I had learned to write memos," he says. Interfaith organizers challenged Gloria to stop "sitting at the computer half the day writing memos, and just go out and talk to people. I gave in right away because I could see the advantage."

Gloria explains, "I can sit up here and say you have to do this and that, but you know what, if you don't want to, if you don't like me, if you don't like the way I'm talking, you're not going to do it. I realized that if you work with teachers in a more relational way they'll do things for you that they normally would not. Parents are the same way."

The individual meetings that were the hallmark of the IAF model were infused in Alliance School culture as a strategy for identifying and cultivating new relationships and leadership among parents, teachers and administrators. Alliance Schools received ongoing training from Austin Interfaith organizers on organizing methods, so that they would be able to bring more members of the school community into the school's improvement work.

Core teams were used in Alliance Schools to surface and address school improvement concerns. The core team provided leadership in conducting conversations that solicited views from the larger school community. At Maplewood Elementary School, for example, "One of the big things we did was organize a potluck," says fifth-grade teacher Amanda Braziel. "We presented the questions: 'What do you see as barriers to your child's education? What do you think Maplewood is doing right and how could we change?' A lot of issues arose from those questions and so when we would meet as a core team, we would talk about how we could work on those issues."

Core teams also worked to integrate parent and community engagement activities into the routine of schools. Weekly parent-principal coffees and parent academies kept parents informed and created a regular dialogue with school faculty. Joaquin Gloria believes these activities helped to "break down some of the barriers so parents see school as a place where they can come and actually talk to somebody, where somebody will listen, and something will come out of the conversation." Parent academies introduced parents to district policies, standardized tests, and academic standards for each grade. At Ridgetop, faculty also organized curriculum nights on each core subject to introduce parents to the content and skills that their children learned in class.

In addition, parents and school faculty conducted annual neighborhood walks to meet students' families in their homes and discuss what was going on in the school. The neighborhood walks provided a way to build more parent involvement. "You look for leaders," Gloria says. "People in the community who have a passion for after-school care, they have a passion for . . . having enough volunteers in the school, for . . . having enough involvement or knowing enough about math or reading or whatever it is. And you take down those names and you tell those parents, 'Well, in the future we might ask you to come to a meeting.'"

Consistent with the IAF's belief that all issues come out of the local base, core teams defined the issues and strategies for improvement. But they did so with guidance from education experts with whom the organization had developed relationships. Austin Interfaith's statewide network created the Texas Interfaith Education Fund (TIEF) to provide research support and training opportunities to local affiliates. Parent leaders attended these training sessions, along with teachers, principals and members of Austin Interfaith congregations.

TIEF sessions were run like graduate school seminars, with small group discussions of issues related to IAF campaigns—budget cuts, state financing options, and health-care-reform strategies, in addition to new curriculum and instructional reforms. In these sessions, core teams talked informally with a wide variety of school-reform experts such as Howard Gardner, Richard Elmore, and Richard Murnane of Harvard University and Lauren Resnick of the Learning Research and Development Center at the University of Pittsburgh. These educators' ideas on children's learning styles, school organization, instructional leadership, and teacher professional development informed Alliance School activities.

Carrie Laughlin, a researcher at the Interfaith Education Fund, describes the IAF's "learning community" approach: "We read materials and we talk about them. Does this ring true? Does this relate to your experience? Each small group puts together a presentation based on their conversation that they present to the guest and the broader group. They ask questions, and they tell stories about their work, and how it either supports that academic's theory or doesn't." Academics loved the experience, Laughlin says: "[One author commented] 'I'm in a room with a hundred people who have all read my book very carefully and have analyzed it and thought about it, and connected it to the real world. You know,' he said, 'I can't get this anywhere else.'"

As the number of Alliance Schools grew, Austin Interfaith worked with educators, including the teachers' union, to infuse professional development sessions with IAF principles and community organizing skills, such as how to conduct one-on-one meetings with parents and other teachers. Fifth-grade teacher Amanda Braziel recalls, "During my first year [at Maplewood] all of the Alliance Schools in Austin had a teacher in-service day. We got together in vertical teams, pre-kindergarten through high school, and we met at a high school and we just really talked and got to know each other and brainstormed issues that we needed to deal with."

Through the Maplewood Elementary School's core team, Braziel became involved in fighting district cuts to art and music teachers at the school. She helped plan an action outside of the school that drew media coverage, and worked with Austin Interfaith organizers and leaders to present the issue to the school board. The work deepened Braziel's commitment to the school. She explains, "We just started doing all these things, and it really fit in with my core beliefs about what school and teachers and parents in the community should be about, and how we should all work together. The Alliance School model was just such a neat concept and I loved it."

Much of Austin Interfaith's education organizing focused on schools, bringing new schools into the network and supporting principals, parent leaders, and core teams. Local organizers also helped schools to apply for ICF grants, helping bring an additional $1.9 million in funds to district schools between 1998 and 2008. At the district level, Austin Interfaith organized to protect the Alliance Schools and expand district understanding and support for the vision behind the Alliance School work. Austin Interfaith held individual meetings with school board members and district staff to cultivate them as allies and recruit them to attend the TIEF training sessions and regional conferences.

John Fitzpatrick, a former member of AISD's board of trustees, believes these training sessions fostered greater understanding by public officials of the needs of district constituents. For Fitzpatrick, the opportunity to meet regularly with Interfaith leaders provided insight "into a community that I do not belong to and that I do not come from. It's been extremely helpful to have them show me what's going on for over half our kids and families, and to expose me to a very different world than the one I grew up in."

Like OCO, Austin Interfaith staged large public accountability sessions with district and municipal officials in which education issues were presented along with other organizational demands regarding health care, immigration, and so on. Austin Interfaith worked with district and municipal leaders to create and fund a new teacher pipeline program to address shortages in bilingual and special education teachers; new parent support specialist positions for high-poverty schools; and after-school, summer school, and ESL programs.

Through its efforts to cultivate city officials as allies, Austin Interfaith developed an ongoing relationship with AISD superintendent Pascal Forgione. Appointed in 1999, Forgione came to the district from a position as U.S. Commissioner of Education Statistics, and believed strongly in using assessment data to align standards and instruction in schools. He was impressed by the IAF's emphasis on adult learning and leadership development. In Austin Interfaith, Forgione saw a partner that could educate parents about their school's performance and generate demand and support for improvement.

Forgione explains, "I went into a school recently and I showed them the data: reading down, math down, writing down. And guess what they told me: 'We love our school. We don't want you to send our teachers away.' Well, everyone wants to love their teacher, but if the teacher is not getting the kids to learn to read, that's not a good teacher. I don't care if she hugs you all day. That's where you've got to build capacity, and that's where Austin Interfaith is good. They bring extra resources, and they bring parent involvement. I think it's a healthy thing."

The organization's relationship with Superintendent Forgione led the district to adopt Alliance School community engagement practices as part of its improvement plan for the district's lowest-performing schools. The district also hired a former Alliance School principal and organizer, Claudia Santamaria, to train school-based parent support specialists to implement Alliance School practices in high-poverty schools.

As with Oakland, Austin's story is unfinished. Austin Interfaith's strategy of relational organizing to transform the cultures of low-performing schools and protect these schools through system-level organizing shows promising results. Data show increased parent and community involvement and higher levels of trust, collaboration, and morale among teachers in schools that were highly involved with Austin Interfaith. Moreover, analyses of student performance data show a significant positive relationship between the level of engagement in Alliance School activities and student test scores.

Nonetheless, Alliance Schools have struggled in recent years against the pressures of standardized testing. Frequent testing and test-preparation activities are encroaching on the time school faculties spend on relational practices, decreasing the number of participating schools to eleven schools in 2006. Even highly engaged Alliance Schools like Ridgetop, notes Joaquin Gloria, find it difficult to maintain the time for neighborhood walks. As the space for organizing diminishes, Austin Interfaith has pursued other methods to build its education work. Lead organizer Doug Greco reports: "We're not moving away from schools, but we're starting to do more education organizing through our congregations and teachers union where we have more space to do the house meetings and parent academies that build the Alliance work."

PARENTS ACADEMICALLY LINKING WITH SCHOOLS

In Miami, the organizing strategy combined an instructional reform with community support to low performing schools. Following seven years of organizing to address local issues related to neighborhood safety, People Acting for Community Together (PACT) turned its focus to public education.

"Education issues had come up before," recalls former PACT executive director Aaron Dorfman. "But by [1996], the organization had reached a level of maturity where taking on a countywide issue and something as significant as school reform became possible. We could move beyond the local neighborhood victories and easily winnable demands."

Every spring, PACT holds an annual public accountability meeting in which the organization's demands are presented to local officials. As part of the planning process, organizers and leaders conduct individual and house meetings to identify priority concerns of PACT's member congregations. In 1995, education was a consistent theme across PACT congregations. Immigrant families from Haiti and other Caribbean countries and South American countries reported that schools were not teaching their children to read.

Children from immigrant families were not the only ones who were not learning to read. Data showed that 44 percent of fourth graders in the district were performing in the bottom quartile on the statewide assessment test, compared with 25 percent in a national sample.[13] PACT believed most of these low-performing students were low-income children of color.

PACT responded to parents' calls for action by creating an education committee to explore the issue. The committee comprised clergy and congregation members, among them parents, grandparents, and educators with extensive teaching experience. Helen Stankiewicz, a retired schoolteacher with two grandchildren in the Miami schools, joined the group because of her grandson's struggles in school. He had been displaced by Hurricane

Andrew and was having difficulty with reading. Stankiewicz recalls that the committee's first task was to identify what schools were doing to support student literacy. Committee members visited schools and talked to teachers about the programs they were using. They learned that there was great variation in instructional programs and very little accountability for performance.

Stankiewicz and others on the committee began researching alternatives. On a visit to schools in neighboring Broward County, committee members discovered Direct Instruction, a program that emphasizes phonics instruction and explicit instruction in reading skills. Formerly known as Direct Instruction System for Teaching Arithmetic and Reading or DISTAR (or SRA), the program had been widely implemented during the 1970s and 1980s in Florida and nationally. By the early 1990s, inductive, student-centered literacy-development approaches had replaced the teacher-directed phonics-based approach.

PACT leaders were drawn to Direct Instruction's traditional instructional method. "Direct Instruction went back to the original thinking about reading," explains Gloria Whilby, a congregation leader and former education consultant with PACT. "Parents understood it because that was how they had learned to read."

The education committee visited a Direct Instruction school in Houston, Texas, and came away convinced that, in Helen Stankiewicz's words, "when Direct Instruction is used by disadvantaged children in disadvantaged neighborhoods, there is great improvement." The committee's assessment was supported by research on the program's effectiveness. A number of evaluations had identified Direct Instruction as an effective program in improving reading instruction for low-income children of color.[14]

That year, PACT launched a campaign to persuade the district to include Direct Instruction on the list of literacy programs that schools could choose to implement. It was an uphill battle. District leadership favored a whole-language instructional strategy, in which students were exposed to a variety of reading materials and helped to develop reading skills by making meaning of texts, rather than through explicit decoding instruction. Maria Prieto, a reading specialist at South Pointe Elementary School recalls that, at the time, "everybody was whole-language-oriented . . . it was like saying a bad word to mention phonics." The superintendent expressed no interest in meeting PACT's request.

PACT used classic organizing tactics to build district support for Direct Instruction. The education committee conducted a power analysis and identified the school board, which was responsible for appointing the superintendent, as the key entity on which to apply pressure. PACT met with individual school board members and district staff to introduce the Direct Instruction program and share evidence of its effectiveness. The organization then staged a three-hundred-person rally to demand the superintendent's support for implementing Direct Instruction in Miami-Dade schools. PACT subsequently mobilized 130 leaders to a school board meeting, again to demand support from officials for the program. As pressure mounted, district officials agreed to add Direct Instruction to its list of approved literacy programs.

Emboldened by its victory, PACT requested district funding so that low-performing schools would have resources to implement the program. Leadership transitions on the school board had brought a new superintendent who was more open to the instructional strategies behind Direct Instruction. The district developed its own phonics-based reading program, and agreed to contribute roughly 40 percent of the funds needed to pay for implementing Direct Instruction in schools. District staff worked with PACT to recruit high-poverty schools to participate in a pilot effort. Based on a previous agreement between the district and the teachers' union, these schools were required to have support from 80 percent of school staff prior to implementing the program.

Five schools implemented the program during the 1996–1997 school year, followed by seven additional schools during the next school year. These schools learned of the program through "word of mouth from teachers," Stankiewicz says. The program was popular in schools; a survey conducted by PACT in 1999 found that 92 percent of three hundred teachers in the twelve schools felt positively about the program.

Favorable reports from the pilot schools attracted the attention of a state senator who suggested that PACT seek state funds for broader implementation of the program. To build a state-level campaign, PACT sought the help of its sister organizations—other affiliates of the DART (Direct Action Research and Training) network in Florida. Together, the DART affiliates began to apply pressure to state officials. DART affiliates mobilized one thousand community members to a public accountability meeting in Tampa. DART members "went to the legislature and testified before the education appropriations committee . . . We even worked with the state to develop their request for proposals," Stankiewicz recalls. The combination of tactics won the support of the state commissioner of education and key members of the state legislature.

In 2001, the Florida Legislature appropriated $7.25 million to fund Direct Instruction in five urban counties, with $2.3 million designated for Miami. The legislation required participating schools to work with a community organization with an identifiable base of local residents or parents. Fifteen schools in Miami voted to implement Direct Instruction during the 2001–02 school year, and entered into a relationship with PACT.

Until the Direct Instruction campaign, PACT had worked from a model in which "you win a victory, and then move on to the next issue," Stankiewicz says. But as PACT became involved in education organizing, its approach began to shift. PACT was faced with a choice: "We had to continue to monitor reform or risk losing it."

The challenge of effective implementation shaped PACT's evolving approach to education organizing. "To win something in education that people care about takes a longer term commitment," observes Aaron Dorfman, who became executive director of PACT in 1997. "With our transit campaign, we passed the thing and now it's in place. We've got to monitor it to make sure they don't steal the money. But the change was won and we move on. In education, you can make a little progress, but the system seems to want to revert back to mediocrity. We've found we need more continuous involvement."

PACT turned to its base of parents and congregation members to monitor the implementation of Direct Instruction. The organization trained twenty-one congregation leaders in the methodology of Direct Instruction to serve as PALS (PACT Academically Linking with Schools). PALS leaders were assigned to schools that were close to where they lived and were coached in how to be supportive. Stankiewicz recalls the goal in PALS was to "go in the schools so that [teachers and principals] know who we are, and if there's something they need to say, or need to talk about, they can." PALS observed classroom instruction and attended professional development sessions in the schools and the district.

PACT leaders used their relationships with school staff and their familiarity with school- and classroom-level implementation to relay principals' and teachers' concerns to district administrators and advocate on their behalf. "They were very much into knowing, 'Now that you've implemented the program, how can we help you?'" recalls one principal. "Are things running smoothly, are the teachers okay? Are the parents okay?" PACT interceded with the district on behalf of schools, winning commitments to maintain the program across principal transitions, and to override a hiring freeze to fill a vacancy in district-level reading coaches. PACT also secured extra books for school libraries from SRA, the publisher of Direct Instruction.

Though Direct Instruction was a cornerstone of PACT's strategy for improving literacy, organizers and leaders understood that "Direct Instruction is not the only solution to what's wrong in the schools. There are a lot of other problems," Dorfman says. One of the chief issues for PACT was the lack of support for teachers. Based on recommendations from the National Institute for Direct Instruction, PACT negotiated with state officials to allow state funds to be used for new districtwide staff positions to help schools implementing the program. The district hired a district-level coordinator and three "super coaches" who spent a half-day in each school every week, observing and supporting teachers using the program. The district also provided professional development for school-level reading leaders and funds for schools to free up experienced teachers to serve as school-level coaches.[15]

As PALS developed, PACT began to integrate the work into its organizational activities. "We have a natural relationship with twenty-six schools so we wanted to build on the success that we had and see where else we could take it," Dorfman says. PACT held award ceremonies as part of its annual public meeting to acknowledge students' exemplary achievement and asked principals and teachers to share their work.

At one of these events, the organization decided to celebrate one child from each classroom making progress in raising reading achievement. Gloria Whilby, who was in charge of the PALS program, recalls:

> We got [the publisher] to donate a book for each child. In all my time, there was nothing more gratifying than to see three, four generations of family members coming out to celebrate that one child who could read. They came out on a Saturday morning, all dressed up in their Sunday best. And the children were more proud of getting a certificate than getting a prize because it was a validation that they could read.

These activities were designed to facilitate implementation of Direct Instruction. In four schools, however, PACT introduced a third level of support focused on building parent leadership and power to address other problems in the schools. PACT's education organizer worked to build parent committees, drawing on PACT's congregation-based model of relational organizing. An organizer conducted individual meetings with parents to recruit interested parents to form a school-based committee and organized house meetings to identify issues. The idea was to build local campaigns around the specific concerns of parents at the school, based on the belief that parent organizing could help to surface and address other problems that stood in the way of success. Dorfman explains: "We are pragmatic. Our issues work is always grounded in the experience of parents and members at the time."

PACT selected schools on the basis of three criteria: they were (a) implementing Direct Instruction, (b) located near PACT congregations, and (c) committed to supporting the parent organizing effort. Three of the four schools with parent committees were in the first cohort of schools implementing Direct Instruction. In these schools, parent committees led successful campaigns to improve bus service, secure facilities improvements, and prevent strip clubs from opening near schools.

In most cases, the organizing was nonconfrontational. "The group of parents just goes and sits and meets with the principal and says these are our concerns," Dorfman observes. "Usually we just talk to the principal and usually they recognize that the issue is valid and they follow through, because they agreed to the project in the first place." Organizers also worked directly with parent teacher associations, because "PTA people often just feel ineffective and are frustrated that they can't get as much done as they want."

In 2005, after almost a decade of organizing in Miami-Dade County, PACT's education organizing hit a wall. A new superintendent implemented a new reading-instruction program in the district, eliminating Direct Instruction from all twenty-six schools. Though PACT fought to preserve the program through large public events and behind-the-scenes negotiations, they were unable to persuade the superintendent to maintain the program, even for the district's lowest performing students. The loss was a shock to PACT, prompting Dorfman to say: "I feel like we've truly been outorganized for the first time."

The conflict between PACT and the district was different from the earlier philosophical disagreements over children's literacy development. The superintendent's opposition was pragmatic; he wanted a uniform reading program across the district so that student mobility between schools would not undermine academic progress. The new leadership also reacted negatively to PACT's pressure tactics, which were perceived as an attempt to strong-arm the district into backing down. In spite of PACT's opposition, the district moved ahead with its plan.

PACT organizers and leaders were furious. "[The superintendent] has totally consolidated power," Dorfman said at the time. "He has pushed through one reading curriculum districtwide. Houghton Mifflin is it. The district is going around and picking up all other teaching materials. It is totally centralized decision making, which is frustrating and counter-intuitive.

Even we never pushed for that. We always said let the teachers vote. Let there be a few tools in the toolbox."

When Direct Instruction ended, PACT dismantled PALS and its school-based organizing. Losing the fight to keep Direct Instruction had taken an emotional toll on PACT organizers and leaders. "It was like someone slapped you in the face when you were not expecting it," Whilby recalls.

In schools, educators responded with weary resignation. Maria Prieto reports "Next year we're all supposed to start on Houghton-Mifflin. Maybe it's a wonderful program, but does it do what needs to be done for our kids, especially those in the lower grades and those who can't read in the upper grades? Everything that PACT has done is being undone for next year, at least in Dade County. We're all devastated that we can't do it next year, but that's the way it goes."

Despite the end of PACT's ten-year campaign, data suggest that the organization's work had a positive impact on schools. An analysis of Miami-Dade County schools show that schools implementing PACT's strategy of community engagement and Direct Instruction made encouraging gains; they showed higher levels of teacher commitment, norms of peer collaboration, and sense of community and safety than comparison schools not involved in the effort. Not surprisingly, effects are stronger in schools with a longer period of implementation. In addition, performance on state-mandated standardized tests between 2001 and 2005 shows substantial gains for the lowest scoring students; these gains exceed those of comparison schools and the district overall.

WHEN REFORMS WORK

We caution the reader against comparing strategies and outcomes across urban contexts. Schools, communities, and organizational conditions vary widely across our sites. Miami, for example, is the fourth-largest urban school district in the country, dwarfing Oakland and Austin in comparison. Austin's fiscal health far exceeds that of both Oakland and Miami, and the city has a much larger percentage of affluent students than is typical for urban districts. Leadership stability in these districts varied widely. Oakland has gone through a period of great turmoil. In contrast, Austin's superintendent was in place for ten years. Other factors, such as a statewide fiscal crisis in California and a series of hurricane-related disasters in Florida, weakened the capacity of districts and schools. In Texas, schools experienced pressure to improve test scores earlier and perhaps more intensely than schools and districts in other states. Such pressure may have increased educators' interest in forming alliances with Austin Interfaith, although testing practices later weakened the effort.

The interplay of strategy and context defines local campaigns. Successful organizing campaigns are site specific; they are not easily transferable across sites. Indeed, organizing groups in other districts have found it difficult to implement the strategies highlighted here, particularly in the absence of a statewide organization that can generate the financial resources and political space for school innovation. In Milwaukee, for example, MICAH's efforts to work with schools using the Alliance Schools model faltered in the face of competing demands on principals' time. EPOP's school-based parent organizing in Philadelphia often faced intense opposition from principals and teachers. Small schools work by organizing groups in Philadelphia and New York City has been much more localized in focus than the work in Oakland.

The challenge of organizing is that campaigns defy replication. Organizers must figure out what will work in their setting, and amass the political power and organizational expertise to move demands for reform effectively. In this respect, OCO, Austin Interfaith, and PACT brought substantial organizational capacity to the work: all three were led by highly experienced organizers. Indeed, lead organizers in Oakland and Austin had more than a decade of experience in district- and state-level work. This high level of experience enhanced the organizations' ability to create political space for schools to undertake reform, to define successful interventions, and to balance the competing demands of district and school-level organizing campaigns.

Creating the Space for Reform in Schools

Early on in OCO's organizing, leaders realized that more than a good idea was required to change the quality of instruction in Oakland's flatland communities. The organization was an old hand at city politics, and the defeat at Jefferson Elementary underscored the need to approach education reform politically as well as educationally. OCO took a series of tactical steps: it cultivated influential allies, engaged hundreds of individual teachers, developed a vision of new educational opportunity in the district, and applied external pressure on the district to support its organizing demands.

In Miami, PACT pursued a similar political strategy, enlisting even the *Miami Herald* to run a free half-page advertisement with the headline: "If your child can read this, thank PACT." *Herald* articles chronicled PACT's organizing to win district approval for Direct Instruction, reviewed the debate between whole-language-based reading instruction and phonics-heavy programs, and described the research that supported the phonics-based approach underlying Direct Instruction.

But statewide networks played crucial roles in creating space—both political and financial—for schools and districts to undertake reform. OCO, Austin Interfaith, and PACT were backed by statewide networks that were also staffed by highly experienced organizers, including the network founders. These organizers mobilized essential political muscle with state-level officials. The IAF, PICO, and DART national networks secured state funds and political attention that helped their local organizing affiliates build grassroots support for reform. Districts and schools used these funds to pay for activities related to the reforms in each site: small schools in Oakland, Alliance Schools in Austin, and Direct Instruction in Miami.

All of the networks provided training opportunities and cross-organizational sharing that facilitated the spread of effective strategies. But in Texas and California, statewide networks included other organizations that were also deeply involved in education organizing. Austin Interfaith and Oakland Community Organizations were thus able to draw on a deep reservoir of organizing expertise and political experience that informed not just what campaigns looked like, but also how the enterprise of school reform was conceptualized. Austin's initial work at Zavala drew on lessons from an IAF affiliate in Fort Worth. In California, OCO's strategy of home visits was developed by a sister PICO organization, Sacramento ACT (Area Congregations Together).

In addition, factors in the statewide context likely facilitated the success of organizing strategies. In particular, Austin Interfaith's success in recruiting teachers and principals to join the Alliance School reforms in Texas was undoubtedly swayed by the political realities of working in a "right to work" state. Educator unions in Texas are weaker in number and influence than their counterparts in other states, and the local teachers' union, Education Austin, is an organizational member of Austin Interfaith.

Understanding How Schools Change

As we noted in chapter 1, the evolution of education organizing across the past two decades reflects a deepening understanding by organizers about the institutional context of schools and the reform levers most likely to reap substantial improvement. The OCO, Austin Interfaith, and PACT campaigns all targeted core areas of school capacity through organizational, cultural, and instructionally oriented reform strategies.

Oakland Community Organizations' initial experiences with schools led the organization to pursue a districtwide strategy of reform. In Austin, early efforts at school-based organizing taught the group to seek active principal participation in the effort. Both groups developed approaches to school-based organizing that intentionally developed a new accountability relationship between educators and community members, based on knowledge of each other's motivations and shared commitment to act in the interests of the school community.

Similarly, in Miami, PACT began organizing with a belief that it could win on the Direct Instruction issue and then leave the issue to develop campaigns on other educational concerns. Growing awareness of the complexities of implementation led PACT to initiate a strategy of school-level support. PACT's work to support educators through PALS and parent organizing ultimately extended far beyond the boundaries of a purely instructional intervention. Educators in low-performing Miami schools, beleaguered and underappreciated, felt acknowledged, celebrated, supported, and inspired by PACT's efforts on their behalf.

In schools where organizing groups were deeply involved, principals and teachers saw a new capacity for problem solving develop in parents, and between parents and educators in their schools. "What they actually do is organize the frustrations and the things these parents would like to see changed here," observed Julio Carrera, the principal of South Hialeah Elementary School in Miami-Dade County. "So [parents] can present [ideas] to me, not screaming, not with outrage, not poking fun at me and saying, 'I don't like this, I don't like that.' But focusing [their proposals] in a more realistic way and negotiating. 'We have seen this and we think that something like this should happen, what is it that you're able to do?' For me, it makes my job a little easier because, in actuality, what the parents want is what I want."

A capacity for problem solving is essential to the change process, but how schools use this capacity determines whether improvements actually materialize and who they benefit. As Michelle Renée and her colleagues observe, successful equity reform involves both creating a supportive political and normative context, and choosing the right technical interventions to put in place.[16]

Consistent with the community organizing belief in participatory democracy, the school-level organizing campaigns described in this chapter focused on issues selected by local participants. Organizers facilitated the organizing process, provided training on organizing skills, and offered assistance in researching campaign issues and demands. These forms of assistance were guided by the larger educational vision in each site. In Miami, local organizing reflected PACT's goal of supporting educators' efforts to implement Direct Instruction while addressing parents' concerns about other problems, such as student safety on the walk to and from school. Although Direct Instruction has sparked some controversy among educators for its prescriptive instructional approach, it was introduced by PACT based on community members' assessment of their schools' needs, and was widely supported by teachers and administrators in local schools.

In Oakland, organizing efforts were guided by a vision of personalization, deep parent and community engagement, and a collegial professional community. Teams received ongoing training from OCO and considerable coaching from BayCES. Indeed, the uniqueness of the OCO-BayCES partnership helped BayCES secure funds from the Bill & Melinda Gates Foundation to create an "incubator" to support new school teams as they went through the school-design process.

The educational focus of Alliance School activities was loosely prescribed; teams had full autonomy beyond the core expectations of leadership development and parent and community engagement. Members of school-based organizing teams were expected to participate in five-day training sessions developed by the Texas Interfaith Education Fund. These sessions introduced educators and community members to philosophies and reform strategies of expert educators, and in this way, aimed to inform Alliance School core teams' activities about prevailing theories of school improvement.

How well schools could carry out the visions that the organizing groups had for them is obviously a matter of degree. Schools were not equally effective, and there are examples from every site of less-than-successful schools. Yet in schools where the groups were consistently and highly involved, teachers reported a focus on achievement-oriented culture that was significantly higher than teacher assessments in comparison schools.

AN INTERPLAY OF STRATEGIES

Decades of failed reform underscore the importance of approaching school improvement from both the top and bottom of the education system. Strategies focused at the top of the system—at school boards and district superintendents, municipal- and state-level leaders—are needed to create a context that supports the school-level change process. Such support is important because low-performing urban schools often have little internal capacity or will for change.

Writing of this problem, scholars Charles Payne and Miriam Kaba observe: "The worst schools suffer from deeply rooted cultures of failure and distrust, are politically-conflicted, personality-driven and racially-tense, have difficulty learning from their own experiences, have difficulty following through even when they achieve consensus about what to do, have shallow pools of relevant professional skill, unstable staffs, and exist in a larger institutional environment that is itself unstable and ill-equipped to do much more than issue mandates and threats."[17]

If this is the reality of low-performing urban schools, school-improvement efforts have very little chance of success without external action to press for, nourish, and protect the reform process. In most urban districts, widespread low performance and entrenched political relationships collude to maintain the status quo. In Oakland, Austin, and Miami, organizing groups provided an outside force, independent of the school system, to break the logjam between districts, educator unions, and other political players. In all three sites, groups provided both a vision and language for key district or state decisions, drafting the small-schools policy in Oakland and creating the program guidelines for Direct Instruction in Miami, as well as collaborating in a host of district-level interventions in Austin.

But the odds are not very high that district-level organizing campaigns will of themselves generate school-level improvements. Mandates and threats from the top of the school system rarely work unless they are accompanied by deliberate and sustained effort to build the capacity for implementation in schools.[18] School faculty and staff must support the vision, feel connected to colleagues and peers, and have the skills necessary to implement reform effectively. In the absence of such engagement, new innovations are too often minimally understood, indifferently embraced, or simply opposed by tired educators who know that this, too, shall pass.

Oakland Community Organizations, Austin Interfaith, and PACT began their efforts at different levels of the system. Austin's Alliance Schools emerged from state-level organizing; OCO's small schools campaign developed from the organization's struggles to address overcrowding in a large, failing neighborhood school; and in Miami, the campaign for Direct Instruction began with a district-level focus. Regardless of which level of the system groups targeted initially, all three sites pursued strategies that combined system-level demands with intensive school-based organizing. In the next chapter we explore in greater depth the question of how groups build the political space for reform through coalition-building strategies.

CHAPTER FOUR

Moving Toward Equity Through Alliances and Coalitions

The problem with school reform is not educators' unwillingness to try new things. Urban schools and districts often have a great many programs in play at any given time, yet districts have notoriously short attention spans for implementing and sustaining reform programs long enough to produce meaningful school improvements.[1]

The challenge, Jeffrey Henig and his colleagues write, "may be less one of gaining attention and commitment than of sustaining attention and commitment, less one of reorganizing educational bureaucracies than of organizing whole communities so that the education enterprise keeps moving in the right direction even when attention and commitment flag." Responding to this challenge requires "sufficient political support to maintain positive momentum in the face of various forces that can block, contain, or gradually erode promising initiatives."[2]

As we noted in chapter 2 reforms can take years to take root and come to fruition. In turbulent urban school contexts, the time frame from defining and introducing a reform to implementing and taking it to scale can be a matter of decades, not years. Recent research suggests that sustained educational improvement is more likely among districts with high levels of *civic capacity*, which Henig and Clarence Stone define as the capacity of community members to solve problems through deliberative and broad-based effort.[3] Such civic capacity is mobilized through broad coalitions in which diverse stakeholders reach agreement on desired reforms and then marshal their respective political and organizational resources to support the agenda.

Studies of civic coalitions suggest, though, that reform coalition efforts often do not involve public education's core constituencies—public school parents and youth from poor communities and communities of color. Research on civic capacity in eleven cities by Stone and his colleagues found that coalitions typically involve government officials, local business leaders and civic elites. Parents of public school children were rarely included, and high school–age youth completely overlooked. In the absence of these perspectives, Stone and his colleagues found that civic coalitions composed of "elites" perceived fewer problems in the school system than did coalitions with community constituents, and that the coalitions of civic elites tended to frame education problems as the product of inadequate governance structures, rather than of fundamental inequities in resource distribution.[4]

Historically, community organizing groups have demonstrated ambivalence about participating in and leading coalitions, because they frequently require compromising on organizational values and norms, while demanding significant investments of staff time. Organizing groups also note that participating in coalitions convened by mainstream groups with significant institutional power risks inadvertently reinforcing the status quo and traditional power dynamics. For some groups, particularly those following in the Alinsky tradition of organizing, participating in coalitions is philosophically and fundamentally at odds with building their own organizational power. In a 2001 study by the Institute for Education and Social Policy, an IAF (Industrial Areas Foundation) organizer from the Washington Interfaith Network (WIN) in Washington, D.C., observed, "What's our self interest? . . . WIN enters an alliance only if it enhances our power."[5]

Increasingly, however, organizing groups view involvement in cross-sector partnerships as an effective way to move their education reform agendas forward. Organizing groups in our study have turned to building long-term coalitions, assembled from multiple constituencies, to push and sustain system-level reform; Community Coalition co-convened the Communities for Educational Equity coalition to win curriculum reform, for example, and Chicago ACORN assembled a diverse task force to pass the Grow Your Own legislation. As organizing groups adopt coalition building as an intentional strategy for augmenting their power, legitimacy, and access, they must remain vigilant that their values and interests are not compromised. Organizing groups are leveraging their strengths—an unwavering focus on equity, the ability to build consensus, and deep and authentic roots in communities—to craft new civic coalitions that can broaden the base of support for reform, create more comprehensive and compelling visions for school change, and generate systemic strategies at the district or state level.

This chapter examines four cases of civic coalitions, ranging from loose partnership efforts in Philadelphia and New York City to deep, broad-based, and sustained civic coalitions in Los Angeles and Chicago. In all four cases, organizing groups formed the core of the coalition effort. These coalitions proposed new curriculum and instructional programs, new approaches for teacher recruitment and induction, and new strategies for developing and financing schools facilities.

COALITIONS DEFINED

In the world of organizing, the term *coalition* is often used loosely. Some organizers believe their groups inherently function as coalitions because they bring together their member organizations—faith-based institutions, community-based organizations, and schools. Others describe ad hoc alliances or partnerships as coalitions.

All of the campaigns we studied were shaped by sustained partnerships with educational experts that helped organizing groups to define their education reform goals and refine their campaign strategies. Some organizations developed strong relationships with education advocacy organizations and university partners, providing the groups with access to education expertise and data. Other organizations conducted their own research in consultation with highly experienced education-reform organizations.

In addition to these partnerships, in several sites groups pursued what researcher Amanda Tattersall has described as "support," "mutual support," and "deep" coalitions.[6] In her typology, *deep* coalitions involve groups in defining a common and broad social vision, developing a long-term strategy for change, and sharing resources at multiple levels. *Support* and *mutual support* coalitions, in contrast, tend to focus on common goals on a specific issue and possess fewer shared structures and less deeply embedded joint decision-making processes.

CIVIC COALITIONS IN FOUR CITIES

The coalitions in our study varied in breadth of membership, depth of participation, scale of vision, and members' plans for continued work together. Who was involved and for how long was determined by the groups' goals. In Philadelphia and New York, support coalitions formed to access expertise and intensify the political pressure on education officials to prioritize local demands for new school facilities and high school creation. Coalitions convened by community organizing groups in Los Angeles and Chicago were particularly broad-based, and included local district or municipal leaders in addition to civic, advocacy, and educator organizations. In Los Angeles, efforts centered on moving a new curriculum policy; in Chicago, the coalition focused on creating a statewide teacher quality program. In this section, we look at how and why organizing groups built these coalitions.

High School Transformation in Kensington, Philadelphia

In 2001, the Pennsylvania legislature authorized a state takeover of the School District of Philadelphia in response to the schools' chronic budget shortfalls and dismal performance. Governor Tom Ridge, a supporter of vouchers and private-sector involvement in schools, hired for-profit Edison Schools to create a blueprint for the takeover. Ridge also signaled that Edison was under consideration to assume control of as many as seventy failing schools as well as several central office functions. Community organizations, advocacy groups, and unions vocally opposed the proposed privatization through rallies, sit-ins, lawsuits, and angry testimony at public hearings. In the end, incoming chief executive officer of the School District of Philadelphia, Paul Vallas, nixed Edison's role in managing district schools. Instead, Vallas and the state-appointed School Reform Commission awarded contracts to run forty-five low-performing Philadelphia schools to a mix of for-profit and nonprofit managers.

The battle over privatization brought together organizing and advocacy groups, unions, and school-reform groups and fostered relationships among these diverse stakeholders. Youth United for Change (YUC) developed an alliance with the Philadelphia Student Union (PSU), a youth organizing group with chapters in schools outside of YUC's neighborhoods. Both YUC and EPOP had longstanding relationships with the Philadelphia chapter of the national Cross City Campaign for Urban School Reform (or "Cross City Campaign"), as well as with Research for Action, a nonprofit research institute, and the Philadelphia Citizens for Children and Youth, a prominent advocacy group in the city.

These alliances provided YUC with important access to educational expertise. Since YUC's inception in 1993, the organization had mounted successful campaigns that improved facilities and safety, won resources for school libraries, and strengthened curriculum. But the group was looking for ways to impact teaching and learning more deeply.

With support from the Cross City Campaign, YUC and PSU youth leaders visited new small schools in Oakland, and later in New York City, Providence and Chicago. YUC and PSU organizers and youth leaders were intrigued by the potential of small schools to address the violence, absentee-ism, and low expectations that characterized the large failing high school in their neighborhoods. The question was how to bring this strategy to Phila-delphia. Nationally, support for small schools was growing—in 2001, the Carnegie Corporation of New York and Bill & Melinda Gates Foundation both identified small schools as the cornerstone of their education-reform funding strategy. But these foundations were not active in Philadelphia, and so the opportunities for pushing a small school strategy were unclear.

In August of 2002, the new district CEO Paul Vallas announced a major capital investment plan to spend nearly $2 billion to replace and renovate aging school buildings. Vallas proposed building nine new high schools, all limited to 800 or 1,000 students. The leaders of YUC's Kensington High School chapter saw the capital plan as an opening to engage the district in replacing this failing school with a campus of new small high schools. YUC leaders led Vallas on a tour of their school to impress him with the need for a new building; PSU similarly advocated for the inclusion of one of its schools in west Philadelphia. In December, the School Reform Commission announced the final capital plan, including new buildings for both schools.

The Kensington YUC youth leaders began an intensive action research process to develop a proposal for reinventing Kensington as small schools. They led a "listening campaign," interviewing more than three hundred students about ideas for a new Kensington. Based on these data, the youth leaders proposed creating four small theme-based schools that would share a library, athletic facilities, and extracurricular activities.

Youth leaders received support for their efforts from Research for Ac-tion and the national Cross City Campaign, which arranged a site visit to small schools in Chicago to deepen YUC's understanding of the factors necessary to make small schools effective.[7] Their investigations convinced the young people that Vallas' proposal to create 800- to 1,000-seat schools was not ambitious enough. The personalization and relationships that made small schools successful could only be achieved with student bodies of no more than 400 students. But school-site autonomy over curriculum and deep community engagement were also crucial elements in the small-schools reforms in other districts, and YUC hoped to bring these ideas to the Kensington campus. YUC leaders shared an initial draft proposal with the principal and teachers from the Kensington campus, and with parents and other community leaders to gain support. In March, YUC presented Paul Vallas with a formal proposal for creating new small schools on the Kensington and Olney High School campuses.[8]

As youth organizations, YUC's and PSU's prior organizing had taught them the need for adult allies to amplify the power and influence of young people's voices. The organizations began a process of recruiting influential organizations to support their campaign. PSU and YUC both joined the Education First Compact, a coalition convened by the Philadelphia Education Fund to encourage broad civic engagement in school reform. The Compact included allies from the antiprivatization battles—Philadelphia Citizens for Children and Youth, EPOP, Research for Action, and other organizing groups, as well as school district officials and teachers union representatives.[9] Both the Compact and the Cross City Campaign endorsed the youth leaders' small-schools campaign. Research for Action worked with Compact members to develop a position paper outlining a districtwide policy on small schools.[10] EPOP helped YUC leaders to build support among elected officials.

Believing that the local community had a vital stake in reinventing the school, YUC also reached out to residents and community organizations in the Kensington neighborhood. The group presented their plans to neighborhood associations, community-development corporations, and parent-teacher associations (known as Home and School Associations in Philadelphia). Meanwhile, as the district moved forward with its facilities plans for Kensington, it had begun to assemble a planning team consisting of a student, a teacher, a clergy representative, and a community resident, all chosen by the Kensington high school principal. YUC intervened to convince the district administration to increase the number of students on the team and to include representatives of active community organizations, including Norris Square Civic Association and the New Kensington Community Development Corporation (CDC); The Lighthouse, a local community center; and Aspira, a youth-development organization serving the city's Latino community. Members of the expanded Kensington planning team informed the district that they unanimously supported YUC's proposal for four small schools, one of which would be housed in an annex to reduce the overall number of students on the campus. The planning team set about finding a suitable site for the new facility and met with district officials to present the case for the additional facility.

In a parallel effort, the William Penn Foundation, a local foundation that had long supported both YUC and PSU, proposed engaging a nationally-recognized school-planning firm to augment the nascent planning team's efforts by facilitating broad community input into the high school redesign planning process. The firm, Concordia LLC, presented its community-based design process to the two youth groups and their allies, who agreed to press the district to contract its services.

In February 2005, the school district announced a "Small Schools Transition Process" to create new small high schools across the city. The district's plan made the redesign of Kensington official, but it imposed a compressed timeline of less than six months for the process. Though district officials continued to consult with YUC, many of the community constituencies that YUC had sought to engage were left out of the process.[11] Without broad community input and involvement, YUC feared that the new schools would not reflect the vision and priorities of the local community. YUC and its allies also believed that the district's proposed vocational themes for the small schools communicated low expectations for the academic achievement of students of color.

YUC consulted with EPOP, PSU, Concordia, and the Norris Square Civic Association to develop a strategy for inserting a community voice into the redesign planning process. In June 2005, YUC and PSU held a joint action to demand the district's commitment to work with Concordia, and its support for a range of proposals for Kensington and the west Philadelphia campus where PSU was working. The action won a commitment from the district's chief academic officer, Gregory Thornton, to contract with Concordia to facilitate community engagement in the school redesign process because, as Thornton noted at the meeting, "Small schools add value, but small schools will not do it alone . . . We need to use the intelligence and hard work of these young folks as we move forward."[12]

With time growing tight—the new schools were set to open in September—Concordia facilitated meetings involving nearly 150 community residents, young people, and parents that produced a "Kensington Community Mandate" and recommendations for the new schools' governance, scheduling, curriculum, student support services, partnerships, and facilities sharing.[13]

In September 2005, three small theme-based schools opened in the original Kensington building; and an annex was planned to house a fourth school. (Though construction was delayed, the district broke ground for the annex in 2008.) The themes of the new schools—performing arts, business and culinary arts—were proposed by YUC students, based on the results of their survey and listening campaign. Working together, YUC and Concordia established a "sustainability circle" of youth leaders and community representatives to monitor the redesign process. Initial data from the school district show that from 2003–04 to 2005–06 student attendance on the campus rose by 10 percent, and the number of campus students planning to attend college rose by 25 percent.

Resolving School Overcrowding in the Bronx

Overcrowding and dangerously rundown school buildings were the focus of the Northwest Bronx Community and Clergy Coalition's early education campaigns, and have remained a central issue throughout the group's education work. In the mid-1990s, District 10, which contained most of the schools in the Northwest Bronx, was among the most crowded of the city's thirty-two geographic sub-districts, with numerous schools at more than 140 percent of capacity. As was true across the city, many of these buildings were crumbling after years of deferred maintenance stemming from New York City's fiscal crisis.

In the early 1990s the School Construction Authority (SCA), an agency created to oversee school facility repairs and new construction in New York City under the joint oversight of city and state officials, began construction on two new elementary schools to ease overcrowding District 10. One of these, P.S. 20, was three years behind schedule by 1995 and had become known as the "sinking school" because of substandard infill at the construction site. The other, P.S. 15, was also behind schedule but opened in September 1995 regardless, with construction continuing around students.

NWBCCC's newly established education committee met with the SCA later that fall to discuss the progress of the two schools as well as dangerous conditions in other local schools—but to little avail. Allegations of corruption, nepotism, and incompetence on the part of the SCA were emerging; a girl in Brooklyn had been killed when a poorly-built school roof collapsed, and revelations of asbestos contamination in elementary schools had angered parents across the city. NWBCCC leaders and organizers turned to publicity; they scheduled a tour of P.S. 20 for parents, district officials, and elected city officials on the day of the August 1996 construction deadline and invited print and television reporters.

The *New York Times* and *Daily News* both covered the tour, along with several Bronx newspapers. The *Times* described the scene this way:

> When the steel and concrete outlines of a new four-story school began rising from the east side of Webster Avenue in August of 1991, residents of the Bedford Park section of the Bronx were hopeful that relief would soon come for their overcrowded schools.
>
> By 1993, the year that Public School 20 was due to open, reports surfaced that the building was sinking into the landfill on which it was built.
>
> Yesterday, the day the school was supposed to be ready again, carpenters were still drilling, hammering and cleaning, and 100 angry parents and children—joined by elected officials, including the Bronx Borough President, Fernando Ferrer, and the City Comptroller, Alan G. Hevesi—showed up to express their dismay at yet another delay. Officials of the city's School Construction Authority, which is building the school, have set and missed seven deadlines since construction began on the terra cotta building.
>
> "We are not surprised that it is not finished today," Lois Harr, a parent and a director of the Northwest Bronx Community and Clergy Coalition, told the crowd of angry, placard-waving parents gathered in an unfinished hallway of the school. "The S.C.A. has wasted too much money, delayed too many schools and left too many children in overcrowded classrooms."[14]

During the tour, the SCA president promised that work would proceed as quickly as possible. Both articles quoted skeptical local educators. District 10 superintendent Irma Zardoya told the *Times*, "I told the SCA in April, you have to make me a believer, because P.S. 15 was a disaster. They assured me that this school would be ready today. Well, they have not made me a believer."[15]

More articles followed in November 1996 when NWBCCC leaders grew frustrated at the SCA's lack of response to safety concerns in the two schools. A number of students receiving special education services had managed to pry open windows on upper floors and crawl onto ledges. When the SCA president ignored the NWBCCC's demands for repairs, the organization invited SCA trustee Paul Atanasio to the Bronx, along with the press. The *New York Times* quoted angry parents, along with the principals of both schools, and reported on Atanasio's promises to secure the windows and make other repairs.[16]

Through their research on the city's school construction process, organizers and parent leaders learned that the local school district superintendent had limited power to resolve facilities problems. In 1996, the NWBCCC reached out to district officials, hoping that an alliance would provide access to more information about facilities. District leaders were receptive to a partnership because it gave District 10 leverage and political backing to pressure the SCA into repairing a number of schools' facilities. One former district official observes, "There were times when [district leaders] couldn't go out there publicly and talk about an issue . . . because it was either with the [New York City Schools] Chancellor or against the [Board of Education] . . . and they were able to do that better than [the district could]."

The NWBCCC maintained its media presence as it continued to push for an end to local overcrowding. As part of the campaign, the NWBCCC created potent visuals of parent dissatisfaction through large rallies, school tours, and testimony at school board meetings. Leaders talked to the press about the appalling conditions and reiterated the group's demands for new space. Sympathetic mayoral candidates, Bronx politicians, and other notables, including the Reverend Al Sharpton, appeared at their rallies and spoke to the media. Between 1995 and 2005, more than three dozen articles citing the groups' school facilities work appeared in the citywide papers, with many more in smaller outlets.

In 1998, the NWBCCC succeeded in winning funds through the city's facilities capital plan to pay for six new school buildings and to lease additional buildings. Bruce Irushalmi, deputy superintendent of District 10, credits the funds with enabling the district to create a total of fourteen thousand new school seats.

Securing the funds was only part of the solution. Dense residential and commercial development in the area meant that there was little space for new school construction. Moreover, even if there was space, the School Construction Authority had proven so inept that the new schools might take years to build. If existing structures would not solve the problem, then a new strategy was needed.

The NWBCCC had arisen from community struggles to stop the wave of arson that swept the south Bronx during the 1970s. As the group organized to rebuild the Bronx, it had spun off a number of local community housing development corporations (CDCs). The CDCs obtained grants from local banks, drawing on community reinvestment funds, to purchase and redevelop abandoned city properties into low- and mixed-income housing developments, which, through a turnkey strategy with the city's housing development agency, were then leased back to the city. Now the NWBCCC organizers and leaders decided to bring this development strategy to schools.

In 1998, the NWBCCC entered into a coalition with the Pratt Center for Community and Environmental Development (PICCED), New York University's Institute for Education and Social Policy, and a number of prominent community development corporations to develop what it called a "nonprofit leasing program."[17] Though other community organizations had attempted to do something similar, most had used private developers. The idea of nonprofit development was appealing to Northwest Bronx leaders because of its potential to generate local jobs and strengthen neighborhood-based institutions.

Through the new coalition, the School Construction Working Group (SCWG), NWBCCC leaders met with city education officials to present the program and its benefits. NWBCCC built partnerships with nontraditional allies such as the New York City Bar Association and Business Partnership, as well as with banks and two national community development finance institutions—Local Initiatives Support Corporation and the Enterprise Foundation—to define a joint agenda for facilities financing and development reform. The group also began exploring how to use new federal funds that Congress had made available through school-financing tax breaks.

But in 1999, events in the city's political landscape derailed the effort. Conflicts between the mayor and school chancellor over school privatization (which the mayor wanted and the chancellor opposed) led to the chancellor's ouster. A year later, new leadership in the White House changed the prospects for obtaining federal school construction funds. The loss of crucial allies within the school system, combined with a new political moment, unraveled the SCWG.

In 2001, the NWBCCC returned to a local organizing strategy, focusing on protecting the capital funds allocated for new schools and school repairs, as well as on building political support to convert a nearby and largely abandoned National Guard Armory into new school space. The NWBCCC spent the next half decade advocating for the Armory's redevelopment into school, community and retail space, enlisting PICCED to draw up plans and recruiting a developer. With local politicians, retail and building trades unions, and community institutions, the NWBCCC formed the Kingsbridge Armory Redevelopment Alliance (KARA) to press for living wages and union protections and ensure that the redevelopment would reflect community needs. In 2006, after long delays and fights about jurisdiction, the Bronx Overall Economic Development Corporation released a request for proposals for the redevelopment. Local politicians, including former Bronx Borough President Adolfo Carrion, credited the NWBCCC with influencing the language of the request for proposals and the resulting designs, all of which included space for community groups and schools.

In the summer of 2006, to the consternation of local elected officials and the Kingsbridge Alliance, the Department of Education revised its estimate of school capacity needs in the Bronx, announcing that no new schools would be built on the Armory site. NWBCCC responded with a report, produced by researchers at the Annenberg Institute for School Reform (AISR), accusing the city of "planning for failure" with unacceptably low projections of student retention as they progressed through the school system. The city's facilities-planning estimates assumed that roughly two-thirds of students would drop out of school before they finished high school, even though the Department of Education had invested substantial resources to increase rates of high school graduation in the Bronx. Noting the disjuncture between projected "survival rates" of 36 percent and high school graduation goals of 80 percent, the NWBCCC-AISR report asserted that the gap in seats amounted to "the difference between high school graduation, college and successful careers, or the school to prison pipeline or dead-end jobs in the low-wage service economy for more than 10,000 Bronx youth . . . If that gap is not filled by the provision of . . . real spaces in which to learn, thousands of our Bronx high school students will pay a terrible price."[18]

Since then, the NWBCCC and its allies have continued to push for new school facilities to reduce continuing severe overcrowding in Bronx schools. In 2008, the NWBCCC won a commitment from city officials to site two new schools on and adjacent to the Armory. As the battle over the priorities for the armory redevelopment continues, the organization has continued working through the KARA alliance on a community benefits agreement that ensures that the redevelopment will bring union jobs to the community.

College Preparation for All in Los Angeles

In Los Angeles, poor facilities conditions in local schools propelled the Community Coalition and its youth organizing component, South Central Youth Empowered thru Action (SCYEA) to join a citywide effort to win voter approval for a school construction bond. Once the bond passed, the Community Coalition led an effort to force the district to distribute funds equitably.

Following the school facilities campaign, SCYEA turned to instructional problems in the high schools. Young people involved in SCYEA's local high school organizing committees reported their schools offered many classes in cosmetology and floor covering, but few of the college preparatory courses (called the A-G curriculum) necessary to gain acceptance to the state's highly regarded University of California or California State University systems.

In 2001, after an extensive survey of students, SCYEA youth began examining the master schedules at their own high schools. "We learned that at Fremont that they had nine cosmetology classes and four chemistry classes," recalls Marcus McKinney, a high school student at the time. An independent analysis by researchers at UCLA's Institute for Democracy, Education, and Access found similar results: schools in Los Angeles' low-income neighborhoods offered 20 percent fewer college preparatory A-G courses than schools in higher-income areas.[19]

Drawing on this analysis, SCYEA released the following statement: "Schools in South Los Angeles do not prepare students to enter college or obtain livable wage employment. Current school-reform efforts focus on standardized testing over preparing more students for college and preferred careers. SCYEA believes that a movement led by students, parents, and community members is necessary to win community-driven school reform."

SCYEA's report identified three core reform issues:

Disappearance Rates

Every year, our high schools lose thousands of students. Each school begins with a HUGE freshman class, which dramatically shrinks every school year through graduation time. About 61% of South LA students 'disappear' before they reach their senior year. We call this the "disappearance" rate because the official transfer and drop-out rates do not account for this enormous loss of students.

Penitentiary Tracking

In the Los Angeles Unified School District (LAUSD), 61% of South LA students "disappear" and there is an alarming rise in the number of students forced into special education. The LAUSD has placed 1 in every 5 African American students in special education, where students are three times more likely to have untrained teachers and to drop out. Many of these students end up in prison, where most of the population did not complete high school.

College Eligibility

According to 1999 state records, only 12% of students graduating from South LA high schools went on to attend California's public four-year colleges. Statewide, only a quarter of African American and Latino public high school graduates were even eligible to apply to a UC or Cal State University (most of them are missing one or two required courses).[20]

SCYEA's initial organizing focused on persuading local school officials to implement three main reform demands: (1) "locate 'disappeared' students and put them back on track to graduate"; (2) "stop forcing 'dead-end' classes on low-achieving students" and assigning students to special education programs because their reading skills were poor or they were behind in their coursework; and (3) inform students of college requirements and "make college required courses available to all students and place them on track to complete the classes within 4 years."[21]

School-based organizing committees led efforts to improve college awareness on high school campuses and to increase student access to counseling so that they would have information about what courses they needed to take. These efforts achieved a series of "small wins," such as counseling fairs during lunch hours. But the wins did not stop the flow of South LA students into low-wage service-sector jobs.

In early 2004, independent of the Community Coalition's local organizing efforts, California State Senator Richard Alarcón introduced a bill in the state legislature that would mandate the college preparatory A-G curriculum for all students statewide. Working with Education Trust-West, a policy research and advocacy organization, SCYEA members traveled to Sacramento to testify in favor of the bill. The bill never made it out of committee, but the experience prompted the Education Trust-West to convene educational justice and advocacy groups from across the state to discuss next steps. Collectively, the groups decided to focus their efforts at the district level, hoping to generate bottom-up change.

In Los Angeles, a confluence of events created an opportune moment for bringing together local stakeholders on the issue of college access. Two local advocacy organizations, the United Way of Los Angeles and Alliance for a Better Community, released the *Latino Scorecard 2003: Grading the American Dream*. The Scorecard, which examined the social and economic conditions of Latinos within Los Angeles County, drew attention when it assigned the district a "D" on public education for its low graduation and college-going rates.[22]

To develop an action agenda to follow up on the *Scorecard*'s findings, Alliance for a Better Community met with the Community Coalition to discuss priorities for local education reform. Though the list of potential reform initiatives was long, the Community Coalition, with years of organizing around A-G under its belt, saw an opportunity to build support for increased rigor in the high school curriculum. In June 2004 the two groups co-convened a roundtable of Los Angeles–based organizations to discuss how the district might be held accountable for providing students with optimal supports for their post–high school careers.[23] Thirty-five organizations attended the event, including research organizations, advocacy groups, community organizing groups, parent organizations, student organizations, universities, and legal institutions.

The roundtable led to the formation of a grassroots coalition that would ultimately become known as Communities for Educational Equity (CEE).[24] The coalition consisted of twenty-five organizations, including research entities UC/ACCORD and the Education Trust-West, advocacy organizations such as the Mexican American Legal Defense and Educational Fund (MALDEF) and the NAACP, and representatives from then-school board president José Huizar's office and Richard Alarcón's office. Within the next few months, the coalition reached consensus on a vision of college access for all Los Angeles students and gathered data, held community forums, built new alliances, and assessed the local political landscape through a power analysis.[25] They met with key stakeholders, including vocational education organizations, the Los Angeles teachers' union, and Los Angeles school board members to gain their support.

At a CEE retreat in February 2005, member organizations resolved to focus on winning a school board resolution to make A-G coursework the standard curriculum for all students in the district. The decision was reached in negotiations with José Huizar's office, which was already a part of the coalition.

The coalition argued that a college preparatory curriculum policy had important implications not only for educational equity, but also for the city's economic future. The twenty-first-century workforce, they asserted, requires young people to possess high-level math, science, and technology skills. Representatives of the building trades in Los Angeles, for example, observed that many prospective candidates were unable to pass the math exam to qualify for their apprenticeship program. Increased rigor was thus not simply about college prep, but about "work-prep" and "life-prep."[26]

The formation of CEE catapulted SCYEA's college-access organizing onto a larger stage. For the Community Coalition, the campaign had started with a relatively small group of youth organizers and leaders working with loosely allied organizations to demand increased educational opportunities in their local schools. Five years later, the fight for what CEE called "the A-G campaign" involved a rare coalition of diverse constituencies across Los Angeles that sought to generate a major change in districtwide policy.

Working closely with José Huizar's office, CEE drafted a school board resolution mandating the A-G curriculum for all LAUSD students, beginning in the 2008–2009 school year. In the weeks leading up to the vote, CEE won support for the resolution from then-superintendent Roy Romer and State Superintendent Jack O'Connell, as well as key leaders from the Los Angeles Trade Tech and Building Trades Council. The Los Angeles City Council voted unanimously in support of a symbolic A-G resolution.

Meanwhile, CEE's aggressive media outreach resulted in more than one hundred published stories in the local media, with editorials in all of the major newspapers on the issue (some in favor, some against). CEE organized three mass mobilizations in the month and a half prior to the final school board vote to demonstrate the depth of the grassroots support for the resolution.[27]

Despite the intensive organizing effort, a week before the vote, prospects for the passage of the resolution seemed uncertain, with Alberto Retana, the Community Coalition's director of organizing, predicting an "uphill battle." CEE had secured the unequivocal support of only three of the seven board members.[28] The vote had already been postponed once because board members felt they had inadequate information to vote on the proposal. There were concerns, in the words of school board member Marlene Canter, about "unintended consequences," such as an increased dropout rate.[29] And not all of the board members were comfortable with the language of the resolution, which mandated A-G for all students, rather than giving students a choice to opt into the college preparatory track.

On the day of the vote, June 14, 2005, the *Los Angeles Times* reported that hundreds of students had gathered outside the school board building, "chanting 'Give us life prep, not a life sentence.'" The *Times* noted that many of the students and community members at the meeting were members of CEE, which the newspaper credited as the "grassroots organization that brought the idea to Huizar and [schools superintendent] Roy Romer a year ago."[30]

The atmosphere that evening was tense, but the resolution passed with a 6-1 vote. The new policy phased in the A-G requirements and stipulated that A-G would become the default curriculum by the 2008–2009 school year, meaning that all LAUSD students would be expected to complete a college preparatory curriculum in order to graduate.

As school board president José Huizar remarked to the *Los Angeles Times*: "This is one of the most significant reforms this district is embarking on in the last 20 years. The payoffs will be huge, the impacts will be huge . . . [W]hat this is about is providing thousands of students an opportunity to attend college—an opportunity denied to them with the current policies and practices."[31]

Rethinking Teacher Preparation in Illinois

Chicago ACORN's early education organizing focused on training parents and local school council members to become more confident, ask more sophisticated questions, and understand the language of education. As part of a training series on math instruction, parents reviewed data on the disparity of student educational outcomes between their schools and those in more affluent communities. The gap in student achievement led parents to examine the issue of teacher quality in their schools.

In 2001, Chicago ACORN released the first in a three-part series of data analyses documenting the problem of teacher inexperience and high rates of teacher vacancies and turnover in low-income communities of color.[32] These reports uncovered substantially higher rates of inexperienced teachers, and teacher turnover and vacancy in schools in neighborhoods where Chicago ACORN worked compared with Chicago public schools as a whole. Large numbers of teachers in Chicago ACORN neighborhoods were teaching without proper certification in their subject area; in some schools, more than half of the regular classrooms were staffed by teachers who lacked elementary teacher certification.

Chicago ACORN's research studies and public testimony focused attention on the disproportionate effect teacher turnover had on schools in low-income neighborhoods. Chicago ACORN leaders catalogued the number of uncertified teachers and full-time substitutes in each local school. Parents demanded to know why brand-new magnet schools could be opened fully staffed with certified teachers, while schools in Chicago ACORN neighborhoods were forced to rely on long-term substitutes to fill unstaffed classroom positions. Their testimony at a school board meeting in February

2001 attracted the attention of both major Chicago daily papers.[33] Chicago ACORN president (and veteran leader) Denise Dixon, a mother of three children in the Chicago Public Schools (CPS) system, recalls, "We were so forward about what we wanted for our children, what we needed, that press picked up on it. It was pretty cool to be heard, to actually have a solution to the problem, and not like we're just complaining. We're saying, this is wrong, and this is how you fix it. It's pretty amazing."

The *Sun-Times* filed a Freedom of Information Act request for teacher credential data and ran a five-part series in the fall of 2001 on the shortage of certified teachers.[34] The series devoted an article to the inequity between schools entitled "Teacher Woes Worse in Poor Schools," and credited Chicago ACORN's research for revealing the phenomenon.

Chicago ACORN's subsequent reports on how quickly new teachers left their neighborhood schools were covered by the *Sun-Times* and by *Catalyst*, an influential local school-reform magazine.[35] *Catalyst* devoted one of its monthly editions to teacher recruitment and retention and published follow-up articles on the struggles of poor schools to hang on to the teachers they had managed to recruit.

Through a combination of public pressure generated by media coverage, testimony at school board meetings, and behind-the-scenes meetings with the district's human resources staff, Chicago ACORN convinced the district to intensify its teacher-recruitment efforts in Chicago ACORN neighborhoods. The district assigned an experienced teacher recruiter to the subdistrict, charged with helping principals to improve teacher recruitment efforts. Chicago ACORN supported the district's efforts by attending new teacher-recruitment fairs and hosting new teachers on a tour of the neighborhoods where Chicago ACORN members lived.

These recruitment measures succeeded in filling teacher vacancies, but they did not slow the exodus of new teachers from the schools. Gwen Stewart, a grandmother and a leader in the North Lawndale neighborhood chapter of Chicago ACORN explains, "Part of the problem is that new teachers only stay for a short while. They're young, Caucasian, and new to Chicago. It's culture shock when they walk outside the building."

The experience taught Chicago ACORN that the problem of teacher quality in their schools stemmed from a deeper and more intractable issue: the majority of new teachers, coming from white middle-class neighborhoods, never intended to stay in low-income neighborhoods. "It is not a pipeline problem of too few teachers being trained in the state," says

Madeline Talbott, formerly head organizer of Chicago ACORN and now of Action Now. "Rather, too few teachers are being trained who want to work in our schools." Young white teachers worked in high-poverty schools long enough to gain experience, and then switched to jobs in suburban districts closer to home. These teachers were unfamiliar with and unprepared for working in schools serving low-income communities of color.

Talbott explains: "Here's what we began to understand, which helped *Catalyst* and CPS to focus on the same: teacher turnover is the cause of vacancies in otherwise easy to fill positions, such as elementary teachers and high school social studies teachers. It only occurs in neighborhoods where no teachers from that very community are being trained to be teachers— low income schools, especially of color, especially African American."

Faced with continuing high rates of turnover, Chicago ACORN began to explore ways to attract teachers who would stay in their schools. An allied organizing and service group, Logan Square Neighborhood Association (LSNA), had developed a program called Nueva Generación. LSNA engaged parents in local schools as school volunteers, parent mentors, and tutors. Nueva Generación was an extension of this parent engagement work, and allowed parents to build on their commitment to local schools by obtaining the certification to work as teachers.

Through the Nueva Generación program, parent members of LSNA could attend classes at Chicago State University and earn teaching certificates to become bilingual educators in their neighborhood schools. The program was widely viewed as a success. Amanda Rivera, a district official and former principal in Logan Square neighborhood school, observed that the parents brought a "comfort level and knowledge of the community" that new teachers from traditional teacher education programs often did not have.

Chicago ACORN saw the Nueva Generación model as a strategy for transforming the pipeline of teachers into low-income neighborhoods. In conversations with other stakeholders, organizers and leaders realized that the program had potential to influence teacher training not only in Chicago, but across the state, given that schools serving low-income children of color in other Illinois districts faced the same problem.

From their work on Chicago's local school councils, both LSNA and Chicago ACORN had developed strong relationships with two school-reform intermediaries, Cross City Campaign for Urban School Reform and Designs for Change. With funding from the Ford Foundation, the four groups convened a teacher quality coalition called Chicago Learning Campaign (CLC). The CLC sought state legislation to establish the Grow Your Own teacher program, based loosely on LSNA's experiences with Chicago State University. The CLC proposed creating local partnerships between community groups and universities across the state to train community residents and teacher paraprofessionals to become teachers.

As seasoned players in the city and state political landscape, Chicago ACORN and its allies in the CLC set about building a broad coalition to push the effort. Passing state legislation, they reasoned, would be much easier if all the organizations that would have a hand in carrying out Grow Your Own programs were on board from the beginning. So CLC members reached out to the school district, local universities, community colleges, unions, and foundations. Chicago ACORN and LSNA met with the state legislators for their respective neighborhoods, with whom they had long-established relationships, and recruited more organizing groups into the collaboration. With Madeline Talbott as the main facilitator, the CLC assembled a broadly representative Grow Your Own Task Force.

As one of its first activities, the task force convened a summit in Springfield, the state capital. A variety of stakeholders were invited, including parents, teachers, universities, philanthropic foundations, and school district officials, as well as state legislators from key legislative districts. The effort proved to be especially successful in capturing the attention of policy makers, and in building political support for the initiative. Talbott recalls: "The way [politicians] generally look at this stuff is they look for the unions and the universities and the school districts. Now they are weighing in and we've got the unions, universities, and school districts. So far we are looking good and [we've] got grassroots on top of that, which [helps] enormously . . . Everybody is starting to jump on board like it's a downhill train." Even legislators who did not support the effort, Talbott says, "made a decision not to oppose GYO when they got a feel for who was at the table and what kind of support it had."

Following the summit, members of the task force worked behind the scenes to draft new legislation. The Grow Your Own Teachers Act passed during the 2004 legislative session. The governor signed on, authorizing the creation of local consortia across the state, comprising universities, school districts, and community organizations. Consortia were charged with recruiting and supporting neighborhood residents who had demonstrated a commitment teaching in hard-to-staff schools to participate in the teacher preparation programs.

Because of a fiscal crisis in Illinois, the GYO Task Force had to wait until the following year to press for a budget appropriation. In the interim, the task force, led by its new director Anne Hallett, who had previously led the Cross City Campaign for Urban School Reform, worked to cultivate support among universities, community groups and unions in high-turnover districts across the state, to ensure that the appropriation would be sufficiently large to pay for the program, and that local consortia would be ready to act once the program once funded.

Task force members also worked with officials at the state department of education to draft the rules governing the program. Chicago ACORN, LSNA, and the other organizing groups pushed to require the participation in each consortium of a community organizing group, which would take primary responsibility for recruiting candidates. Without the continuing involvement of strong community organizations, task force members worried that teacher training institutions might use GYO funds to re-create the kinds of programs already in place.

In 2005 the Illinois State Legislature approved an initial appropriation of $1.5 million in planning grants to ten consortia, and has provided additional appropriations of roughly $3 million in each year since (reaching a total of $11 million by 2009). Talbott, Dixon, and the board, staff, and members of Chicago ACORN continue to play a leading role in the Grow Your Own initiative through their new affiliation with Action Now. To date, eight of the twelve public universities in Illinois participate in GYO, and sixteen consortia across the state are supporting cohorts of future teachers.[36]

BUILDING NEW CIVIC CAPACITY IN URBAN SCHOOL DISTRICTS

If local organizing develops new social capital in communities, coalition-building strategies aim to leverage community-based social capital into new political power to make larger and more ambitious reform demands. As the preceding examples illustrate, organizing groups participate in a variety of coalitions—from a set of loose partnerships to deeper, more broad-based groups. In each case, these coalitions were essential to achieving reform. Coalition strategies helped expand the pressure on education officials to accede to local demands. They also provided essential leverage in moving system initiatives. Consistent with the findings of Jeffrey Henig and his colleagues, coalitions that involved a broader range of constituency groups had more influence and capacity not only to engage decision makers, but also to respond to, anticipate, and address challenges in the educational and political context.

Regardless of the coalition structure, when building or joining coalitions, organizing groups face the challenge of ensuring that the social capital mobilized is used to shift power dynamics and improve equity. Community organizations must thus work in ways that counter the dynamics and pitfalls of traditional coalitions, which are likely to marginalize community perspectives.[37] Organizing groups participating in coalitions in our study played a vital role in bringing community voices into reform discussions and in creating inclusive coalition cultures, so that equity demands remained front and center in the effort.

Establishing a Place for Community at the Reform Table

Reform coalitions naturally prioritize the concerns of those who are present over those who are not. Reform coalitions in urban districts are traditionally dominated by the workplace concerns of educator unions, as well as by private-sector interests in privatizing school functions, reducing bureaucratic restrictions, and centralizing management and control. These constituencies are often white and middle-class, and in many cases neither parents nor employers of students in the public school system.

Including parents and youth of color and representatives from low-income and/or immigrant communities at the table does not necessarily change whose interests are promoted through the work. Organizing groups may bring new constituencies to the table, but influencing the normative beliefs that undergird how coalitions operate is a fluid and complex process. Coalitions are dynamic entities shaped by relationships among member organizations, as well as the interplay of discursive and oppositional activity through which their members arrive at a collective vision and strategy.

Though the organizing groups in our study used research conducted by "experts," each organization framed schooling problems in terms of the experiences of community members whose lives were directly impacted by overcrowded schools, run-down facilities, low academic expectations, and high rates of teacher turnover. The populist character of these frames, combined with statistical evidence, brought a level of legitimacy that helped groups exert greater control over coalition agendas, strategies, and outcomes. In New York City and Philadelphia, the NWBCCC and YUC defined coalition goals from the outset. In Los Angeles and Illinois, where coalitions were broader in scope, the Community Coalition and Chicago ACORN drew on their local experiences to influence coalition partners. As

Los Angeles school board president Monica Garcia observes of the Community Coalition: "They will get up, expose a reality, and then provide what they think is their solution and then include folks in that."

Coalition member organizations each bring their own unique strengths to the reform effort, but the work must operate from a sense of "community mandate," says Alberto Retana. Observers in Los Angeles note CEE's deep and authentic connection to its constituency—parents and students—as a critical factor in the coalition's ultimate success, one that separated CEE's work from more traditional advocacy efforts. Community Coalition, along with Inner City Struggle, an organizing group in East Los Angeles, mobilized extensive turnout from their respective neighborhoods in support of the A-G curriculum resolution. Young people from SCYEA and Inner City Struggle, some of whom had been involved in the fight for A-G for four or five years, received ongoing briefings about CEE's efforts and canvassed their neighborhoods to build grassroots awareness of the proposed policy. Youth also raised awareness about the policy resolution at local high schools through class presentations and cultural productions featuring visual and digital art, music, theater, and poetry to educate their peers on the need to improve the quality of their schools. Leading up to the school board vote, SCYEA members collected roughly 5,000 of the 13,000 signatures for a petition supporting the A-G resolution and served as key media spokespersons on the need for increased rigor in the curriculum.

The addition of "people power" helped coalitions to win support from key political players, including district leadership and local elected officials. "I am pretty convinced that no amount of intellectual framing and data and research that we could have provided would have moved that district," observes Russlynn Ali, then-executive director of the advocacy organization Education Trust-West. "We needed the 800 plus Latino and African-American parents [and youth] to mandate rigor. It was organizing unlike anywhere else I've seen in the nation."

Shaping an Inclusive Coalition Culture

Charles Kadushin and his colleagues note that when coalitions convene, conflict and differences in power "typically are either ignored or minimized in the initial call for 'everyone to come to the table.'"[38] Yet ignoring conflict creates "serious problems" in the long term. In this respect, community organizing groups may be particularly well prepared for the complexities of coalition building. Organizers and leaders are trained to build relationships, identify self-interest, and to act as skillful and effective communicators and negotiators. The methodology of community organizing emphasizes the development of concrete, winnable demands put forth through consensus. Experienced in this process, organizing groups are accustomed to navigating differences in power and negotiating through conflict to arrive at a common vision.

In Los Angeles and Illinois, where coalitions were broad-based and sustained for several years, members observed that the Community Coalition and Chicago ACORN's participation set an open and respectful tone in the group. In Los Angeles, the skilled facilitation and collegial leadership style of organizer Alberto Retana helped the coalition navigate political and personal dynamics within and outside of the coalition, and bring different partners to a shared vision. "[He] was able to keep the meetings on the issue and if there was any division, he was very skillful at helping to get the core questions and concerns addressed," recalls Sandy Mendoza of the United Way. Similarly, in Chicago, Amanda Rivera, the Director of Induction and Mentoring Programs for the Chicago Public Schools, was impressed by Madeline Talbott's ability to "bring people together" and create an "inclusive process," one that helped her to "appreciate [the culture of] organizing."

In both Los Angeles and Illinois, staff organizers played highly visible roles, more so than in YUC and the NWBCCC. The respective roles of organizers and leaders varied among the different coalitions, likely due to contextual factors such as the scope and intensity of the coalition effort and other strategic considerations. Though the NWBCCC's vision defined the SCWG, for example, parent leaders were the dominant voices in the coalition effort. Similarly, in Philadelphia, youth maintained a presence at all levels of the small-schools campaign. While leaders were clearly present in Los Angeles and Illinois, interview data suggest that staff organizers were perceived by other coalition members as crucial to shaping the culture and focus of coalition efforts.

Moving Systemic Equity Reform

John Gaventa and Heidi Swarts argue that the impact of successful organizing can be measured in terms of the resources the groups generate, the level of representation groups achieve in decision making, and the extent to which the group's work shifts the paradigm in how a problem is conceptualized and addressed.[39] Certainly each coalition achieved substantial impact: fourteen thousand new school seats in the Bronx, four new college-oriented high schools in the Kensington neighborhood of North

Philadelphia, mandatory college preparatory curriculum in all Los Angeles high schools, and $11 million in funds for sixteen consortia across Illinois to prepare new teachers for jobs in low-income communities of color.

Commitments of new policy and funding are one marker of organizational influence in district, municipal, and state decision-making processes. Another marker is the degree to which groups develop ongoing relationships with officials who influence both public and behind-the-scenes actions. In New York and Philadelphia, groups formed deep and continuing connections with educators, and enlisted them as behind-the-scenes allies to the efforts. District 10 leaders shared data and ideas with the NWBCCC and were receptive to NWBCCC proposals for new school facilities sites and leasing development strategies. Likewise in Philadelphia, local and city-level district officials listened to YUC proposals for revamping the Kensington high school campus and involved the organization at each stage of the redesign process.

In Chicago and Los Angeles, where coalition efforts included district and community leaders, educators played more overt roles in the coalitions. In these efforts, community groups faced the challenge of applying pressure while preserving the interests of their allies in the system. Al Bertani, formerly the chief officer for professional development in the Chicago Public Schools, observes that Chicago ACORN "was able to maintain a posture as a friendly critic or critical friend of the system while recognizing that building an alliance with the system would help them advance their goals."

Chicago ACORN and the Community Coalition's years of organizing developed both knowledge of the existing power structure and relationships with political players. The groups used their knowledge and relationships to propose strategies that leveraged the collective strength of the coalition—including its inside allies—to push for systemic, rather than incremental, reform. As Madeline Talbott observes, the role of Chicago ACORN and Action Now in the coalition was not just to put forth the notion of Grow Your Own as a valuable program. These organizations' role was also to bring expertise in Chicago politics to the table, to "look at what we have to do *politically*, beyond what we have to do programmatically, in order to succeed."

BEYOND THE VICTORY: CHALLENGES TO SUSTAINED REFORM

Along the spectrum of coalition efforts, what can be achieved is clearly dependent on contextual factors as well as the internal dynamics of groups.

Community groups that built sustained efforts were led by staff with long histories of work and long-standing relationships within the advocacy community, as well as extensive knowledge about the political interests of local district and municipal officials. These relationships and knowledge equipped them to build cohesive reform efforts with broad and ambitious visions.

Like the work discussed in chapter 3, organizing in these four cities is an unfinished story. All of the organizations are closely monitoring their victories. They are also grappling with how to maintain pressure at the system level and to create a presence at the school level to prevent the "watering-down of reform's equity-minded aspects" that diminish the prospects for substantial educational change.[40] The NWBCCC and local officials continue to advocate for building new schools on the abandoned Armory site, following the NWBCCC's 2007 report on inconsistencies in city officials' education facilities estimates. In Philadelphia, Youth United for Change and its allies are calling for genuinely small schools, challenging the district's decision to implement 600–800 seat schools while continuing to organize young people on the Kensington high school campus.

In Illinois, following passage of the GYO act, Chicago ACORN wrestled with the higher education institutions in the task force to ensure that the state funds would not flow directly to these institutions. "We understand we may have to compromise, but we're going in fighting for how much we can get," observed Madeline Talbott during the negotiations over how the program would function. "Having worked with [higher education institutions] for a few years in the fight to get funded, we understand how they really operate, that they have good intentions, but once the money starts flowing, if there are no restrictions . . . they will just slurp up the money and do what they've always done with it."

CEE in Los Angeles has worked with district staff on the A-G implementation committee to ensure that the necessary resources and supports are in place for the reform to be successful. Joanne Kim, an organizer at the Community Coalition observes: "Our job is not to figure out every detail of how the district is going to do this. That's what they get paid for. Our job is to maintain the pressure and also to make recommendations on what the community thinks is especially important, instead of bureaucrats dictating what they think is important, in terms of student achievement and other important measures of success."

In 2009, CEE secured a $1.75 million grant to continue to engage community, civic, and business partners in a collective effort to keep the district accountable for providing all LAUSD students with access to a rigorous college preparatory curriculum. CEE is building local organizing collaboratives in clusters of high schools and their feeder elementary and middle schools. The Community Coalition, as one of the lead organizations in the South Los Angeles Collaborative, is working to develop a model career academy at Locke High School and to push the district to take such best practices to scale.

Charles Kadushin and his colleagues have observed that the cooperation required in a successful coalition of multiple organizations is, at best, an "unnatural act." Moving from temporary, relatively focused issue coalitions to coalitions advocating for more general, abstract goals and visions can be challenging, for "even if a social ill is perceived as a common adversary, individuals and organizations with different ideologies, professional perspectives, or self-interests will differ on how to address the problem."[41] Philosophical tensions are inherent, as are funding tensions among coalition members.

Such questions loom large for these groups. But as Reneé, Oakes and Welner point out, the challenge may be less one of sustaining these reform coalitions as they are, and more of sustaining the work of community organizing from which "a new force or (preferably) set of forces could arise to sustain a hospitable political and normative environment" for reform.[42]

CHAPTER FIVE

Responding to the Challenges of Scale

When the Illinois State Legislature passed the Grow Your Own Teachers Act in 2004, Chicago ACORN organizers and leaders were elated. Even though the state budget was already stretched, and coalition members knew that funding for the program that year was unlikely, key players were lined up in support of the bill and a funding appropriation during the following fiscal year was expected.

After the victory, the Grow Your Own task force convened to assess its work. In those meetings, former Chicago ACORN head organizer Madeline Talbott recalls realizing that the group could not simply declare victory for its neighborhoods and walk away. "There was a moment when we thought you win the funding and then you just get funded for your neighborhood and let everyone else do what they want, but we don't think that anymore," she says.

Talbott and her community organizing partners saw the opportunity to influence teacher preparation far beyond simply the creation of a handful of neighborhood-based teacher pipeline programs. As she noted at the time:

We think we've got to set this up right and control it as much as we can. This is about more than just getting highly qualified teachers who will stay in our schools . . . We now believe that the community organizations have a role to play in the development of the teachers so that there are teachers in our schools who respect the students and the community, and don't get that belief beaten out of them along the way. We have the chance to change the way institutions of higher education operate going forward, and we're very excited about it. It's just kind of overwhelming.

The imperative of improving educational outcomes for large numbers of children has drawn organizing groups into monitoring and implementing reform programs, taking on roles in schools far beyond how they have traditionally operated. ACORN has a national reputation among organizing groups for its exclusive focus on policy-level campaigns. Now, Talbott says, she doesn't "believe that you can win and have it mean anything unless you're prepared to climb into some of the schools and implement it."

"Climbing into schools" pulls organizing groups in competing directions, and in this chapter we explore those directions in depth. On the one hand, as Talbott notes, groups face the challenge of making sure their campaign victories will be implemented authentically and meaningfully at the local school level. On the other hand, the goal of equity pushes groups to seek reform across ever-growing numbers of schools through strategies that aim for district- or statewide scale.

Definitions of scale typically consider the number of classrooms, schools, or districts reached by a reform effort.[1] Drawing on scholarship by Cynthia Coburn at the University of California at Berkeley, we argue that reaching for scale encompasses the challenge of implementation—fostering mastery, understanding, and ownership of reform within schools and districts—as well as the challenge of building organizational power to move reform in a wider political landscape.

The competing pressures of depth and spread are what Coburn calls "interrelated" dimensions of scale: "[S]caling up not only requires spread to additional sites but also consequential change in classrooms, enduring over time, and a shift such that knowledge and authority for reform is transferred from external organizations to teachers, schools, and districts." Efforts at scale must attend to the "nature of change; issues of sustainability; spread of norms, principles, and beliefs; and a shift of ownership such that a reform can become self-generative."[2]

Education organizing in every site considered in this study reflects the ongoing tension between competing priorities for depth *and* breadth. Beneath this tension lies a fundamental dilemma: if participation and leadership development are the foundation of community organizing's vision for a strong and vital democracy, then reforming schools cannot be engineered by parachuting in new models of reform from above, as district leaders and education reform organizations often do. Reforms must be constructed locally by educators and community members in ways that build on their respective domains of knowledge and expertise, while cultivating a sense of collective efficacy within a school community and a shared accountability to the goal of improved student outcomes. As we noted in chapter 3, community organizing groups can help to catalyze these forms of local capacity when organizations are deeply and consistently involved in schools.

At the same time, concentrating organizing resources on a small number of schools will not shift the disparities in political power and economic capital that have educationally impoverished huge portions of the U.S. population for much of our nation's history. More powerful approaches are needed to drive a new political agenda that realigns policy and resources so that children from low-income communities, immigrant families, and communities of color receive the quality education they need and deserve. These approaches often entail coalition- and alliance-building activities at a level of the system that is far removed from organizing activities in local schools.

This chapter explores how the interplay of depth and breadth shapes school-reform organizing. Sites in our study worked to embed reform in schools by confronting the beliefs of educators and community members that stand in the way of equity-based reform, and by proposing innovations at the school and district level that embody a set of countervailing beliefs about student capacities, the role of communities in the educational process, and the relationship between schools and communities they serve.

Our discussion of scale also considers the role of state-level organizing in protecting and expanding successful education-reform programs and strategies. We highlight statewide campaigns in Wisconsin and Texas as examples of how organizing networks build and exert statewide power through a process of citizen education and engagement. We conclude with a discussion of how organizing groups are responding to the organizational capacity challenges that accompany efforts to move reform to scale.

ROOTING REFORM: ISSUES OF DEPTH, INTEGRATION, AND ACCOUNTABILITY

What is authentic and meaningful education reform? Reforms are often conceptualized in technical terms—that is, in terms of the procedural mechanics of how new strategies or practices for school improvement work. Whether or not these reforms actually produce desired outcomes depends on prevailing beliefs and political relationships within the community and educational system.

Depth

A long history of research suggests that reforms are more likely to produce deep and lasting change if they engage the normative beliefs and operational structures that shape how school systems work.[3] By *normative
beliefs*, we mean educators' explicit and implicit operating theories about
how students learn and how instruction should be delivered, as well as their
assumptions about student capacities to learn and the role of families in
the learning process. *Operational structures* are the procedures and mechanisms through which schools and districts enact normative beliefs. Classroom scheduling, lesson planning, faculty meetings, and parent-teacher
conference routines are operational structures through which schools and
school systems communicate a set of beliefs about the roles, expectations,
and capacities of participants. These normative beliefs and operational
structures shape educators' actions in schools: how teachers and principals
work with each other, how they organize and deliver instruction, and how
they interact with students and families.

In chapter 3, we examined Austin Interfaith and Oakland Community
Organizations (OCO) efforts to change the normative context of schools.
Both organizations challenged educators' *and* parents' beliefs about their
respective roles in student learning and how schools should function as
organizations. Doug Greco, lead organizer at Austin Interfaith, explains,
"Our approach is to work with the adults in schools to teach them and
engage them in the democratic process, and build schools that are communities of learners and mentoring institutions, so that teachers and parents
model the habits and practices of democracy and learning for students."
Drawing on the organizing principles of power, accountability, and participatory democracy, Austin Interfaith and OCO built new patterns of behav-
ior in educators and between school faculty and community members.

Austin's Alliance School work was characterized by leadership development activities, community walks, house meetings, and school improvement campaigns. The purpose of these activities was to contest the apathy,
frustration, and sense of helplessness so common among the educators and
parents of students in low-performing schools. In their place, Austin Interfaith organizers hoped to build what Professor Susan B. Empson at the
University of Texas at Austin calls the "infrastructure" for school-level improvement. She says, "It can't just be a principal telling teachers what to

do, it can't just be one teacher who's enthusiastic about teaching math in a new way and wants to experiment. And it can't just be parents insisting that the school do a certain thing. It has to be all of them working together and creating a shared vision."

In Oakland, OCO helped to define a new vision of schools as collegial, personalized, and "academically rigorous learning environments for urban students who do not currently have access to them."[4] OCO then promoted this vision in new small schools through parent leadership training and parent involvement in the school-design process. Rick Gaston, principal of the Castlemont Business and Information Technology High School, notes: the resulting cultural norm in small schools emphasized "empowering the full spectrum of voices from across our school community . . . Rather than just thinking of things from a principal and teacher's perspective, [I've learned] to always reach out and try to include and empower the parent community."

In urban districts, reform efforts typically impose new operational structures—new classroom observation or performance assessment procedures, for example—to prod schools along the path to improvement. Community organizing groups have positioned their reform efforts differently, working instead to confront normative beliefs and then propose new structures (or reshape existing ones) to embed an alternative set of beliefs in schools.

The extent to which organizing campaigns yield lasting change depends on the degree to which new beliefs are sufficiently integrated not only within schools but also across multiple levels of the school system. Numerous studies have documented the ease with which reforms are thwarted or uprooted by changes in the local context of schools.[5] Reforms proposed by community groups must withstand the transitions in staff and administrators as well as shifts in organizational priorities that are inevitable in any context, and even more frequent in low performing schools. To what extent do district leaders understand and practice relational behaviors in Austin? Or define teacher quality in terms of community knowledge as well as professional expertise in Illinois? District officials' agreement with the organizational and instructional theories underlying proposed reforms increases the likelihood that they will protect and sustain the work.

Integration

Chapters 3 and 4 provided examples of how organizing groups are shaping new district policies, district-level support structures, and funding initiatives to promote school-level change. In Austin, Miami, and Oakland, where we found evidence of positive school- and student-level effects, organizing efforts generated new districtwide staff positions and professional development opportunities to help schools implement reform.

Yet in these sites, groups faced considerable obstacles in establishing what Cynthia Coburn calls "normative coherence," which ensures that district-level policies, procedures, and professional learning opportunities are consistent with reform principles and practices. In large part, these difficulties stem from the dysfunctional and fragmented structure of districts Early on in the small-schools reforms, OCO's Ron Snyder observed in frustration: "Not only do you have to create the schools, but you have to create the system that supports the schools . . . Human resources, budget, curriculum offices all operate independently. They don't talk to each other, so there's no integration in what they send out to the schools and what they expect the schools to do."

Difficulties in building normative coherence also stem from competing views of how schools change and what constitutes effective educational practice. In Texas, the Alliance School model struggled against competing theories held by district- and state-level leaders about the role of testing in school improvement and student learning. By the early 2000s, statewide accountability pressures had created "a difficult situation for community organizing," observes Angela Valenzuela, a researcher at the University of Texas at Austin. "The [Alliance School] model depends on relationships with [principals] because you need to be able to actually reserve a room usually at school, and you need to develop a set of programs and activities with the parents. I've heard principals saying 'We just can't do this right now. We have to focus on the benchmarks.' or 'We have to focus on the TAKS test.'"

In 2002, the Austin superintendent adopted Alliance School community engagement practices as part of the district's reform plan for its lowest-performing schools. The district created new "parent support specialist" positions and provided professional development opportunities to help principals and teachers in these schools work with parents effectively. But the cycle of test preparation and testing undermined implementation of these new community-engagement strategies. Valenzuela says, "Anyone who comes into a school now is going to see that they're not as welcoming because—unless you've specifically been invited—they don't have time for you. Everything is squeezed out.

Accountability

In any reform, district support is not simply a matter of whether leaders share the reform vision, but also of the extent to which leaders feel accountable to the needs and concerns of the constituency behind the reform. Building new accountability relationships between school system leaders and community constituencies is a core mission of community organizing groups. Direct action in the form of rallies and mass attendance at school board meetings are often used to demonstrate the size of the constituency that is concerned about an issue and to remind educational leaders of the organization's capacity to raise a public fuss when commitments are not fulfilled.

Accountability relationships are not static. Demands for accountability must be continually asserted to maintain a sense of responsibility among long-standing leadership and to ensure that emerging leaders will prioritize community needs. OCO's repeated mobilizations were crucial to sustaining support for the small-school reform from district leaders and three successive state-appointed administrators. In contrast, Austin Interfaith's difficulties in preserving space for the Alliance School work, and PACT's struggle to maintain the Direct Instruction program, suggest a weaker accountability relationship between district leaders and community organizing constituencies. In this respect, PACT's experiences with Direct Instruction are instructive.

In its initial organizing to win Direct Instruction, PACT pursued an aggressive strategy with school board members, holding individual meetings to present their argument and seek board members' support. Miami-Dade County officials eventually endorsed the program, adding Direct Instruction to the list of preapproved curriculum programs that schools could implement. The district later added a second phonics-based curriculum to the list of preapproved programs, in a sign of its support for the Direct Instruction approach to literacy development. The district also added new staff positions to foster implementation of Direct Instruction through school-based coaches, three district-based "super coaches" and a district-level administrator for the program. As the district took on more responsibility for supporting the program, PACT turned its attention to school-level activities and statewide education campaigns.

Three years later, however, the district stance toward Direct Instruction shifted with the appointment of a new superintendent who brought a different management theory about school-level autonomy and instructional coherence. When the incoming superintendent decided to implement a new literacy program, PACT struggled to rally support for Direct Instruction among school board members. "After years of working with supportive superintendents, we had ignored the need to keep relationships of power with school board members," former executive director Aaron Dorfman says. Once the superintendent "decided to forge ahead with removing Direct Instruction, we didn't have enough power in relationship to him to stop it."

Changing the Rules of Engagement

Defining scale in terms of depth, integration, and accountability makes clear just how difficult a task organizing groups face in catalyzing widespread and sustained reform. The operational challenges multiply as the number of schools involved in reform grows. OCO's success in stimulating a districtwide strategy of small-school creation in Oakland precipitated a rapid growth in new small schools, from six schools in 2001 to forty-eight in 2008.[6] As the number grew, OCO organizers found they could not keep up with the demands. There were not enough organizers on staff for OCO to assign an organizer to each new school. And the intensive support with relationship-building and problem-solving required by the start-up schools quickly overwhelmed organizers. Confronted with the limits of its own capacity to keep pace with the reforms, OCO shifted its strategy to provide district-level leadership development training for parents and educators and to train design team members through a partnership with the district's small-schools office. The idea was to "get people coming to us, instead of us trying to figure out how we get there," Ron Snyder says.

The increasing involvement of community organizing groups in reform implementation reflects growing awareness among organizers and leaders that, to achieve lasting change, education campaigns must penetrate schools more deeply than merely putting reforms in place. Groups that have done so include not only Austin Interfaith, OCO, and PACT, but also organizations that traditionally focused on district-level policy campaigns, as well as youth-led organizations with a history of very specific school-improvement campaigns. YUC's Andi Perez observes: "It used to be that you go, you negotiate, and you have your action. Now we're organizing community organizations to be a consistent voice in the reform, understanding that along with the research that small schools are better, comes research that community engagement makes schools better."

Historically, the push for equity led policy-oriented groups and youth-led organizations to focus on the next big win, rather than to get involved in monitoring implementation of previous victories. "Most of the time, the victories that folks win aren't at the scale that's really needed," explains organizer Alberto Retana, who also notes that organizing wins on books, security, and student-teacher relationships might be important but monitoring small victories drains organizational resources.

Taking on more complex educational issues has shifted the kinds of relationships groups are building with schools from sporadic involvement to more continuous engagement. YUC and SBU are now core partners in the new small schools they helped create in Philadelphia and New York City. In Los Angeles, CEE coalition members are working closely with district officials to define indicators of high academic expectations and instructional rigor in support of the new A-G policy. And Chicago ACORN is deeply involved in professional development to figure out "how you get classroom-to-classroom visits for teachers and parents to eliminate the isolation and encourage peer-coaching and conversation," according to organizer Madeline Talbott. "We're doing this so we'll be in position in the hard-to-staff schools so that when they get a critical mass of Grow Your Own teachers, we'll be able to impact the whole culture of the schools."

SPREADING REFORM: BUILDING POWER TO INFLUENCE STATE-LEVEL POLITICS

As Cynthia Coburn points out, scale requires collective ownership, "so that [the reform] is no longer an 'external' reform, controlled by a reformer, but rather becomes an 'internal' reform with authority for the reform held by districts, schools, and teachers who have the capacity to sustain, spread, and deepen reform principles themselves."[7] Reforms must be integrated into the daily life of schools and districts so that they are not "add-on" activities but are instead viewed as integral to how schools organize and carry out their work. This understanding of "deep" scale necessitates the type of sustained engagement with schools and districts described above. Increasingly, however, the work of developing ownership of reform also involves state-level organizing targeted at winning the support of state-level political leaders and departments of education.

Though state departments of education have historically been weak, state roles in educational policy expanded substantially following the passage of the No Child Left Behind Act in 2001. States assumed increasing influence over district educational policies through their roles in defining educational standards and performance goals and assessing, monitoring, and reporting on how schools meet these performance goals.

All the sites in our study have organized to build power to influence state-level politics. Campaigns have been developed to protect local reforms from incompatible state-level demands, such as those imposed by high stakes testing in Texas. State-level organizing also responds to the limited capacity of urban districts to sufficiently address community demands for equity and school quality. On issues of teacher quality, school construction, and school financing, in particular, states are increasingly the target of organizing because reform requires a level of resources, capacity, and influence beyond what many urban school districts can muster.

Chicago ACORN, for example, turned to a statewide strategy of Grow Your Own teacher development after three years of local organizing to address teacher turnover. By developing a state-level strategy, Chicago ACORN hoped to gain more resources than the Chicago Public Schools could provide and to make use of political opportunities in the state context created by No Child Left Behind to influence the system of teacher preparation.

The Grow Your Own campaign in Illinois provides one example of how organizing groups exert state-level influence through strategic coalition building. Chicago ACORN and its allies built a statewide coalition that included community groups, education-reform organizations, teacher training institutions, the teachers' union, and Chicago school district officials to push for the new teacher pipeline program. These coalition members were deliberately recruited by Chicago ACORN and its allies so that the coalition would represent the range of constituencies with influence and credibility among state-level leaders.

State-level alliances are common in community organizing, particularly between organizing groups and research and policy organizations that provide expertise relevant to organizing campaigns. Members of the national organizing networks—ACORN, DART, the Gamaliel Foundation, IAF, and PICO—also wield state-level influence by building and mobilizing affiliates in strategic legislative districts. During the course of our study, the Gamaliel Foundation created new affiliates across Wisconsin to build statewide power. In Texas, our research followed the Industrial Areas Foundation's mobilization across the state to demand reform of the state's high-stakes school accountability system. We turn to how and why organizing networks developed these strategies next.

Statewide Organization-Building in Wisconsin

During the period of our study, Milwaukee Inner-city Congregations Allied for Hope (MICAH) and its parent organizing network, the Chicago-based

Gamaliel Foundation, implemented an ambitious expansion strategy across Wisconsin. In the span of a decade, the network formed eight new organizations under the umbrella organization WISDOM. The network's goal was to build regional (metropolitan) power and statewide power to address systemic inequities across the state.

The third-oldest organization in the Gamaliel Foundation, MICAH was founded in 1988. The organization began with a strong organizational identity of being rooted in the core of Milwaukee. "They drew a line around the black and Hispanic community, chose the name, Milwaukee *Inner City* Congregations Allied for Hope, and said, 'This is where we are. Because if we create a citywide or countywide representation, white people will come in and take over and it won't be our organization,'" recalls Greg Galluzzo, executive director of the Gamaliel Foundation.

MICAH began education organizing in the early 1990s, negotiating with the district and local colleges to improve the recruitment of teachers of color in district schools. In the mid-1990s, the organization won state funding for class-size reduction in early elementary grades for Milwaukee schools.

In 1998, the organization challenged the local school board and state legislative leaders on a proposal to reduce busing costs by requiring children to attend neighborhood schools. Milwaukee is the second most segregated city in the country, and the district has been under a court-ordered desegregation plan since the 1970s. The school district also has one of the most extensive school choice programs in the country, with roughly a fifth of the district's students traveling from the city to attend schools in the surrounding suburbs. Transportation costs for students traveling across the district, as well as to the suburban schools, are paid jointly by the district and state.

MICAH saw the end of busing as a threat to equity in the district, fearing that a return to neighborhood zoning patterns would effectively end all hopes of integration and consign low-income African American children to low-performing schools. Without the option of busing for students who opted out of their neighborhood school, families that lacked the means to drive their children to school would have no choice but to let their children walk through dangerous streets to poorly performing, central city schools. The magnet and specialty schools that had been a cornerstone of within-district integration would thus be closed to inner-city children.

"The mayor, the bipartisan legislature, the newspapers, everyone thought it was a great idea. We were the only people in town who had questions about it," recalls David Liners, a former organizer with MICAH. "We decided to look carefully into everything about this initiative. We reviewed every document that came out."

Because the Neighborhood Schools Initiative involved district as well as state resources, MICAH's advocacy targeted local school board members and members of the state's powerful joint finance committee. MICAH leaders testified at school board meetings and legislative committee hearings and held rallies and media events. At these events, MICAH called for the district to continue the policy of paying transportation costs so low-income families could send their children to more successful schools in the district and surrounding suburbs.

MICAH drafted a position paper outlining their objections to the district's plan, which was released as a press statement. Coverage in the *Milwaukee Journal-Sentinel*, along with letters to the editor from several MICAH leaders, put the school board on the defensive. Other organizations, including the teachers' union and the American Civil Liberties Union, echoed MICAH's concerns about segregation and children's safety walking to school at the hearings. The final plan, while still emphasizing neighborhood schools, preserved busing and made provisions for students who moved mid-year. Aaron Schutz, a member of MICAH's education committee and a professor at the University of Wisconsin summed up the campaign: "MICAH drew a line in the sand over the issue of equity, and the Milwaukee Public Schools backed off."

The neighborhood school initiative exposed the contours of a deep and intractable problem facing the Milwaukee public schools. Like urban communities across the country, Milwaukee's tax base had declined steadily since the mid-1970s, as middle-class families moved from center-city neighborhoods to communities in the city's outer ring and suburbs. The city faced recurring budget shortfalls in education spending, along with great disparities in spending between district schools and schools in surrounding affluent communities. Compounding the resource scarcity and disparities, the Milwaukee school district was required by law to pay the per-pupil costs of Milwaukee students who chose to attend schools in other districts.

As in other states, Wisconsin has experienced intensifying pressure to reform its system of school funding. (Five states in our study—California, New York, Pennsylvania, Wisconsin, and Texas—have faced lawsuits arguing that their funding formulas violate constitutional guarantees of the educational rights of urban students.) Two-thirds of Milwaukee's education spending, on average, is provided by the state under a statewide plan intended to equalize school funding among school districts by reducing local property taxes. In practice, the plan has favored wealthy districts that are more likely than poorer districts to rally voter support to circumvent revenue caps.

In 1999, MICAH expanded its organization to reach across municipal boundaries to recruit wealthier and largely white congregations into the organization. The move reflected the Gamaliel Foundation's assessment that MICAH would not be able to influence metropolitan politics without an organizational base in more affluent and politically connected communities that surrounded the city.

Greg Galluzzo explains: "MICAH did a lot of good things. We won a 25 percent set-aside for contractors that worked for the city, shut down a lot of drug houses, fixed up a couple of schools. Then we took on a campaign to pass a referendum to get more money for schools. Half the city is white, half the city is black. White people are sending their kids to private school. They vote in greater numbers than people in black communities. We tried to pass the referendum and we lost. Without organizing the whole city, there are certain things we can't do." As Galluzzo aptly observes, Wisconsin's low-income families, immigrant communities, and communities of color are concentrated in cities that dot the southeast part of the state, yet much of the power over what happens in these urban communities rests in the hands of white elites who live in wealthier suburban areas.

In 1999, in a strategic response to this dynamic, Gamaliel initiated a new statewide network in Wisconsin, called WISDOM, which provided the space for MICAH and other Gamaliel affiliates across the state to connect with one another and to collaborate on statewide campaigns. MICAH's lead organizer, Ana Garcia-Ashley, stepped down from her position to lead the expansion effort and began building Gamaliel affiliate organizations in strategic locations across the state. By creating new "metropolitan" affiliate organizations that spanned urban-suburban communities, Garcia-Ashley aimed to make MICAH more powerful. "We had lost so many state fights and I was tired of losing," she says. "I was tired of only being powerful as long as we stayed on our own turf, as long as we didn't step out of MICAH's territory."

Gamaliel's expansion strategy was heavily influenced by the policy vision of Myron Orfield and David Rusk, now researchers at the Institute on Race and Poverty at the University of Minnesota Law School. Orfield and Rusk proposed a strategy of regional equity organizing to address growing disparities between affluent suburban communities and poor inner city and edge-city communities. Their ideas resonated with Gamaliel's leadership, and particularly for Galluzzo, who had seen a similar pattern of defeat repeat itself across Gamaliel organizations. "We knew we would always lose," Galluzzo says. "The poorest people are paying the highest tax and they are the ones subsidizing the property tax base. [For example, in Milwaukee] money was being taken from their drug treatment programs to support a new baseball stadium. We stopped it from being taken from the county, but we couldn't stop it overall because we weren't powerful enough."

By the early 2000s, the Gamaliel Foundation had adopted a strategy of "metro equity" organizing across all of its affiliate organizations. With this new approach, Gamaliel aimed to develop campaigns that prevent "urban sprawl by significantly stopping the flow of public or private money away from older communities at the center of the region into sprawling, segregated suburbs."[8] Reflecting this organizational vision, then-education organizer Christopher Boston of MICAH explains: "We're trying to build a powerful organization that's diverse in terms of culture and race, denomination, age, socioeconomic status; a mix of all people. This is the way a lot of our congregations are, and the way the work has to be to succeed. If you're an organization only of poor people, then it's always a case of 'us versus them.'"

At the state level, WISDOM focused on three major issues: school funding, treatment alternatives to prison for nonviolent offenders, and immigration reform. MICAH anchored these state-level efforts, particularly the effort to reform the state school financing system. MICAH member Lois Glover served as president of the statewide network, and MICAH leaders co-chaired the statewide WISDOM education committee, bringing leadership and mobilization capacity to the statewide network's campaign for more equitable school funding formulas.

Locally, as the longer-term school funding fight stretched out, MICAH searched for education issues that would keep its leaders connected to the organization. David Liners says, "With schools you have to act locally, but by definition, if you only act locally, you will hit your head on a wall. On the other hand, it's a recipe for disaster if we're only trying to do mega stuff because it becomes too far removed from everyone's life." Under Liners's direction, MICAH mounted a successful campaign to create school-level "mobility coordinators" to work with families to reduce student mobility in schools.

Tyrone Dumas, an administrator in Milwaukee Public Schools' Office of Diversity and Community Engagement who worked with MICAH on the Neighborhood Schools Initiative observes, "From September of a given school year to June of the following year (a complete school year), we could see thousands of address changes in the district—about a 50 percent mobility rate in some schools in that time period. MICAH, the Social Development Commission and other community based organizations worked with us to figure out how to look at that problem and find some solutions. Other than the housing issue, what can we do within the school district or system to try to ease the burden on those children?"

In 2003, Ana Garcia-Ashley left WISDOM to start building a national campaign for Gamaliel on immigration reform. David Liners moved from MICAH to take over leadership of WISDOM's work. Liners expanded WISDOM and helped initiate a new statewide school funding coalition called the Wisconsin Alliance for Excellent Schools (WAES), in partnership with policy and advocacy organizations in the state.

With Liners's deep relationships with MICAH leaders, MICAH continued to be a force in the statewide work. Described by observers as the "community action wing of [the] whole campaign," MICAH sent busloads of people to actions on funding in Madison, the state capital, and mobilized leaders to attend public hearings across the state.[9]

At the state level, the funding campaign became increasingly technical in nature. In 2005, WAES initiated a study to assess the actual cost of education in Wisconsin schools. Remembering this, David Liners asks, "What do teachers cost? What do buildings cost, what does gasoline and heating oil cost? All those things that go into it, how big should classes be according to our own standards? . . . We're looking for a base number, and then we're looking to layer on how much more you need to add for special needs students. How much do you have to add on for English language learners? How much more do you have to add in for children in poverty, particularly children in concentrated poverty situations?"

To keep the work rooted locally, WISDOM affiliates held neighborhood forums on school funding issues to inform parents about the campaign. At the time, Liners observed: "One of the difficulties we face right now is until that moment comes that you've actually got that opportunity [to get the funding], it's hard to figure out how to keep our folks engaged. There's not something for everybody to do every month. There's not something necessarily new to learn every month. So part of the thing is, well, how do we use time well then? We don't want to keep sitting around having strategy meetings about strategies that may or may not ever come about."

Locally, MICAH was in disarray. After Liners's departure, the organization cycled through two lead organizers and two presidents within eighteen months. In the midst of these transitions, a former organizer from another organizing network led a failed effort to convince MICAH's board members to pull away from Gamaliel. For Galluzzo, MICAH's internal struggles exposed an overarching challenge of organizer recruitment, retention, and development, not just within Gamaliel network, but across the field of community organizing as a whole.

Greg Galluzzo explains:

> We work with Catholic priests who run churches of two, three, five thousand people, and if you send in a pretty inexperienced person, you'll lose them. Those congregations will walk away. You have to present a very professional, sophisticated person who can hold their own with doctors, lawyers, Lutheran ministers. [But Gamaliel, like the other organizing networks], doesn't have a bunch of organizers on the shelf just to put in there . . . What we need is a system where a gifted person who wants to do this work is given all the back-up he or she needs to become successful. That back-up is helping them raise money, helping them turn out leaders, helping them cut issues, helping them manage a board, and helping them write bylaws, helping them do the legal stuff. There's a very wide range of things that a person has to learn."

In 2005, MICAH appointed education organizer Christopher Boston as lead organizer for the organization. Boston, a young organizer with roots in a MICAH member congregation, was also trained as a pastor. He began the work of rebuilding the organization, starting with recruiting new leaders onto the education committee to replace those who had moved on to work with WISDOM.

Boston led a three-year campaign to secure state funds to expand the number of school nurses in Milwaukee public schools. MICAH leaders met with health-care providers, school officials, and education experts to discuss the impact of access to health services on student learning. The organization built partnerships with local city and state health agencies and succeeded in winning support from the governor to include a funding increase for school nurse positions in the FY 2007–09 state budget.

High-Stakes Accountability in Texas

In contrast to the Gamaliel Foundation's network-building strategy in Wisconsin, the IAF's organizing in Texas relied on an existing base of established affiliates. The Texas network arose from local organizing by Ernesto Cortes in San Antonio, where he founded Communities Organized for Public Service (COPS) in 1974. Across the next quarter century, Cortes and his colleagues—Sister Christine Stephens, Joe Higgs, Sister Mignonne Konecny, and others initiated new organizations across poor communities in Texas, including one in east Austin. In 1990, these IAF affiliates united in a statewide network called the Texas Industrial Areas Foundation (TIAF).

The Alliance School work in Texas was created through TIAF's statewide organizing in 1992, and has remained one of the network's most prominent examples of successful education organizing. In 2004, Austin Interfaith took a lead role among the Texas IAF organizations in initiating a statewide campaign to protect the Alliance School work by challenging the use of test scores as the primary accountability measure of student learning.

Texas was one of the first states to adopt a high-stakes accountability system in which student promotion and graduation were linked to performance on a state-mandated test, known as the Texas Assessment of Academic Skills, or TAAS. Though test scores across the state improved steadily over the 1990s, the state also experienced a number of testing scandals. In 1999 the Texas Legislature moved to address concerns about inflated scores by mandating inclusion of test scores from special education and bilingual students and instituting a new and more rigorous test called the Texas Assessment of Knowledge and Skills, or TAKS.

Under the leadership of superintendent Pascal Forgione, the Austin school district instituted beginning- and midyear diagnostic assessments to help schools prepare for the annual standardized exam. The diagnostic testing aimed to provide teachers with timely and accurate information on student performance and counter the effects of high student mobility in district schools. As Forgione puts it, "There are so many kids changing schools that you can't just use the data from last year because you've got about thirty percent of your kids who weren't in your school last year."

But educators in Alliance Schools believed that the intense pressure to improve test scores was edging out the relational practices that had previously helped to raise student performance. At Pickle Elementary School, principal Claudia Santamaria observed, "The parent conference time that we used to spend getting to know parents and talking about what we knew about their kids from their progress in previous grades, turned out to be talking about taking a test and then talking about the results of that test."

Santamaria left Pickle Elementary School to become an organizer with Austin Interfaith, and began holding individual and group meetings with teachers, administrators, and parents in the Alliance Schools to discuss their experiences of district's testing regimen. From these conversations, a core group of leaders stepped up to begin exploring issues of assessment and school accountability. Austin Interfaith leaders consulted with education researchers at the University of Texas at Austin to learn more about high-stakes accountability systems and alternative forms of assessment. Based on these consultations, Austin Interfaith leaders devised a plan to protect Alliance Schools from the pressures of testing activities by creating a new "sub-district" of schools within the Austin school district. Sub-district schools would be freed from administering periodic diagnostic tests in exchange for demonstrating their capacity to meet the district's school improvement benchmarks. Seven Alliance Schools were interested in the proposal, and teachers from those schools began meeting regularly with Austin Interfaith leaders to build a campaign.

During the 2004–05 school year, Austin Interfaith leaders, including parents, teachers, and university researchers, pressed district leaders to endorse the sub-district concept. The organization met with school board members and spoke at school board meetings. One of the researchers, Professor Susan B. Empson from the University of Texas at Austin, recalls presenting testimony "about the role of assessment and instruction and the need for assessment that was formative and provided teachers with information they could use."

An expert on young children's mathematical thinking, Empson was critical of the district's benchmark testing for its rigidity and for failing to provide useful information to teachers: "Everyone was very concerned about making sure their kids pass reading, so they weren't thinking that much about math. There was also a lot of top-down direction, a lot of top-down prescription for what should be going on in the classroom down to what they called an instructional planning guide, which is a daily sequence in each subject [for classroom activities]. In the schools that [were] not performing up to standard, teachers perceived the district to expect them to follow it lockstep."

Austin Interfaith's sub-district proposal was not well received, Empson recalls. "I didn't sense on the part of the district that that kind of experimentation would be applauded. Their sense of needing the answers yesterday, and then every three months after that, didn't leave schools and teachers any room to try out anything new, or to even ask new questions."

The school district would not agree to release Alliance Schools from district mandated assessment tests. District officials expressed concern about whether alternative assessments would yield reliable data about student performance and argued that the district lacked the authority to make such a move on its own. "We cannot ignore the state system," said one district official. "We cannot act to opt out of it, but you can go to the legislature and see if you can get somewhere with alternative assessments. Now if you get somewhere with the legislature, then we can talk."

Stalled in Austin, in 2005 organizers turned to a network strategy. Austin Interfaith presented the idea for the sub-district at a statewide conference of IAF groups. "We had twenty leaders from Austin to do the statewide seminar," notes Claudia Santamaria. Four of the leaders were principals from the prospective sub-district schools, and the rest were teachers, pastors, and leaders from the congregations. "They presented the sub-district planning idea to the entire network that Saturday morning, and talked about how we need our sister organizations to be in conversation with their legislators." At the statewide conference, and in follow up local trainings called "civic academies," IAF leaders discussed the implications of high stakes testing, along with other network wide issues, such as education financing and health care.

Over the next few years, TIAF network leaders met individually with elected state officials to seek their support for reforming the statewide accountability system. Other organizations in Austin had proposed legislation for holistic assessment of students by including class grades and teacher recommendations in decisions about student promotion. Austin Interfaith periodically met with these organizations, inviting representatives to share their reform proposals with Interfaith leaders. Two particularly vocal organizations were the NAACP and the League of United Latin American Citizens, headed up by Angela Valenzuela from the University of Texas at Austin.

TIAF also mobilized leaders to maintain pressure on the Austin school board. In 2005, network leaders attended a school board meeting, following the statewide testing day. Claudia Santamaria recalls, "We stood up, and we had signs and children. We talked about the legislative work that we're continuing to do, and how we had collected thousands of pictures of children statewide and delivered them to the governor's office, saying 'These are the faces of the kids that are getting shortchanged in health and education.' We shared that with the board and said that we realize that they need a constituency not just locally, but at the state level and that we are committed to being that constituency if they work with us as well."

In 2007, the state legislature created a "Select Committee" to study the impact of high-stakes testing on Texas schools. The committee held hearings across the state during the next two years. An IAF affiliate was present at every one of these meetings to push the organization's agenda. "We're not anti-testing," explains TIAF's Sister Christine Stephens. "We're anti-'teaching to the test,' and only teaching kids how to take tests. Kids are coming out of schools knowing how to take a test, but not knowing anything else. They're not learners, they're test-takers."

IAF leaders called on state leaders to "create an accountability system that is diagnostic, rather than punitive, and takes into account students growth, rather than using a single assessment to judge whether students and schools pass or fail." One affiliate, Border Interfaith, shared the results of three public "listening sessions" with El Paso parents, teachers, and students, reporting that "teaching to the test leads to disengaged students and puzzled parents, without preparing students for higher education learning and assessment."[10]

In March 2009, Select Committee members introduced a proposal in the Texas State Legislature to reform the state's accountability system. The bill, which was passed by the legislature in May, will replace the use of a single test-based measure for judging student performance with a system that incorporates a variety of performance indicators to measure how well schools are raising student achievement and preparing students for college or the workplace. In addition, under the new system, passing the annual exams will not be the sole gatekeeper for students in third, fifth, eighth, and eleventh grade to advance to the next grade.[11] Reporting on the bill's successful passage two months later, the *Austin-American Statesman* observed, "Gone are many of the school reforms ushered in by then-Governor George W. Bush, such as a prohibition on promoting a student to the next grade if he or she failed to pass the Texas Assessment of Knowledge and Skills. That promotion decision will now be left to the school and parents."[12] The accountability bill also includes $10 million in state funding for long term job training initiatives, such as Capital IDEA, which Austin Interfaith created ten years ago, to train low-income adults for in-demand jobs such as nursing, network technology, and teaching in the areas of bilingual and special education.

Exerting State-level Power

Both the Gamaliel Foundation and the Texas IAF pursued statewide organizing to achieve education reform on a broader scale. In Wisconsin, the statewide campaign emerged from organizers' assessment that local campaigns had no chance of producing substantial change in a context where political power rested outside of municipal boundaries. In Texas, the statewide campaign formed to address the political reality that testing policy is set by the state. Organizing only at the district level could not defuse the testing pressures experienced by Alliance Schools.

As multi-issue organizations, both Gamaliel and IAF initiated their state-level work by building broad reform agendas that extended beyond the schools. In Wisconsin, WISDOM sought treatment alternatives for minor prison offenders and immigration reform as well as school reforms. In Texas, the IAF defined a "stand with families" platform that reflected the work of local organizations on affordable housing and job training, while also proposing a school financing plan to increase state revenue without implementing regressive sales taxes that disproportionately impact middle- and low-income families. These broad reform agendas widened the organizations' appeal across the state. The agendas also represented the organizations' core belief that issues of schooling, housing, jobs, and health care are connected, and that addressing them effectively demands expanding democratic control and power at the levels of government where decisions about resources are made.

In chapter 4, we noted that coalitions leverage community-based social capital into new political power to make more ambitious reform demands. A similar dynamic exists for state organizing, although the work is carried out on larger stage. The basis of statewide power is local work to educate community members about their self-interest, the needs of their communities, and the larger issues of equity, justice, and democracy. In this sense, state-level work is defined by the local civic engagement that happens through conversations during neighborhood canvassing and in house meetings, as well as in formal training opportunities created by groups.

Both the IAF and Gamaliel Foundation use leadership development trainings as the basis for leader engagement. "Leaders in our congregations and schools want to understand how their experience fits into a larger context," says organizer Russ Louch of Austin Interfaith. Civic academies created by the IAF allow for extended discussion among leaders about reform issues. "Do they understand the intricacies of how testing works, and what's possible for changing it? We lay out what the accountability system is, what the effects are on schools and kids, and we ask: How do you see this? How does this connect to the economy and your own economic situation? Are our kids being prepared for jobs and college?"

As community members become more knowledgeable about issues, they are more likely to participate in local politics, hence exerting civic power at the polls in ways that expand political accountability for their communities through the threat of *pressure* politics.[13] Former staff director Clay Smith of the Northwest Bronx Community and Clergy Coalition explains the concept: "Part of the implicit message that we bring to the table when we meet with bureaucrats or elected officials, is that if you don't do this, we're going to make sure everyone knows that you didn't do it and people are likely to vote against you."

In Wisconsin, WISDOM drew extensively on MICAH's organizational resources and relationships because the other affiliates in the state-wide network were so new. In other sites, though, longstanding statewide organizing networks provided considerable support to their local affiliates. The IAF has twelve affiliate organizations across Texas, PICO has twenty affiliate organizations in California, and DART has ten affiliates in Florida. Though DART is younger than IAF and PICO, its Florida affiliates participated in PACT's campaign to secure state-level resources for Direct Instruction, and the DART affiliate in Daytona Beach continues to implement Direct Instruction in thirteen schools in the Volusia County School District.[14]

Staffed by senior organizers, statewide organizations brought expertise and knowledge about state legislative and budgeting processes, along with important political relationships. When confronted with the state takeover of Oakland schools in 2003, for example, PICO California provided crucial backing to OCO by mobilizing its affiliates to discuss the issue with state-level political leaders. Jim Keddy of California PICO explains, "We have a history with the secretary of education, who knows us [and] trusts us. So when we go to her and say: 'The state takeover of Oakland schools could squash something that's really important,' she says, 'How can I help?' instead of 'Who are you?'"

RESPONDING TO THE CHALLENGE OF A
MULTIDIMENSIONAL SCALE STRATEGY

Although we have emphasized the need for multilevel strategies to scale up reform, achieving both depth *and* breadth is extraordinarily difficult. Organizing groups are usually small, with a handful of paid professional staff. Sites in our study ranged from having five organizers on staff to two. In most cases organizers were spread across organizing campaigns on a wide variety of community issues, such as access to health services and transportation, in addition to the development of high-quality schools.

Simultaneous campaigns at the school level and systemwide (whether targeted at the district, municipality, or state) require balancing different and sometimes conflicting types of organizational activities. Are organizers holding individual meetings to cultivate new leadership among parents or teachers or distributing flyers to mobilize community members for a city hall rally? Are they researching strategies for education reform, or driving long distances to attend state-wide meetings?

John Baumann, one of PICO's founders, lays out the optimal scenario for the interplay of multilevel strategies: "Small is beautiful, and out of the small grows something that becomes big and powerful . . . We might be able to get some legislation changed, but it's always going to be important that the local group take ownership and implement it locally in their community." Because the work draws on the same pool of volunteer leaders, multiple parallel campaigns run the constant risk of defusing the energy and time of even the most passionately committed parents, youth, and community members, and can create confusion in organizational identity. Campaigns focused on winning resources, as most district- or state-level campaigns aim to do, follow the arc of government budget cycles. These campaigns move quickly, and require deep knowledge of the issues and the confidence and skills to take on district- and state-level players.

The Gamaliel Foundation's expansion across metropolitan boundaries surrounding Milwaukee, and across the state of Wisconsin, was a pragmatic response to shifts in the state's economic and political landscape. Yet the expansion strategy raised wide-ranging challenges for MICAH. MICAH organizers observed that the network's expansion strategy monopolized their time and attention, blurred organizational identities, and sacrificed important local relationships. The participation of inner-city pastors dropped off, organizers believe, because African American clergy perceived the organization to be focused on statewide, rather than inner-city, issues.

"People feared that WISDOM would swallow up MICAH," recalls lead organizer Christopher Boston. "MICAH brought all the resources, power, and people. In our adoption of some statewide issues, we were really neglecting a lot of local stuff."

Scholar and Gamaliel activist Robert Kleidman has observed that statewide and metropolitan organizations face a fundamental dilemma of "how to retain participatory democracy while creating larger groups that encompass more people and a wider geographic area . . . As more key decisions are made at the regional level, more effort is required to encourage widespread participation in meetings, training, and public events."[15] Though Kleidman discusses Gamaliel Foundation efforts, these tensions are familiar to organizers across the country. PICO's John Baumann sums up the core challenge: "We've got to keep cultivating new people . . . We need always to be bringing new people in."

PART THREE

IMPLICATIONS FOR COMMUNITIES AND SCHOOLS

CHAPTER SIX

Increasing Community Capacity

Organizers in the PICO national organizing network believe that "organizing is not simply about solving problems. It is about empowering people, having choices, and beginning to dream of new ways of doing things." Their words cut to the heart of community organizing's theory of change: *the process of building power to create lasting social change begins with the intentional development of leadership among ordinary people at a grassroots level.* Organizing groups tap into community members' sense of justice by challenging them to consider the "world as it should be," versus the "world as it is," and to take the steps necessary to move closer to a more just and equitable society. In this sense, education organizing campaigns are intended not only to change schools, but also to develop new leadership skills in individuals and to harness the collective leadership of members in ways that increase the capacity of communities to create broad and lasting systemic change.

The notion of community capacity finds its theoretical foundation in the social capital literature. Scholars have noted how the development of trusting and reciprocal relationships within networks of individuals in communities can generate new opportunities for community members. The premise of organizing is that this social capital (networks and norms) can, when linked to an institutional base, provide the foundation for political action to assert greater control over the use of existing resources, and greater accountability from public and private institutions.

By *community capacity*, then, we mean the development of new leadership skills, knowledge, and aspirations among members, as well as the norms of collective deliberation that enable communities to mobilize social capital for shared goals. Such capacity, we argue, helps communities advocate for better schools, participate in their improvement, and engage a broad array of stakeholders in support of public education. As Mark Warren, Pedro Noguera, and other scholars have observed, strengthening public schools through grassroots organizing occurs in concert with the revitalization of surrounding communities.[1]

In this chapter, we explore the community dimensions of school-reform organizing. In the first section, we discuss how organizing groups work to develop leadership, reviewing in detail the goals of leadership development as well as the methods groups use to meet these goals. We then examine how the process of leadership development impacts individual participants, as well as how this process builds the overall capacity of communities to support successful schools.

DEVELOPING GRASSROOTS LEADERSHIP

Developing leadership is *the* central function of organizing groups. As we noted in chapter 5, organizing groups' organizational power and, thus, their potential to affect systemic change is predicated on the capacity to develop a large base of informed and empowered constituents.

Take the story of Lourdes Zamarron in Austin, Texas. In 1991, Zamarron was an involved parent at Zavala Elementary School, which her three children attended. She did what was asked of her, helping with school events and volunteering in the classroom, until the day she realized that Zavala students were not passing the state-mandated TAAS tests. Then Zamarron became involved with Austin Interfaith, working with the principal, teachers, and other parents on the Zavala core team to introduce dramatic changes into the school—a new health clinic, new curriculum, new planning time for teachers, and a new science enrichment program. Within two years, Zavala's student attendance and standardized test scores had improved.

But the impact on Zamarron's life ran deeper. She lived and raised her children in public housing for twenty-five years, before moving out in September 2008. Two of her children graduated from the University of Texas and her third child is attending Kansas State University. Now a public school teacher in Austin, she believes her experience of leadership in Austin

Interfaith taught her that she did not have to accept things the way they were. She remembers not getting a raise at her previous job and thinking that it was all right. She remembers not having job benefits and that, too, was okay. Becoming involved in Austin Interfaith helped her develop an appreciation for her own power, as well as the collective power that comes from organizing with others. Zamarron looks back and reflects, "The word 'power' was not in my vocabulary. Neighbors changing things did not make sense. But once you have a taste of power you want more. I became a leader teaching others about power and how you can make a difference." This sense of power, Zamarron believes, was crucial not only in helping her own children succeed, but also in standing up for what schools in her community need and making sure that educators in positions of power do their jobs effectively.

Within the lexicon of community organizing, active members are called 'leaders.' Christopher Boston, lead organizer of Milwaukee Inner-city Congregations Allied for Hope (MICAH), explains that the organizer's job is to "grow and develop leaders, but [not to] hold their hand all the time." Organizers support and guide members in their leadership development process, challenging members to take on leadership roles, while checking in consistently so that leaders know support is available when needed. "They don't say here's the agenda and now do it," explains Angela Baker, a parent of five children and an Austin Interfaith leader of over ten years. "They teach you how to do it, how to be involved."

Organizing groups foster leadership among members through a variety of informal and formal organizational structures. A common practice is to encourage new leaders to take on responsibilities right away to gain experience. Sister Mignonne Konecny, a long-time lead organizer for Austin Interfaith, asserts the guiding philosophy of many organizers: "If they are going to learn, they must *do*." At the same time, new leaders are not left to fend for themselves. Teresa Anderson, former president of the Northwest Bronx Community and Clergy Coalition (NWBCCC), observes that mentoring and coaching new leaders is a core purpose of organizations. As leaders become experienced, she says, "We push them to mentor a newer leader. We say 'Yeah, you're great, but you'd be even greater if you gave away your skills to somebody else who's coming into the circle—teach them the ropes, take them under your wing and push them a little bit to be more forceful and to start getting the bigger picture.'"

Ongoing mentoring and coaching are complemented by formal mechanisms for leadership development. For organizing groups affiliated with national networks, structured opportunities for leadership development occur most typically through national and regional trainings. For example, MICAH, an affiliate of the Gamaliel Foundation, provides training locally to its members, but leaders also access training through the regional and national network. WISDOM, the statewide Gamaliel network in Wisconsin, integrates a training component in its quarterly meetings. Nationally, MICAH leaders participate in Gamaliel's extensive menu of training options, including: a week-long leadership training, held four times a year; a three-day training specifically for clergy whose congregations are members of Gamaliel affiliates; a three-day advanced training for experienced leaders, held once a year; and a leadership development training specifically for female leaders.

Other national organizing networks—ACORN, DART, IAF, and PICO—offer similar slates of training opportunities for adult leaders to learn more about the fundamentals of organizing. Trainings last from several days to a week, and are designed to be intensive experiences. Sessions focus on skills development, but more importantly, for many members they represent the first in-depth exposure to the concepts that undergird the methodology of organizing. Sessions can be deliberately provocative, as trainers agitate members to reexamine and reconstruct their core beliefs. In addition to grounding leaders in key organizing concepts, these trainings serve another important purpose—to foster a sense of community within the network, forge a sense of shared identity and culture, and to build loyalty to the organization.

Not all organizing groups are affiliated with national networks. Youth-led organizing lacks a national network infrastructure, and as a result, youth organizing groups often create their own training sessions. Youth United for Change (YUC) runs a week-long training in the summer for new leaders, while the Community Coalition has an eight-session intensive training, called the Leadership Academy, for its new youth members. Both YUC and SCYEA, the Community Coalition's youth organizing component, employ popular education approaches designed to build critical consciousness in young people about the connections between their individual experiences and broader social problems. YUC's training series integrates organizing skills and education issues into a larger discussion of social and economic policies, while SCYEA's training focuses more squarely on education problems and roots issues of educational justice in the context of a racial analysis. NWBCCC and its youth affiliate Sistas and Brothas United (SBU) hold monthly trainings, on a semester schedule, called the Leaders of Tomorrow School. There are introductory sessions for new leaders and intermediate-level sessions for more experienced leaders.

Though groups have diverse avenues for leadership development, several themes hold constant. Leadership development efforts across groups focus on building three key areas of skills and understandings in members: an understanding of power; organizing skills, such as public speaking and relationship-building through one-on-ones; and content expertise on school-reform issues.

Developing an Understanding of Power

Effective organizing requires an analysis of how power dynamics shape schooling conditions and community life. Organizing groups challenge leaders to explore and dissect issues of power on multiple levels and through multiple perspectives. Conversations about power center on themes of building awareness of personal power; recognizing the potential of collectively held power; and understanding power in the context of race, class, and faith.

Many individuals, especially those from traditionally marginalized communities, hold negative views of the word *power*, viewing it as a coercive force used for personal gain, often to the detriment of their families and communities. As Christopher Boston of MICAH observes, "A lot of people don't even know what power is. They are apprehensive about the word *power* because they look at it as a certain group of people having it and them not."

A common refrain of community members is an experience of feeling powerless before joining the organization—the sense that they could not speak up about their concerns to teachers, school officials, or policy makers, and that if they did speak up, no one would listen. Before joining Sistas and Brothas United, says Yorman Nuñez, a youth member, "I never thought, residents—you know, regular community people could just go and actually meet with politicians. I thought, we were us, they were them, and that's the way it was."

In response, organizing groups begin by teaching members to view power as the capacity to act in ways that demonstrate agency and self-determination. Developing this sense of personal power is a dominant theme in leadership trainings. At the start of one network's week-long training, for example, the lead trainer tells the new cohort of leaders: "We will engage you about what you need to do to become a more powerful person. For most of us it is about identifying the stuff inside us that prevents us from becoming powerful."

Discussing power in such explicit terms helps members recognize the ways in which they are powerful and, more importantly, to translate that sense of personal power into action. Organizers routinely point out that the Latin root of the word *power* means "to act." Without power, asserts a network trainer, "values are nothing more than hollow declarations. Real evil is powerlessness."

To underscore this message, organizing groups define and contrast institutional power with community-based power. At ACORN's national leadership training, called Leadership School, the trainer engages the group in an exercise called "What Is Power?" In the session, the trainer elicits as many ideas as possible about sources of power (money, status, education) to arrive at the concept that poor people can build power through organization building.

These themes shape leadership development activities with public school parents as well. A parent organizer with the Eastern Pennsylvania Organizing Project (EPOP) introduces the concept of power to new parent leaders coming into the organization. "I talk to them about how they have power by being parents," she says. "If they're not happy that they have every right to complain. Now, one person complaining is not really going to be heard. If you have 60, 70, 100, 200 parents complaining about the same thing, and demanding change, you are going to see results."

All organizing groups believe that understanding and deconstructing issues of power is central to leadership development, but there are thematic differences in how organizing groups frame power in their leadership development process. In general, all organizing groups acknowledge the linkages between race and economic outcomes. But groups emerging from the Alinsky tradition have tended to emphasize an economic analysis of social injustice. In contrast, groups like the Community Coalition in Los Angeles have situated the struggle for power in terms of race and class. Alberto Retana, the Community Coalition's director of organizing, observes, "Whatever conversation we have about skills, whatever conversation we have about building power, we want a race and class analysis to be at the center."

Leadership development exercises in the Community Coalition push young people to examine the economic and social disparities that both characterize and divide "black and brown" communities. Students are taken on tours to compare wealthier, predominantly white communities with their own neighborhoods. During the tours, the students have an assignment: to document the range of services and resources that exist in each neighborhood. The results are predictable, yet stark nonetheless. Clive Aden, an alumnus of SCYEA observes: "We have a liquor store on every corner; and in Beverly Hills, they have grocery stores. We've got check-cashing places; in Beverly Hills, they have banks . . . We've got fast-food restaurants; and they've got dine-in restaurants." Other SCYEA leaders concur with Aden's observations, adding that schools in Beverly Hills look like country clubs, while schools in South LA resemble prisons.

Exercises such as these are common in other youth-led organizing groups as well and provide participants with a platform to reflect on the implications of economic and social disparities and how to go about changing them. With a deeper understanding of the ways in which mainstream institutional power manifests itself to diminish the positive social and academic outcomes for young people of color, students begin to see the necessity of building "people power" within their own community to challenge the status quo. Though education organizing is the arena for action, the goal of stimulating larger societal change undergirds the work.

Among institutionally-based groups, an analysis of race and class is present, but the imperative of taking action is also situated within the context of faith. At a DART national training, for example, the concept of power is explored within a larger discussion of the commandment to "love thy neighbor." The trainer shares scripture to delineate the connection between individual and collective power, and to underscore the point that living the commandment successfully depends on harnessing the power that comes from building an organized constituency. At another institutionally-based network's training, Biblical stories are used to distinguish unilateral power from relational power. In contrast with unilateral or coercive power, relational power is associated with mutual respect and accountability. The possibilities of relational power are infinite and transformative, the trainer asserts, because such power is rooted in love of self and others.

Learning Organizing Skills

A sense of agency and self-potency are necessary to act. But leaders need also to develop the skills that support collective action. Organizing groups provide a range of supports to expand members' skills in the mechanics of organizing, including public speaking and negotiation skills, facilitation skills, relationship building through one-on-ones, and campaign development. Though these behaviors are implemented in a community setting, organizations that work closely with educators—such as Austin Interfaith and OCO—also teach principals and teachers the same set of skills.

Among community organizing groups, members are encouraged to take primary responsibility for the full range of an organization's public activities. Evidence for this type of distributive leadership within organizations was supported by our surveys of adult and youth members of organizing groups.[2] Beyond attendance at large events, which most members report, 30 to 50 percent of adults and 50 to 85 percent of youth report taking a significant role in core group activities, such as conducting outreach to recruit new members into the organization, planning or facilitating meetings, making decisions about the group's demands, and developing campaign strategy.

Many groups utilize a system of rotating facilitation to give members experience in leading meetings, guiding discussions, and building consensus. Explains Bea Bernstine of OCO, the goal is to "help bring up other people so that if there's a meeting, I should not always be the one leading it. We need to encourage new leaders to lead meetings, etc. Now, are they really timid about it? Yeah, so why don't you lead with them or have one of the experienced leaders lead with them? Having an 'experienced leader' work with a new leader helps the new leader know what should be expected, how they can react, etc. This way it won't seem so difficult the next time." Within SBU, the practice of sharing leadership is called "stepping up, stepping back." As organizer Amy Cohen observes, "We all have to play a role in helping [new leaders] to succeed. That builds leadership in everybody, not just in the person who's leading the meeting, but also in the people who are thinking, 'How do I support this person? What role can I play to help us succeed collectively?'"

One-on-Ones. Building relationships based on trust and accountability, through what most groups call *one-on-ones*, is a skill all organizing groups aim to develop. One-on-ones are purposeful, focused conversations that leaders or organizers initiate with prospective members and a variety of other stakeholders, including educators, public officials, and allies. These conversations are designed to recruit new members, to identify and understand the issues facing community members, and to pinpoint an individual's self-interest in addressing those issues. One-on-ones also foster mutual responsibility and a sense of shared interest as the basis for what organizing groups term *public* relationships between members. Though institutionally-based membership groups tend to emphasize the role of one-on-one meetings in their organizing approach, all groups view these kinds of meetings as important.

For community members and educators, the process of learning how to conduct one-on-ones meetings is often a defining dimension of their development. Alliance School teacher Amanda Braziel observes, "I think I already possessed some natural leadership abilities, but Austin Interfaith helped me build on those by teaching me to sit down and have one-on-one conversations with parents, community members, and other teachers to find out what makes them tick and then, kind of go from there and figure out who would be a valuable leader in what area."

Public Speaking. Public speaking and negotiation skills are particularly important skills for emerging leaders, since they determine how effectively leaders will represent the interests of the organization when interacting with public officials (or other targets). Sessions with decision makers are rehearsed carefully, both to support leadership and to avoid errors that can undercut the organization's power. Preparation for speaking and negotiating roles can be intensive, with organizers helping leaders to rehearse their remarks and anticipate questions and/or challenges that might arise. Ofelia Zapata, a parent involved with Austin Interfaith, recalls preparing for a briefing with district officials: "We went through my story (or testimony) and practiced it again and again. I don't know how many hours the organizer put in, but we put in a lot of hours. I was extremely shy and so nervous that I would cry. Standing in front of people or even just one person made me cry. I remember meeting with the organizer all the time until I felt confident to deliver my testimony. But the organizer was like my shadow; he was there. He said, "Tell me how you understand it, how you want to present it.'"

In network-based groups with several decades of practice in this method, such sessions are carefully choreographed, with little left to chance. For example, a day before People Acting for Change Together (PACT)'s public accountability meeting in 2004, the organization held a rehearsal at one of its member churches. Speakers practiced their speeches and received feedback from organizers and fellow leaders. During the rehearsal, then-executive director Aaron Dorfman role-played a contentious public official so that leaders could practice their responses to such situations. When difficult moments arose in the next day's accountability session, leaders were prepared to act in ways that preserved their political standing.

Strategic use of the media can help to amplify organizing demands, shaping public opinion about an issue—such as school overcrowding or teacher turnover—and increasing the pressure on decision makers. For this reason, organizing groups routinely incorporate some form of media training into their work to help members develop key talking points and become effective spokespersons for their campaigns.

The skills just described—building relationships and public speaking—are ones that cut across the life of a campaign. The mechanics of campaign work and the art of developing campaign strategy require a particular set of skills that community organizing groups routinely teach members. With minor variations, organizing groups generally emphasize the same core elements of a successful campaign: researching problems to identify an issue that is manageable and winnable, framing the issue in a compelling way for policymakers and the public, identifying reform alternatives and crafting demands for decision makers, negotiating a commitment, and reflecting on the outcomes.

Developing Content Expertise

The organizing campaigns described in previous chapters represent a high degree of professional knowledge about the political context of education and the organizational and pedagogical strategies needed to achieve reform. Though research has always been part of the community organizing model, there is an increasing focus by organizing groups on developing content expertise among leaders, particularly as school reform demands and strategies become more complex. Parents and youth members bring firsthand knowledge of their own schools, but unless they have had other positions within the school system or the world of education reform, they do not have deep content knowledge about how the larger school system functions and the possibilities for reform: "I read the paper for probably five years straight and still didn't know half the things that went on behind the scenes," observes a parent leader with OCO.

To develop content knowledge, organizing groups conduct site visits to schools, hold briefings on school problems, and sponsor forums with education experts. These kinds of experiences help to deepen members' knowledge of school-reform issues and provide a basis for formulating campaign strategy and negotiating demands with policy makers. As the campaigns highlighted in previous chapters illustrate, site visits to model schools and/ or programs help organizations to identify reform strategies, such as Direct Instruction in Miami, small schools in Oakland and Philadelphia, and Grow Your Own in Illinois. Alliances with research organizations also generate ideas for reform. The Gamaliel Foundation's alliance with the Institute for Wisconsin's Future, for example, helped to shape the organization's statewide school finance campaign.

To date, few opportunities exist nationally for organizers and leaders to learn about education reform, outside of the occasional sessions that national networks create for their affiliate organizations. One of the most visible national efforts was hosted by EPOP and Research for Democracy for several years, and introduced organizers and leaders to innovative campaigns in the field and to researchers with expertise in teacher quality, small schools, and professional development.

Learning more about schools and school reform involves not only an understanding of current schooling practices, but also an understanding of the policies from which educational disparities arise. SCYEA complements briefings for members on local school problems, such as the state of school facilities and the problem of college access, with trainings about the historical and political context of public education. In one training session, for example, students play an interactive game in which, for the purposes of the activity, they are designated as either rich or poor. They line up at one end of the room as milestone events in education are announced (e.g., *Brown v. Board of Education*). Students take one step backward or one step forward to illustrate the implications of particular policies for low-income students and wealthier students. The exercise helps students understand the historical legacy of policies that have contributed to sub-standard education for poor communities and communities of color. SBU uses a similar exercise to help members evaluate whether education policies increase or diminish their chances of graduating from high school and attending college.

INDIVIDUAL IMPACTS OF INVOLVEMENT IN ORGANIZING

Though the aim of education organizing is to produce institutional change, the experience of participating in campaigns can profoundly impact on individual members' perceptions of themselves, their skills, knowledge and involvement in schools, communities and family life. Austin Interfaith's Ofelia Zapata says simply, "[Organizing] helped me to realize we could make change and create things, and so [I] really started imagining things I wouldn't have imagined before."

New Leadership Skills

A common perception among outsiders is that people join organizing because of a predisposition to social action. Yet many of the leaders we interviewed said they first showed up at an initial meeting for no other reason than their friend was going and there would be free food. Yorman Nuñez recounts coming to SBU by accident: "I was bored, and my friend took me here. The moment I came here, I was at a school safety meeting and they were talking about meeting with politicians and stuff like that, people in charge and I said that you could not just meet with people in charge and everybody there basically told me, 'Yes we can.' We in fact have a meeting scheduled in a day and that's what we're preparing for. And I was like, 'Wow.'"

In this sense, organizing can stimulate (rather than respond to) the desire of individuals to get involved more deeply in their communities and provide the skills to do so. Consistent with the goals of organizing, adults and youth members report learning and improving on skills in relationship building, facilitation, and public speaking. Tangible leadership and organizing skills were especially evident among youth involved in organizing, who, from a developmental perspective, are still in the process of coming into their own intellectually and socially. Across a wide spectrum of items, more than 70 percent of the youth in the study's survey sample believe their involvement in organizing improved their ability to research a problem, express their views in front of a group of peers, create a plan to address the problem, and contact authority figures to get them to pay attention to the problem.

Ravaut Benitez, a youth leader with SCYEA who went on to attend the University of Wisconsin-Madison on a full scholarship, observes, "When I started here I was very timid, and scared to speak in front of a lot of people. But here I learned that if you really believe in something, don't be afraid to speak about it, and to show how you really feel." It's not surprising that young people involved in organizing would begin to see themselves differently and recognize themselves as leaders. Yet many of the policy makers they are attempting to persuade do so as well. Yvonne Torres, a former regional superintendent in the Bronx, observes "One of the things that I find I can measure is . . . the *way* that they have conversations with me. If the kids can sit at a table and have conversations with me around this is the research, this is where we want to go—I mean, that doesn't come out of the sky . . . [SBU has] organized the kids to be good thinkers. They are not afraid to speak to adults and share their thinking."

Like the young people surveyed for this study, adults involved in organizing also report enhanced leadership skills. More than 65 percent of adult survey respondents say their ability to develop relationships improved substantially as a result of their involvement in organizing. Austin Interfaith's Angela Baker observes, "You learn to deal with public officials in such a way that it's not [like] they're your master or something and you're some little servant. You learn to deal with them as equals, and you're comfortable with that."

About half of the adults surveyed report that their ability to speak in public and to plan or run a meeting had improved. Ronn Jordan of the NWBCCC recalls his evolution as an effective public speaker, "When I first got involved, I was just pissed off about [the condition of schools in the Bronx] and I wasn't one of the people that wanted to be up in the front to talk about this. I had never spoken publicly before or anything like that." In his early days as a leader, Jordan worked with an organizer to prepare his speeches. Initially, at public events, he would read from the paper version of his speech. Through coaching and practice his comfort level with public speaking improved, and eventually, he says, "I put the paper down and I hit every point that I was supposed to make and realized that I didn't need to stand there and read that."

Increased Knowledge About Local Schools and School Systems

Involvement in organizing increases members' knowledge about decision makers within schools and school systems and their understanding of the intricacies of school policy. More than 80 percent of the youth sample report that, because of their participation in organizing, they know more about school policies, how to make changes in their school, their rights as public school students, and who makes decisions about what happens in schools and school districts. A YUC youth leader recalls, "I used to think little about school and everything that's going on. But when I joined YUC and found out more about the schools, I had a bigger point of view. I feel like I actually know what's going on now."

Among adult respondents of our member survey, 50 percent of respondents say they know more about who makes decisions about schools because of their involvement in organizing. More than 40 percent of respondents know more about school policies, how to make changes in their child's school, and who to go to about schooling concerns. Such knowledge helps members feel better equipped to speak up and advocate for school improvement. Fannie Akingbala, a probation officer and a leader with Austin Interfaith, observes, "When you get more information you feel more secure standing up talking about this is how things work, this is what we need, [and] these are the things that we would like for you to look at with us because we have people hurting in these areas."

Roughly 60 percent of the adults we surveyed were parents of public school students. These parents report becoming more involved in their child's schooling than they had been prior to their participation in organizing. Involvement in schools included participation in traditional parent involvement activities such as attending school events and PTA meetings and talking with their child's teacher.

In addition, close to 80 percent of parents say their involvement in organizing makes them more likely to look at data on their child's school and raise concerns with school and district administrators. These activities extend beyond traditional forms of involvement and are indicative of deeper and more critical forms of parent engagement, based on asserting accountability with educators. Denise Dixon, former president, and longtime leader in Chicago ACORN expresses the transformation in how parents conceive of involvement in their children's school: "My oldest is 21 and went through the public schools. I never once asked her teacher is she qualified. Now I feel empowered to ask, 'What are your qualifications?' I was never able to do that, but you get this sense of power like, 'You can't talk to me like I'm a punk.'"

New Expectations and Aspirations

Involvement in organizing can fundamentally transform leaders' expectations for themselves, in both their personal lives and their academic and professional lives. For young people, in particular, participation in youth-led organizing often alters their perceptions of their own academic abilities, and consequently, raises their educational aspirations.

As Eva Minott, a youth leader from Los Angeles, observes, mainstream society tends to harbor low expectations for young people of color and their future prospects. The disparities between South Los Angeles schools and wealthier schools mean that students at wealthier schools "have everything they need and they go on and become successful when we don't. And they expect us to go into low wage labor and go into the underground economy and expect us to go and clean their cars, fix them, and work in McDonald's or something. They don't expect us to become anything."

To illustrate Minott's observation, some educators were skeptical when SCYEA leaders presented a proposal for integrating student feedback into the teacher evaluation process. Alberto Retana recalls, "[At the] follow-up meeting with our organizer . . . [one of the teachers said] there was no way the students would have come up with that, that this was a college-level analysis [and our] students don't have the capacity to come up with a policy like that."

By no means do all educators have low expectations for their students, and there are many examples of committed teachers and principals who provide a rich and challenging environment for all of their students, regardless of assumptions about race and class. Still, many of the young people involved with SCYEA, YUC, and SBU report that they attend schools with low expectations and few supports for their academic progress.

In contrast, young people perceived youth organizing groups to be characterized by high expectations and adult support for their academic success. This perception is shaped by the extensive support organizing groups provide for students, including access to computers, access to space to work on projects, access to constant tutoring, staff attention to academics, and staff advocacy on behalf of students. Both SCYEA and SBU have an academic coordinator on staff who reviews student report cards and provides services similar to that of college counselors. In addition, SCYEA coordinates an annual college tour of both public and private universities in California.

As a result, 89 percent of youth surveyed indicated that because of their involvement with the group, they are more motivated to finish high school, and 55 percent say they are more likely to take harder classes. As Fernando Carlo of SBU observes, participating in the organization and fighting for better schools motivated him to try harder academically and gave him the skills to produce stronger work: "It's because I got these skills at SBU that I did so well in school, like the speaking, the writing, the expressing myself, the thinking about things, taking criticism—these are all things I've learned from SBU."

Describing a similar trajectory, Julio Daniel, a SCYEA leader, observes: "[Before] I really didn't worry about school too much. I used to skateboard, so I would spend all my time doing that. I'd come home from school. I'd pick up my skateboard and I'd go skate. I wouldn't come home until 9:30, 10 at night. And I would never make time to do my homework. So I mean, that was hurting my grades pretty badly."

After joining SCYEA, Daniel says, "I realized what my priorities were because I knew I couldn't fall back on skateboarding as a career. At the moment, when I was doing it, I thought that I could. I saw it within my reach. It was something very tangible. But it isn't . . . Coming here put everything into perspective, and allowed me to—I don't want to say grow up, but to definitely become more responsible."

Involvement in organizing also increases young people's intentions to pursue college and graduate school. Across the three groups in this study, 80 percent of the young people surveyed expect to pursue a college education, and 49 percent expect to complete a graduate or professional degree as well. The research literature suggests there is often a gap in the aspirations young people profess and their ultimate actions. Additional research on the long-term academic outcomes for young people involved in organizing is needed to assess the extent to which aspirations translate into reality, but at least one group in this study, SCYEA, tracks the academic trajectories of their students, and finds that the college-going rates of their members hover at around 90 percent.

Fittingly, young people involved in organizing express a wide range of future career aspirations, from becoming nonprofit leaders to journalists to artists. Yet, regardless of their career paths, nearly 90 percent of youth say they intend to stay involved in activism. Nearly 80 percent express interest in finding a job in the field of organizing, while 40 percent say they would consider a run for public office one day.

Yorman Nuñez of SBU is one such young person. When Nuñez first joined SBU, he had dropped out of high school and spent his days at parties in abandoned apartments. SBU helped him re-engage with his own education: he got his high school degree and entered college while working at SBU as an organizer. In May 2009 he announced his candidacy for the New York City Council. While still a leader in SBU, he shared this thought: "We're all future elected officials, teachers, lawyers, doctors. Many of us are going to become staff at SBU and make it bigger—have it be all around the country . . . I can't say now that I'm always going to keep up this work in this way. But whatever I do in the future, I'm going to change the world. I'm going to affect it. With my history and background, I don't want to see today's youth grow up in the way I did. I take everything in this organization personally because of that."

Among adult leaders, more than 60 percent of survey respondents believe their involvement in organizing raised their expectations or goals for themselves and for their families. This was particularly true for many female leaders, who may have felt beholden to more traditional gender roles because of family or cultural norms. 76 percent of adult female leaders say they have raised expectations for themselves, and 72 percent say they speak up more to their family about their personal wishes. These behaviors, leaders argue, change how they interact with schools. In the northwest Bronx, parent leader Hilda Borgos observes, "I learned that if I keep my mouth shut all the time, everybody's going to keep stepping on me."

"When I got married," Ofelia Zapata recalls, "My mom said, 'Your husband, he's your voice, he's the one that makes the decisions, he's the one.'

I just never felt I had any part of the decision making. At Austin Interfaith it was the opposite. It was like, 'You are somebody and your voice does count.' And that was real hard for me to understand and believe." After her husband died, Zapata says, "I didn't know what my purpose was—my husband wasn't there. So who's going to speak for me now? And the [Alliance Schools became] an opportunity for me to put some promise in my eyes to what was going around me . . . I have realized that learning the tools of organizing saved my life."

COMMUNITY CAPACITY TO SUPPORT SUCCESSFUL SCHOOLS

Throughout this book, we have argued that community organizing builds and leverages community-based social capital for the purpose of gaining control in the political processes that create inequity and allow it to continue. We have also asserted that, given the relationship between schooling outcomes and community conditions, truly transformative change in the educational futures of young people is unlikely to result from strategies focused on improving schools in isolation from communities. Thus a core question for our research has been to understand whether the process of leadership development in parents, students, and community members that occurs in school-reform organizing contributes to greater community capacity to support school success. In the previous section, we reported our findings on individual leadership skills, knowledge, and aspirations, noting the transformation in personal goals that develops from a sense of power, skills and knowledge. Here we focus on the collective aspects of community capacity, namely, the extent to which community problem solving, community commitment, and civic and political engagement are demonstrated by participants.

Community Problem Solving

More than 70 percent of the adult leaders surveyed for this study say they are more knowledgeable about how to resolve community problems, and are more active on community issues. Leaders assert that their orientation toward community problem solving developed from the systemic analysis of larger social, economic, and political conditions that organizations cultivate through formal training and informal group interaction. This analysis creates a sense of accountability to take responsibility for making change happen and to act in the interests of others.

"When you join a group that's trying to do something, you're accountable to each other for that work, and for the responsibilities you take on in that work," says NWBCCC leader Teresa Anderson. "But it's also the sense of accountability you feel as a member of society, and as a parent. You know, we bring our children into this world, and most of us think, 'Well, this is the world, this is what you get, and we have to deal with it.' But why can't we make things a little bit better for our children? We're all responsible for one another. Our success rests on everyone's shoulders, not just one person—not me, not the organizer, not the Coalition—everyone."

Community Commitment

Among both youth and adults, 70 percent of leaders surveyed for this study say they know more about their community and have stronger relationships with people in the community because of their involvement in organizing. This feeling of interconnectedness draws on faith traditions—"I am my brother's keeper," says one Chicago ACORN leader. It also draws on new awareness of the causes of community conditions.

Clive Aden from SCYEA observes: "I look at things a lot differently now. Before, I really didn't care. I'd see bums walking down the street; I'd see crackheads and alcoholics [and] it wouldn't affect me. I wouldn't even really care about it. But when I finally came in here, it made me look at things in a different way. Because you know, I just felt like looking at these people—that could be some of my friends one day, if not me one day . . . It's just like instead of seeing problems and not doing anything about it, now I would say something about it and do something about it."

Responsibility and commitment to the well-being of the entire community can generate a new sense of power and purpose, particularly in communities where opportunities for meaningful engagement in public life are either absent or dysfunctional. Reflecting on SBU's organizing to end school overcrowding, youth leader Rafael Peña says, "You feel the momentum . . . you're demanding something that's going to benefit you *and* students throughout other schools in each borough. . . . And if you don't win your campaign, then it's going to harm the community."

Civic and Political Engagement

For many leaders, involvement with organizing represents the first time they became politically active. Of adults who took our member survey, 37 percent say they attended a rally or other forms of direct action for the first time through their organizing group, while 47 percent met with a public official for the first time. 40 percent of adults report having conversations with other parents about school issues for the first time through their participation in the organizing group. Interview data make clear that these conversations are critical catalysts for parents to begin seeing themselves as political actors. T. A. Vasquez, a parent leader in Austin, explains the connection:

> You know your neighbors, they know you, they know your kids, I know their kids, but we never really knew what kind of struggles we were really facing. We didn't talk about our hopes and dreams with each other. [When] I had my first "house meeting" . . . we really got down to talking about what needed to be different at school . . . As I started talking to my neighbors it was like I'm not the only one having trouble with my teenage kid. I'm not the only one struggling with insurance. I'm not the only one concerned about the gangs. I mean [other] people were, too . . . I've known this woman for, like, fifteen years and I never even knew she felt the same way I did. And she's willing to step up and say, "Yeah we're going to do something."

Among young people, 87 percent report that they attended a rally or press event for the first time through the organizing group; 69 percent signed a petition for the first time, and 63 percent contacted or met with a public official for the first time. Compared with their peers in a national sample, young people in our survey sample were seven times more likely to have attended an action, three times more likely to have been involved in community problem-solving efforts, and three times more likely to have contacted a public official.[3]

THE PROSPECTS FOR LONG-TERM EDUCATIONAL SUCCESS

In the introduction, we defined a theory of action for community organizing: engagement in organizing builds a new awareness among parents, youth, and community members of their power to create change through collective action, as well as the confidence, skills, and knowledge to articulate their self-interest and speak on behalf of their community. Through successive campaigns, more leaders join the effort, expanding the number of community members who feel powerful and knowledgeable, and increasing the organization's power to build strong accountability relationships with decision-makers. Such relationships help to introduce new policies in districts, shape new priorities for resource allocations, and generate new strategies at the school level that can help children do better.

But successful schools and successful students are not produced through reform that happens in one moment of time. Schools that succeed do so because community engagement and investment is ongoing. For this reason, community capacity and school system capacity are dynamically related. Parents and students who expect more from their schools and have the skills to build strong relationships and engage their peers in problem solving are more likely to meet success when intervening with a problem in school. Similarly, educators who have experienced community power are more likely to listen and address the concerns of parents and students and to work with them on projects for mutual benefit.

Scholar Alejandro Portes and others have observed that the social capital literature pays insufficient attention to the potential of social capital to generate negative consequences for individuals and families through "exclusion of outsiders, excess claims on group members, restrictions on individual freedoms, and downward leveling norms."[4] Portes writes:

> The research literature on social capital strongly emphasizes its positive consequences. Indeed it is our sociological bias to see good things emerging out of sociability; bad things are more commonly associated with the behavior of *homo economicus*. However, the same mechanisms appropriable by individuals and groups as social capital can have other, less desirable consequences . . . While it can be a source of public goods, such as those celebrated by Coleman, Loury, and others, it can also lead to public "bads." Mafia families, prostitution and gambling rings, and youth gangs offer so many examples of how embeddedness in social structures can be turned to less than socially desirable ends.[5]

Our point here is to observe that building community capacity is not the same as building community capacity for *justice*. Community groups are as capable of making choices that exclude community members from benefits on the basis of race, gender, sexual orientation, income, or other difference as they are of crafting alternatives that work to the benefit of everyone. Importantly, organizations' work to define a shared vision of equity and justice is an essential component of community capacity for transformative change.

Our data suggest that deep involvement in community organizing contributes to a profound transformation in individual participants, in both the personal sphere of self and family and the collective, public sphere of group and community. People involved in the core leadership of organizing groups report new skills, new knowledge, and new awareness of their capacity to generate change individually and collectively. They also demonstrate a new and deep investment in community life—a sense of attachment to their community, an orientation toward community improvement, and both the experience of and commitment to long-term civic and political action. Themes of fairness, opportunity, equality, and democratic participation thread through our data. Such new community capacity is a hopeful step closer to the transformation of power relationships necessary to creating the quality schools all children need.

CHAPTER SEVEN

Working with Educators

Earlier chapters have described the ways in which community organizing groups develop and mobilize community-based social capital to build the political power necessary to sustain reform. Organizing groups work at multiple levels, through coalitions and on their own, to achieve impact. Whether working at the school, district, or state level, however, the success of community organizing for school reform hinges on the cooperation of educators.

At the school level, the importance of parent and community participation in shaping reform is well documented. Parent involvement has been viewed as a critical strategy for increasing student achievement since the Johnson administration's War on Poverty programs of the mid-1960s. Educators' views of what constitutes effective forms of parental involvement changed significantly in recent decades. Joyce Epstein's influential typology of parent involvement, for example, initially asserted four major types of parental roles: parenting, communicating with school staff, volunteering in school, and supporting student learning at home. This typology was later expanded to include participating in school-based decision making after the emergence of school-based management/shared decision making in the late 1980s, and collaborating with community-based organizations in recognition of the role of community resources and services in strengthening school programs in the mid 1990s.[1]

The literature on community engagement with district-level power brokers for the most part casts school boards as the site of democratic participation in decisions about schooling. Michael Fullan, for example, has written about communities' effectiveness in opposing reforms that run counter to their values or beliefs about education, usually vis-à-vis school boards.[2] Progressively more school districts are assuming nontraditional governance arrangements, notably mayoral or state control, and there is little research on community or parent participation in proposing or initiating reform at the district level under these kinds of alternative structural arrangements, outside of broad coalition work.

Despite evidence that parent and community participation is important to improving education, at least at the school level, parent involvement has largely focused on volunteering, fund-raising, and other peripheral activities.[3] The emphasis on teacher professionalism of the last few decades has encouraged teachers to work cooperatively and to view themselves as experts with a stake in school decision making, but these reforms have not striven to create space for other constituencies in the work of reform. School professional cultures often reflect middle-class norms and modes of interaction, and while educators are accustomed to middle-class parents advocating for their own children, they often see low-income and minority parents as disengaged and less legitimate participants in schools.[4]

The constituency involvement introduced by community organizing differs substantially in vision, goals, methods, and impacts from traditional forms of parent involvement. Rather than simply participating in the day-to-day life of the school, parents and young people involved in organizing are active agents for change. Instead of focusing on the performance of individual students, organizing efforts aim to generate improvement in schools that will affect a large number of students through increased accountability, access, and quality.

This chapter reviews the relationships organizing groups have developed with educators in the school system, including district-level administrators, school principals, teachers, and teachers' unions. Reflecting on these relationships, we examine when and why educators are receptive to organizing demands for change. We assert that organizing groups and educators are more likely to develop effective working relationships to achieve educational impact when there is a favorable political climate, agreement about school-reform priorities, and mutual understanding of organizational goals, motivations, and culture.

RELATIONSHIPS WITH EDUCATORS

District-level Relationships

As we noted in chapter 1, early education campaigns focused on building the power necessary to negotiate with decision-making "targets" within their local schools and districts. Over time, relationships with district administrators, school boards, schools, and school-reform organizations evolved as organizing groups built increasingly complex reform campaigns. Sites in our study generally positioned themselves as educators' allies. At the same time, they have maintained the independence necessary to hold educators accountable to their demands.

When Chicago ACORN began organizing to address the high rate of teacher vacancies in schools in the North Lawndale community, it staged a mass protest to demand action from the Chicago Public Schools' central administration. Once it gained the attention of district leaders, Chicago ACORN shifted tactics. Madeline Talbott, formerly head organizer with Chicago ACORN and now Action Now, recalls deciding to "climb inside and stay quiet" for several months in order to encourage the district's assistance in improving new teacher recruitment in Lawndale schools. Chicago ACORN leaders and staff worked closely with human resources staff to understand recruitment practices and to exchange data on vacant teacher positions. At the same time, Chicago ACORN staged protests outside of the state board of education offices to demand school performance data mandated by the federal No Child Left Behind Act. By directing protest tactics toward the distal state-level target, Chicago ACORN aimed to maintain a sense of momentum and energy among its membership base without threatening the emerging relationship with the district staff. Al Bertani, former director of mentoring and induction in the Chicago Public Schools, observes that Chicago ACORN was "politically smart enough to position their work in such a way that they could say, 'We know that this is a problem. We know you're working on this problem. We're trying to bring more of a spotlight on it in relation to the neighborhoods that we serve.'"

Chicago ACORN and school district officials cooperated closely where their agendas aligned. Because the district saw promise in the Grow Your Own model, it joined the GYO task force and collaborated with Chicago ACORN and its organizing allies in drafting state legislation for the teacher pipeline program. Similarly in Los Angeles, school board president José Huizar partnered with the Community Coalition and Communities for

Educational Equity (CEE) from the beginning of the A-G curriculum campaign. And in New York City, NWBCCC and the local district superintendent Irma Zardoya recognized their mutual interest in securing new school facilities, and built a collaborative relationship from the outset.

As organizing groups have won larger-scale campaigns, they have wrestled with the strategic question of how to support and monitor reform. Taking on such roles vis-à-vis implementation necessitates a closer relationship with district-level staff than many groups have developed previously. Close working relationships were evident in a majority of sites in our study, as noted in part II. For example, Oakland Community Organizations (OCO) joined the Oakland school district and Bay Area Coalition of Equitable Schools in a three-way partnership to implement the district's new small autonomous schools policy. Youth United for Change (YUC) and Sistas and Brothas United (SBU) are partners in new small schools in Philadelphia and New York; Chicago ACORN and Austin Interfaith have worked with their districts on teacher pipeline programs; in Los Angeles, Community Coalition participates alongside its CEE allies in the district implementation committee established by the A-G resolution. In Miami, People Acting for Community Together (PACT) helped to develop a district-level support structure for schools using Direct Instruction.

School-level Relationships

The development of strong working relationships with schools has been difficult for organizing groups. Schools in low-income neighborhoods are under tremendous pressure and scrutiny and often have little experience with interacting meaningfully with parent or community groups. While organizers and leaders saw their campaigns as ways to help schools win additional resources and improve instruction, many principals and teachers chafed at what they perceived as additional pressure from organized parents.

When SCYEA students were organizing for improved facilities and resources, former Community Coalition director Karen Bass recalls, "We had principals who were mad at us because we pointed out how poor the conditions were in their schools. They took it personally, as opposed to feeding us information off the record so we could bring pressure to bear to help them." In Chicago ACORN's early forays into education organizing, a strategy of targeting principals cost the organization their relationships with some schools. "In certain schools, even though they have a new principal, that history [of conflict] has stayed," Madeline Talbott says. "We had to learn some things the hard way."

The first school-based organizing campaign of the Eastern Pennsylvania Organizing Project (EPOP) at Isaac A. Sheppard Elementary School demonstrated how easily educators can feel threatened by outside scrutiny. When EPOP parents secured crossing guards and police officers for the school and shut down notorious drug houses that lined students' walk home, the teachers and principal were appreciative. But when parents began to ask questions about students' poor academic performance, teachers felt attacked.[5] Teachers felt their jobs were threatened by EPOP's calls for filling teacher vacancies with bilingual teachers to improve communication with the school's heavily Latino community. As relationships deteriorated, EPOP eventually demanded, and won, the principal's dismissal.

The new principal, Tomás Hanna, recalls that "there was suspicion" among teachers. "There was a perception that EPOP had exerted enough pressure on the school and [with] the district, and that the district itself felt that it was a time to make a change in leadership at the school." Hanna, a Puerto Rican from inner-city Philadelphia, felt a sense of connection with the school's Latino population and was open to community participation. He worked with EPOP leaders to address many of their complaints and build a more collaborative environment in the school.

Chicago ACORN and the Northwest Bronx Community and Clergy Coalition (NWBCCC) learned to position their efforts as allies with the power to advocate on behalf of schools' needs. Talbott notes that Chicago ACORN leaders found principals were happy to have the group's support "as long as we were talking about alliances and how we could work together." NWBCCC similarly recalibrated its approach to individual schools by reaching out to the parent coordinators from local schools. Ronn Jordan recalls:

> We pulled together a summit with all of them here and met with them and showed them that the Northwest Bronx Coalition is not just going in and trying to get everybody fired at their school, because our reputation is . . . : "Don't let them in here because they are going to find out what is going wrong here." [Schools] are afraid of us, and so we built this relationship with [the parent coordinators]. Now we are seen as one of their resources. The parent coordinator's job is to help parents with issues that will make them more likely to come in and be a part of the school. They know they can call one of our neighborhood organizers and say this person is having immigration issues or housing problems or whatever it is. They refer people to our community organizers.

The depth of relationship that allows organizing groups to penetrate school structures and norms requires sustained, focused school-based organizing of the type undertaken by the Alliance Schools network in Austin, OCO and, on a smaller scale, PACT. Drawing from their methodology for organizing in congregations, these groups worked deliberately to build new leadership capacity and new relationships in schools as a platform for improving school performance.

In Alliance Schools, sustained organizing produced just this sort of leadership and relationships, particularly among school faculty and parents. Principal Joaquin Gloria explains, "The parents know that it's safe to talk, to ask questions and to probe and push the teachers' thinking. And vice versa—parents know that it's okay for the teachers to push their thinking because that's the environment that we've set up."

In Oakland, Jean Wing of the New Schools Development Group observes OCO's school-based organizing created "a much deeper and more integral and empowering role for parents than just the traditional fundraiser events." In Oakland's Castlemont Business and Information Technology School, principal Rick Gaston believes "having folks like [OCO] to get with regularly help[ed] shape my vision and my understanding about we're trying to do here. It's about democracy, and community involvement, and ...that doesn't always come naturally to our district or school culture."

Relationships with Teachers' Unions

Organizing groups' relations with teachers' unions are complicated and inconsistent. On some issues and in some contexts, natural overlaps in agendas facilitated joint work; in other cases agendas conflicted or were too divergent to support collaboration. Organizing groups and teachers' unions have different relationships with district officials, which can confuse their relationships with each other. Union elections often spark a wholesale shift of priorities when new union leadership comes into power. Such internal transitions can disrupt developing relationships with organizing groups, or conversely, provide new openings for alliance building.

In Miami, the teachers' union was besieged by scandal in the early years of PACT's education organizing, and was too preoccupied with sorting out its internal struggles to be either an ally or an opponent in PACT's Direct Instruction campaign. EPOP and YUC allied with the teachers' union in Philadelphia in a campaign to curtail school privatization efforts in the city. But the Philadelphia Federation of Teachers was involved in a prolonged contract negotiation in 2004, and was largely silent on issues related to either EPOP's organizing or to YUC's campaign for small schools.

The Oakland Education Association opposed OCO's first attempt to create small schools, and the union president continued to speak out against small schools as an expensive strategy that encroached on protections in the teachers' contract. After OCO's unsuccessful effort to create a small school on the Jefferson Elementary School campus, OCO spent the summer of 1999 conducting one-on-one meetings to build relationships with individual teachers and demonstrate that a teacher constituency existed for the strategy of small-school creation. When thirteen Oakland schools faced restructuring under the No Child Left Behind Act in 2005, an OCO organizer worked closely with union building representatives and parents to propose alternative solutions to restructuring.

In Los Angeles, the Community Coalition and SCYEA found support for the A-G resolution from individual building-level union representatives, but not from the leadership of the United Teachers of Los Angeles. Though CEE was unable to convince the union leadership to come on board, the union did not actively oppose CEE's campaign. Organizer Alberto Retana believes the strategy of deliberate relationship building within the union rank and file helped to avert an open conflict between the reform coalition and the union. The union would most likely have blocked the curriculum policy resolution, Retana says, which would have hampered CEE's negotiations with district leadership. Just after the resolution passed, however, a different faction took the helm of the union and has worked with CEE to support implementation of the A-G policy.

Chicago ACORN formed close working relationships with Chicago Teachers Union leadership, successfully enlisting the union's participation in the Grow Your Own Task Force. In 2004 a contentious election brought new leadership to power and weakened the relationships Chicago ACORN had established. Shared opposition to the district's Renaissance 2010 initiative to replace some underperforming or underutilized schools in gentrifying neighborhoods with charter schools helped Chicago ACORN to rebuild those ties. In New York City, the United Federation of Teachers provided some support to NWBCCC's work on facilities and school funding, and actively helped the NWBCCC and its allies win district agreement for a lead teacher program in ten elementary schools.

Arguably the closest community-union relationship developed in Austin, where Education Austin is a dues-paying member of Austin Interfaith.

Texas is a right-to-work state, and teachers' unions do not have collective bargaining authority. The unions thus have far less political power in lo-cal- and state-level politics compared with their urban counterparts in other states. Education Austin, which was the first teachers' union in Texas to merge the NEA and AFT locals, joined Austin Interfaith to work on edu-cation issues of joint concern and to collaborate and build organizational power together. As Education Austin board member Babs Miller observes, because the union is an institutional member of Austin Interfaith, its mem-bers attend IAF trainings and participate in Austin Interfaith's education organizing campaigns.

Miller believes the IAF's methodology of one-on-ones is helping the union attract new members and build deeper relationships with existing members. One-on-ones are ostensibly ways to get to know other people, she says, "but the way IAF does it and [the distinction] between personal and public relationships [was the piece] we were missing in the union. Be-cause what we did in the union up until then was we signed people up to join and that was the end of it. We would send out flyers and send out appeals to join us in some activity, but there was no relationship there be-tween even individual union members within a building, much less relation-ships between individual members and the union office."

WHY EDUCATORS LISTEN

The superintendents, school board members, municipal leaders, and prin-cipals we interviewed offered many explanations for their willingness to collaborate with organizing groups and their regard for them as impor-tant forces for school reform. Educators described community organizing groups as truly bringing in the voices of their constituencies—more ef-fectively than their districts had been able to do, and more deeply than is typical among traditional school reform advocates. A dominant reason for their receptivity, these educators say, is their perception that community organizing groups are engaging community members who historically have not participated in school system decisions.

Organizing groups' roots in communities with poorly performing schools brought passion, tenacity, and a sense of urgency to demands for improvement. Deep and ongoing relationships with community members also positioned organizing groups as credible sources of knowledge about community conditions, and in some cases, led groups to identify novel re-form solutions to address specific needs in local schools. Educators also appreciated the political savvy and power that community groups could exert through their organizing, and acknowledged the importance of external pressure in holding educators themselves accountable to addressing the needs of low-income constituencies.

Credible Voices for Disenfranchised Communities

A key factor in establishing credibility was the degree to which community organizing groups prepared and supported their members—parents, students, and community residents—to articulate their needs. The presence of constituents speaking directly to district officials about their experiences and concerns reassured the officials that organizing demands reflected a broad consensus about schooling needs, rather than the self-interests of a small group of individuals. This consensus took on heightened legitimacy because of its focus on improving poorly performing schools that typically have few advocates. For example, a former Austin school board member describes Austin Interfaith as "really the only voice in this community for poor people and for working-class folks." Another former school board member from Austin offers a similar view: "[What] I think everybody appreciated was they knew that Austin Interfaith actually was connected to the schools it was purporting to represent. With the other [school reform groups] we were never quite sure of this. Not all the board members agreed with [AI's demands, but they] at least saw it as a legitimate organization working with schools and parents to bring what they thought was appropriate for those schools.

Similarly, Paul Vallas recalls his time in Chicago prior to taking the helm of the Philadelphia schools, observing that "a lot of school reformers . . . didn't even live in the city." "Groups like [Chicago] ACORN and EPOP . . . represent some of the most racially and economically isolated district schools in some of the poorest communities," giving them authenticity in their negotiations with the district, Vallas says. In New York City, former assistant superintendent Bruce Irushalmi believes Community Superintendent Irma Zardoya's receptivity to working with NWBCCC stemmed from her perception of the organization as "a genuine community activist group populated by poor people who were advocating for their own children and children in the community."

Organizing groups' relationships with community members, combined with a focus on equity and fairness, provided an avenue for educators to act on their own values in a larger context that they believe too often reinforces privilege and inequity. Research has long noted the highly political

nature of education reform, as well as the presumptive power of more affluent communities to control the outcomes of these political struggles.[6] In
this respect, when there was alignment between organizing demands and
superintendent agendas, superintendents saw organizing groups as helping
create political space for equity-based reform decisions.

A central tenet of organizing is the notion of pressure politics; that is,
the deliberate effort to force decision makers to meet the group's demands
through campaigns that escalate pressure through increasingly public,
large-scale tactics. Though the threat of public embarrassment or damage
at the polls is likely an underlying motivator for any public official, our
data suggest it is not the only dynamic in play. Respect for the organizations and the moral persuasiveness of organizing proposals for change were
also key factors in negotiating organizing demands. "It's not that there's
a fear that Austin Interfaith is going to turn out ten thousand people to
vote against you," says John Fitzpatrick. "It's that this is a big group that
we can work with. We care about their values, we care about who they're
serving, and they've got a track record of accomplishments." In this same
vein, Irushalmi believes that part of the NWBCCC's appeal was that their
demands for participation in school reform decisions resonated with Zardoya's
beliefs about parent engagement. "It was exactly what she was trying to encourage principals to facilitate in their own schools. And it gave her the
opportunity to not only practice what she preached, but also to model it."

Source of Knowledge and Innovative Solutions

District leaders assert that community groups enhance district improvement
processes by bringing knowledge and information about low-income communities and, in some cases, creative ideas for addressing difficult issues. As
Austin's John Fitzpatrick notes, "I make better decisions on behalf of the
entire district because I know a little more about communities of color and
low-income communities. Austin Interfaith helped me understand something I wanted to understand but I didn't have a lot of practical hands-on
experience with."

In the balkanized institutional environment of urban educational bureaucracies, relationships with community organizing groups can help
district superintendents to counter the effects of insular thinking. Paul
Vallas says, "Bureaucracies have a tendency to try to limit the flow of bad
news and increase the flow of good news . . . I need access. I need to get
information through nontraditional ways. And these groups . . . provide
me with that access." A New York City councilman and longtime ally of

the NWBCCC and SBU, shares a similar observation, noting that community organizing groups are "the eyes and ears of the neighborhood." Community walks and school tours arranged by the NWBCCC and SBU allowed him to see conditions firsthand and energized him to push school system officials to address school overcrowding in the neighborhoods he represented.

Knowledge of the school and community context can also help groups to craft new strategies for addressing difficult problems where conventional solutions have proven ineffective. In New York City, surging housing development and in-migration to northwest Bronx neighborhoods created a situation where the school system was unable to find large vacant lots on which to build new schools. The NWBCCC's long history of housing organizing formed the basis of its proposal to develop new school space through a turnkey strategy—involving local community development organizations, banks, and the school system—to develop smaller-scale school buildings on nontraditional sites. Though the NWBCCC's proposal initially failed to generate support among school system officials, it was adopted by the district five years later.

In Chicago, school district officials viewed the Grow Your Own program as a "targeted solution," in the words of Al Bertani, to the challenge of teacher recruitment and retention in the neighborhoods where Chicago ACORN and its allies organized. A state education official involved in the GYO legislation notes that Chicago ACORN's knowledge of its own community, and "research into teacher turnover at the various schools, and primarily in the city of Chicago," led Chicago ACORN and the GYO reform coalition to "come up with a novel way of addressing that problem."

In the case of Direct Instruction, PACT parent and community leaders brought the program to educators' attention and persisted in advocating for the program despite initial opposition from district officials. Data from research and site visits to schools convinced PACT members that the approach was consonant with the needs of the low-income and immigrant students in their community. District-level staff, as well as principals and teachers in Direct Instruction schools, embraced the program with enthusiasm because, as principal Julio Carrera notes, "Progress shot up."

"Critical Friends"

District staff across the sites valued the group's role as advocates, capable of mobilizing substantial pressure for resources and reform. Stanford University scholar Larry Cuban has observed, "When superintendents introduce major changes, such as expanding parental choice, firing slackers, pressing principals to be instructional leaders, or redesigning comprehensive high schools, conflicts are inevitable. Often, they involve dilemma-rich, politically volatile choices."[7] In this context, organizing groups can provide essential support when reform decisions challenge long-standing relationships and political or educational priorities.

Sometimes this pressure can be marshaled as leverage by administrators at the top of the system to move reform down to schools. In Oakland, for example, former Oakland superintendent Dennis Chaconas sought to deploy OCO's mobilization power to build cooperation for his improvement agenda. "If you care about improving the learning experience for poor kids, you have to create advocates outside the school system to be able to force issues of improvement," he says. "If you take a school that is nowhere close to effective and OCO starts to organize parents and builds a strong base, principals and teachers might start to say, 'I might lose my job. I've got to start becoming more effective!'"

Political leverage also provides district officials backing in their advocacy for new priorities with adversaries on the school board, among factions within the district administration, and with state-level leaders. Former Milwaukee School Board member Jennifer Morales observes the role of MICAH's advocacy in protecting the rights of poor families in the Neighborhood School Initiative. "I need [them] to keep hammering on—to say, 'A good, solid public education that prepares children for citizenship and the workforce and all the other roles they have to fulfill . . . [It] is that child's birthright and you are going to make sure that it happens,'" she says. Milwaukee superintendent William Andrekopoulos describes MICAH as a "real advocate at the state level" in supporting the district's budget requests and securing funds for class-size reduction. In New York, Irma Zardoya recalls that as an outside entity with considerable local influence, NWBCCC "leveraged support in addressing mutually identified district needs."

Where organizing groups are able to forge alliances with individual schools, they can play the same type of outside advocacy role as they do on behalf of districts. PACT's relationships with schools implementing Direct Instruction provided both problem solving support and protection for schools. PACT leaders met with teachers and principals and relayed concerns to the district administrators in charge of program; they could, as one principal observed, "go to the district [and] go to regional offices, and put pressure that sometimes we as principals can't." Though high school principals were often wary of SBU's organizing, sometimes viewing its members as troublemakers, some administrators became more supportive once they saw the political leverage that SBU could deliver for their schools. One principal struggling with overcrowding and tension between small schools sharing a large campus encouraged his parent coordinator and teachers to speak out at SBU's press conferences.

Across cities, district administrators emphasize that the same power and independence that allows organizing groups to effectively advocate for district needs is an important source of accountability within their relationships, as well. Austin superintendent Pascal Forgione observes, "Austin Interfaith has got to be my critical friend. They're not my best friend. They've got to be critical. They've got to be the conscience of my community. Sometimes I don't want to hear it; most times I don't mind because we have such shared values. But whether I like it or not, that's their job."

School-reform organizing succeeds when organizing groups and districts are able to negotiate their differences successfully. In large part, as educators note, these successes reflect the savvy of groups in balancing external pressure with open lines of communication. Educators we interviewed were cognizant of the multiple roles organizing groups must take. For example, OCO organized teachers to oppose the state administrator's plans for schools in corrective action under NCLB, even while working closely with the district to create additional small schools. Chicago ACORN mobilized community residents against the Renaissance 2010 plan without jeopardizing the school district's participation in the Grow Your Own task force; and administrators in Philadelphia invited EPOP to train principals in community engagement principles even though EPOP had threatened a lawsuit over a district proposal to revise the formula for dispersing federal Title 1 funds for high-poverty schools.

The importance of organizing groups' willingness to challenge district decisions is a consistent theme across urban district officials. Chicago's Al Bertani describes Chicago ACORN as an "appropriate, friendly critic, or critical friend of what the system has been doing." Zardoya in the Bronx calls NWBCCC "watchdogs; they're catalysts, they push, and they remind you about priorities."

Officials consistently note the importance of having what Michele Cahill, former Senior Counselor for Education Policy in the New York City Schools, calls "strong stamina on both sides for tension." Commenting on OCO, a member of the state administrator's staff in Oakland sums up the art of maintaining an effective accountability relationship: "They understand how to stay in a relationship and keep it constructive so that you can live to fight another battle. You're always kind of pulled right to the edge of breaking the relationship, but it doesn't actually snap. So we may feel like we have a conflict that's irreconcilable but then we come together again as allies when the next threat shows up. And so they keep coming back and we keep coming back even though it feels like we're huge enemies in moments."

GETTING TO IMPACT: FACTORS THAT FACILITATE WORKING TOGETHER

Organizing groups have molded a range of relationships with educators—from intimately working with principals and teachers to create parent-friendly school climates to negotiating with high-level district leaders and partnering in systemic school reform. As the examples above illustrate, through these relationships organizing groups contribute in a variety of ways to the educational enterprise and the goal of improving the academic achievement of all students. Yet, like any relationship, these relationships do not come easily and can be fraught with complications. Under what circumstances, then, would we expect to see relationships between educators and organizing groups yield the greatest level of impact?

Urban schools and districts are complex entities, and efforts to improve public schools are correspondingly complicated. At any given moment, there are multiple reform initiatives in place, as well as the prospect of new programs, all competing for limited time, attention, and funds. Add that to shifting leadership at the district and school level, as well as changing governance structures, and it becomes clear that building effective relationships with educators requires navigating through a constantly changing terrain. Such a task is difficult even in the best of circumstances.

Our interviews with educators and organizing groups revealed that several factors contributed to the process of developing productive relationships between educators and organizing groups. These factors include strategic openings in the political climate for reform, convergence in the school reform agendas of the district and the organizing group, and mutual understanding of organizational goals, motivations, or culture. When these conditions exist, they produce a hospitable environment in which both entities are able to work toward the goal of positively impacting schools and student academic outcomes. When these conditions are not present, school-reform initiatives proposed by organizing groups are often in danger of being thwarted, stalled, or undone.

Favorable Political Climate

The average length of a superintendent's tenure is three years, yet the amount of time necessary to implement new initiatives and see substantial progress ranges from three to five years.[8] As superintendents come and go, they often take members of their staff with them, diminishing continuity in senior district leadership and endangering reforms that are in progress. Principal turnover is especially high in urban districts, and principal departures can spark substantial transition among teaching staff. Complicating the picture further, many large urban districts are embroiled in fractious debates over governance, grappling with competing calls for mayoral control and the authority of local school boards.

In addition to leadership transitions, political and policy battles at the state level and locally over school financing, high-stakes testing, the role of teachers' unions, and the presence of charter schools, to name just a few, are likely to impact the political climate for reform. As we noted in chapter 5, examples from organizing campaigns in Miami and Austin illustrate how the political context can impede the group's education-reform objectives, while the small-schools campaign in Oakland shows how groups can respond effectively to a turbulent political context.

Austin Interfaith's press for authentic assessments and relief from Texas's standardized testing regime was thwarted by the political realities of education in that state. Despite persistent advocacy from Austin Interfaith during the 2004–05 school year, the school district declined to release Alliance schools from district mandated assessment tests, citing concerns about the difficulty of constructing an alternative assessment to the statewide test as well as the external political pressures on the district.

Austin Interfaith fell victim to the political zeitgeist. Benchmarks established in No Child Left Behind pushed schools and district to focus intensely on standardized testing, and Texas, as the home state of then-President George W. Bush, was in the national spotlight, since much of the administration's rhetoric around the Act stemmed from the "successes" Texas had had under Bush's governorship.

In this context, it was clear that Austin Interfaith's push for the sub-district would have a difficult time gaining traction. While they were unsuccessful with their sub-district plan, two years later, with criticism of No Child Left Behind and high-stakes testing mounting, the climate was more favorable for a reexamination of the role of high-stakes testing. After a two year campaign, in 2009, the Texas Legislature created a new statewide accountability system to "deemphasize the TAKS test score, give students more flexibility on class choices, and make a high school diploma count for more."[9]

Yet leadership transitions do not inherently create an unfavorable political environment. In Oakland, OCO's organizing to develop new small schools in the district occurred within a tumultuous political context. Between 1999, when OCO's organizing for small schools began, and 2009, there have been six transitions in district leadership, as well as a state takeover of the district due to the district's severe budget deficit. The small-schools movement flourished within this difficult context in large part because of a network of supportive relationships OCO had built with allies inside and outside of the district. OCO leveraged the political power of these relationships to serve as an active and vocal proponent for continuing the reform, and generated consistently large scale mobilizations to demonstrate the breadth and intensity of community demand.

Organizing groups work to develop organizational power and knowledge of the context so that when the right political movement presents itself, they are ready to act. "OCO was the only group to follow the trends in public education and youth development, and the intersection of those two worlds enough to be right there at the very moment when things were going to the next place," says Greg Hodge, a former school board member in Oakland. "When the school-design piece hit the table, they were able to build on the hard lessons they had learned from their charter school experience, to say, 'No, we want to work within the existing public school system and make change happen in that way.'"

Chicago ACORN positioned the teacher quality work within a national dialogue about teacher quality. Madeline Talbott observes about Grow Your Own: "It's a concept whose time has come. It's a historical moment where it's easy to do. It's a campaign that's like apple pie so you don't have a lot of opposition."

Convergence of School Reform Agendas

When the schooling demands of organizing groups are perceived to be aligned with the goals of educators, and vice versa, the potential for meaningful reform increases. Examples from Chicago, New York, and Philadelphia demonstrate the ways in which groups and districts can create effective inside-outside relationships in support of a common agenda.

Paul Vallas recalls that part of the reason that YUC and the School District of Philadelphia had a constructive relationship was "because there is very little that we disagree on. So they advocate for small schools. I believe in small schools. So they want to break some of the big behemoth high schools into multiplexes and I've always been a supporter of that." At the same time that YUC and the Philadephia Student Union (PSU) were settling on a small-schools strategy for Kensington and West Philadelphia high schools, Vallas's staff were developing a citywide small-schools policy. Because they agreed on broad principles, the district was willing to compromise with the youth organizing groups on details of the plans.

Chicago Public Schools officials were excited about the Grow Your Own model because it addressed one of their critical concerns. In response to the pressures of No Child Left Behind, the district under chief executive officer Arne Duncan's leadership had focused increased attention on the problems of teacher recruitment and retention and was actively thinking about strategies for keeping teachers in struggling schools. "I think we captured ACORN's attention that the district was taking the problem of teacher turnover much more seriously," Al Bertani recalls. The district was especially receptive to the Grow Your Own strategy because it had already set about developing supports for teachers in hard-to-staff schools. Bertani and his colleagues believed that GYO would complement the district's efforts in those schools.

In New York City, Irma Zardoya and Bruce Irushalmi supported NW-BCCC's sometimes-confrontational organizing because they recognized the district and community's mutual interest in securing new school facilities. NWBCCC's early campaigns to push the School Construction Authority to move faster in completing school construction projects drew widespread attention in the media.

Austin Interfaith's proposal to create a sub-district of schools, in contrast, contradicted the reform goals of the school district. Pascal Forgione, who had formerly served as the U.S. Commissioner of Education Statistics, was a strong proponent of educational standards and the use of assessment data to align standards and instruction in schools. Forgione, concerned about the lack of curriculum standards in the district when he arrived, sought to streamline the curriculum and build corresponding assessments. He explains, "I'm a standards guy. I'm not a test guy. I want to teach to the standards. Now certainly alternative assessments are nice, but I've built thirty tests in my life. Well, I know a little bit about testing, and alternative tests are very difficult." Though Forgione supported the Alliance Schools model and often allied himself with Austin Interfaith, he was unwilling to support their request to suspend district mandated benchmark assessments. Even if he had supported the sub-district proposal, it is likely he would have encountered substantial resistance from school board members and state officials.

Understanding of Motivation, Goals, and Culture

Differences in the norms and structures of schools and community organizing groups also mediate the possibilities for reform. Urban school systems function as top-down, bureaucratic, and insular institutions, while community groups generally place a premium on participation and fluidity.

In the cycle of organizing campaigns, reform demands and campaign strategy are developed by groups through some form of consensus-based process, although groups vary considerably in the number of core leaders involved in these discussions. Engaging decision makers in negotiating demands is usually a public process that involves an audience of community members in a meeting led by a youth, parent or community leader. These meetings are often tightly scripted to ensure maximum control over the agenda, and to elicit a statement of agreement from official representatives. Decision making in educational bureaucracies is also scripted, but it is often defined by a chain of command in which the space for negotiation is constrained by political relationships and regulatory controls (see table 7.1).

TABLE 7.1   Cultural differences between school systems
and community organizing groups

	School systems	**Community organizing groups**
Culture	Hierarchical, compliance orientation	Democratic, problem-solving orientation
Decision making	Top-down chain of command: decisions are made by administrators	Participatory and inclusive: decisions are made by the group, generally by consensus
Locus of expertise	School leaders and professional leaders are experts	Community members: everyone has something to contribute
External pressures	Political interests and regulatory constraints	Need to "deliver" concrete victories to constituents on concerns

Source: Seema Shah and Kavitha Mediratta, "Negotiating Reform: Young People's 'Leadership in the Educational Arena,'" *New Directions for Youth Development* 117 (Spring 2008): 44–53.

Cultural differences in the operational norms of school systems and organizing groups contribute to the difficulties in developing effective alliances between the two entities. School and district officials often fear that outside groups do not sufficiently appreciate the complexity of the problems and constraints schools face. Sylvia G. Rousseau, formerly a local district superintendent in Los Angeles, explains that educators are apprehensive of community organizing groups out of the fear that they will come "into your school, riling up students without . . . regard for the good work, in spite of the difficulties, [taking place] in schools."

Irma Zardoya concurs: "There are principals out there that are still distrustful . . . because of the flyers that are sometimes sent out. An incident occurs and a flyer is sent out in the community and a meeting is set up in a different part of the community to talk about the school, and yet administrators and the teachers have no clue as to what's being said about their school or what they can do about it." Organizing groups' willingness to use confrontational tactics to surface and mobilize the collective anger of community member can be particularly threatening to educators at lower levels of educational bureaucracy. Principals worry that local conflicts will prompt retaliatory action against them by higher-ups in the system who want to make the problem go away.

In addition, reform negotiations and partnerships carry an inherent tension between organizing groups' need for immediate action to address urgent school problems, and the limitations of what administrators can do to meet demands for change. Even when there is mutual agreement on the need for reform, constraints posed by political demands and perennial budget shortfalls can circumscribe the possibilities for district action. Tomás Hanna in Philadelphia calls for greater attention to each others' cultural contexts. "[The group] will backdoor you in a minute if they think you are blowing them off," he says. "And you know what? If you're blowing them off, you deserve it. But if you're not and you're really limited and you can't [take action], a heads up would be nice, for them to say, 'You know what, I'm taking it [up the chain of command].' That would be nice."

For their part, organizing groups find it necessary to continually assert their improvement agenda and autonomy within alliances with educators. Christopher Boston of MICAH observes that district-level educators often do not "understand that we're organizing to build power. They want to build relationships with community groups [in order] to get groups to do [the educators'] work. Its like, "You know, if MICAH really wants to be helpful, this is what you could do." Rebecca McIlwain of Austin Interfaith explains, "[We've] got to have that public space where they know we can take them on and we will." Otherwise, she continues, organizing groups risk becoming "cogs in the whole bureaucratic wheel."

When educators and organizing groups both understand the differences in organizational culture, and the motivations for their respective stances, productive relationships of mutual understanding can emerge. Sylvia G. Rousseau observes of the Community Coalition: "I have found them to be challenging, as they should, but it's responsible challenging. Where we find common ground to cooperate, we cooperate. There are times when we're not in cooperation, but I've found . . . that their agenda has been clearly the welfare of kids."

Bruce Irushalmi in the Bronx recalls that respect for the disciplined methodology of organizing led to a strong working relationship with organizers and leaders. "This was a group [that said] 'This is our agenda, these are our demands, and when are you going to meet them?' But the need to do that kind of confrontational conversation was significantly reduced over the years because we trusted each other." Recognizing the group's influence as a community voice, he says, it behooved the district to negotiate differences before going public with a particular stance, so that the NWBCCC and district leadership could speak with "a single voice." In the end, says Irushalmi, "If we invested the time to work with them, the outcome was better for the people we were all interested in."

LOOKING FORWARD

In this chapter we have explored the factors that can support deep and effective working relationships between community organizing groups and school system educators. We have shared illustrative examples from the work of study sites to show how and under what circumstances trust and collaboration can emerge, but it should be noted that there were many more examples of both successful and unsuccessful collaboration than what we have discussed here.

In chapter 2 we observed that across urban districts, superintendents, school board members, and other education officials assert that organizing groups enhance their ability to address the needs of underserved low-income, African American, Latino, and immigrant communities in their districts. We underscore that point here. Despite the potential for confrontation and misunderstanding, urban school system leaders assert—consistently and passionately—that organizing groups help them to fulfill their social and moral obligations as well as their professional mandate to educate all students fully.

Finally, we note that community groups have demonstrated considerable growth in their understanding of and willingness to accommodate the contextual factors that constrain the actions of district and school officials. Educators, too, have come to see the potential of collaboration with organizing groups and have developed more nuanced understandings of how organizing groups wield power. As the educators we interviewed emphasize, both educators and organizing groups need to continue the difficult work of understanding their respective positions so that more effective and productive relationships, capable of generating real change, can form.

Organizing in a New Political Moment

When Barack Obama assumed the office of president of the United States of America in January 2009, it marked a new moment for community organizing in the country's political landscape. Obama brought to the office a deep knowledge of organizing, having worked for three years as a community organizer with the Gamaliel Foundation on Chicago's south side. Obama also brought new visibility to the work. Leading up to the election, his experiences as a community organizer had been widely disparaged by influential Republican leaders and vigorously defended by organizers across the nation. The end result of the political drama was an unprecedented prominence for the field.*

Throughout this volume, we have asserted that community organizing aims to address persistent social and economic inequities that have long defined educational outcomes in the United States. The emergence of community organizing for school reform as a field across the past two decades traces the struggles of parents, youth, and community members to establish their legitimacy—as organized constituencies—in asserting their right to quality schooling and their proposals for educational reform. Underlying these efforts is a deep concern for what organizers and community members (including parents and students) see as *educational justice*. This term

---

*Our thanks and appreciation to Anne Henderson, senior fellow of the Annenberg Institute for School Reform, for her contributions to this chapter.

refers not only to the fair and equitable allocation of resources, but also to the need for close attention to and respect for the interests of low-income families and families of color. We hope this moment of new visibility for organizing will foster deeper and more expansive alliances between organizing groups and educators.

What are the benefits of deeper alliances between educators and community organizations? The stories of organizing in this book suggest the power of organized communities to catalyze change by bringing passion, urgency, political influence, community knowledge, and creative ideas to the table. When communities join with willing educators, these efforts can generate far-reaching reform. Such reforms include:

- *New capacity in districts:* New staff positions were created to implement community-generated proposals for reform, and new relationships were developed that helped districts access existing community resources more effectively.

- *Positive school climates:* Positive changes were reported by principals and teachers in the areas of school safety, parent-teacher relationships, shared decision making, and a focus on learning. In communities with run-down, crowded school buildings, new schools were built and old schools overhauled.

- *Stronger professional cultures in schools:* Improvements were reported by teachers in the form of greater input in school decision making, a stronger sense of collective responsibility, a stronger culture of staff collaboration, collegiality and joint problem solving, and a deeper sense of commitment to their schools.

- *Stronger instructional core in schools:* Higher expectations for student achievement were reported by teachers, as well as increased classroom resources and higher-quality curriculum and instruction.

- *Deeper parent involvement in children's learning:* Greater involvement was reported by parents in both traditional parent involvement activities, such as attending school events and PTA meetings and talking with their child's teacher, and new accountability-oriented behaviors, such as looking at data on their child's school and raising concerns with school and district administrators.

- *Increased motivation and higher aspirations for educational success:* Greater motivation to take harder classes, finish high school, and pursue a college education and a graduate or professional degree was reported by youth involved in organizing. Higher expectations were also reported by parents and adult community members.

* *Improved student educational outcomes:* Increased student engagement and educational outcomes were also evident. For example, schools that sustained deep involvement with Austin Interfaith realized gains in the percentage of students meeting minimum standards on TAAS. The small schools established through Oakland Community Organizations' advocacy are academically outperforming the schools they replaced. Reading gains in PACT schools using Direct Instruction exceeded those in matched comparison schools as well as the district as a whole, and academic progress was greatest for the lowest performing students. In communities that focused on high school reform, schools are reporting higher attendance and college aspirations.

Across the sites, in varying ways, organizing groups built shared, focused conversations among community members about student learning, and worked to support and strengthen the work of teachers and principals. In doing so, organizing presents a highly cost-effective school reform intervention. Operating with average organizational budgets of roughly $200,000–$300,000 per year (in which education is only one part of organizations' overall activities) groups in our study helped to bring about reforms that directly benefited their district's lowest-performing students.

Our research cannot—nor can any research on community organizing—make a causal argument for the role of organizing in improving student educational outcomes. We argue that, given the scale of our study, the consistency of evidence across interviews, surveys, and school administrative data suggests a strong positive relationship between community organizing and improved equity and capacity to support student learning within the urban districts in our study.

Organizing groups face a number of daunting challenges. Chief among them is the need to develop organizing strategies that: combine school and systemic level work; build a "bench" of trained organizers who can replace the generation of leaders currently at the helm of organizing groups; and measure the longer-term impacts of organizing in terms of outcomes for participants as well as in the context of communities.

When the groups we studied began organizing in the early 1990s, most worked at the school level to recruit parents, youth, or community members into a committee focused on resolving pressing school problems, first by meeting with the principal and then by advancing up through the chain of command to the district, municipal, and state level, until organizing demands were met. These campaigns succeeded in replacing ineffective or unresponsive school leadership and bringing critically needed resources to low-performing schools in high-poverty neighborhoods. But the campaigns also revealed the limitations of school-level work in generating sufficient power to address the overarching inequities in resources and capacity that prescribe the possibilities for schools in low-income neighborhoods. By the mid 2000s, organizing groups across the country were involved in campaigns for systemic reform.

Yet in sites where we found improved school capacity and student outcomes, these improvements resulted not simply from school-based or system-level reform strategies, but from the strategic combination of both. These sites pursued strategic systemic levers and complemented this work with some form of school-level support. This school-level work was the most intense and developed in the Austin site. In Austin, our research documents much greater penetration of the school climate and culture than in the other sites.

Not all school-level engagement is equally effective. Our research suggests strategies that build trust in schools and support people acting on that trust together are more likely to see specific victories leverage broader capacity. Gains are also more likely when the organizing is sustained at a high level of intensity. These findings are consistent with the educational change literature and most notably, with research by the Consortium on Chicago School Research on the role of relational trust in providing a foundation for improvement in schools.

We assert that the combination of school- and system-level strategies is essential to improved public schools. Such pronouncements are easy to make, but extraordinarily difficult to carry out. Groups must balance the demands of working at multiple levels of the system without overstretching staff resources and wearing thin the base of volunteer members and leaders. In maintaining member participation across the life cycle of systemic reform campaigns, organizations must also overcome the barrier of professional education jargon that can diminish members' confidence and the lack of those visible wins that serve to build a sense of group identity and power. And as groups take on more-complex initiatives, they must take care to avoid becoming so deeply involved in implementing services that fill gaps in district or school capacity that they are not recruiting and developing new leadership in communities. As Alberto Retana of Los Angeles reminds us, organizing must be "not just about relationship-building, but about building power and pushing the district to do its job."

We caution readers to avoid the trap of conflating scale with replication, assuming both that successful strategies can be exported from one district to another and that the imperative of numbers of schools reached trumps the imperative of depth in reform. While organizers and leaders can learn from the work of others, they must figure out what will work in their particular organizations, communities, and schools on the basis of the interests of members, their staff capacity, and the strategic openings for action in their context. "Yes, you want to learn from people," says Gamaliel's David Liners, "but I think when you try to import somebody else's good idea, a lot of times it just doesn't work." Moreover, as we detail in chapter 5, moving demands across large numbers of schools means very little if capacities, expectations, and outcomes are not changing within those schools.

Organizational capacity is the linchpin of effective organizing, yet this capacity draws on a small and uncertain base of resources. Organizational budgets of $200,000–$300,000 per year may suggest a cost-effective intervention, but the bare-bones budget of most groups can put the work at risk when organizational conditions change. Several organizations in the study experienced extensive internal turmoil during the six years of our research. Turnover in directors, staff, and core leadership hampered these organizations' efforts to build and sustain campaigns.

Organizing groups that led successful campaigns were characterized by a stable core of staff and leaders, and invested extensively in their development. Directors and organizers in some sites had decades of experience in their organizations and communities. The continuity in staff and leaders, combined with ongoing development opportunities, enhanced organizations' sophistication and skill in engaging in multiple constituencies in the reform work. The infrastructure provided by national or regional networks, as well as by local university or advocacy partners, added to this organizational capacity by facilitating cross-organizational sharing of strategies, organizer skill development, data and policy analyses, and additional state-wide mobilization power.

Though all of the national networks have invested resources in recruiting and training new organizers, to date, the demand for organizers far exceeds the supply. The pipeline of new education organizers is even more constricted because the position requires additional levels of expertise. Organizers in this study demonstrated extensive knowledge of the political context of education and of effective organizational and pedagogical re-form strategies. They also demonstrated a high level of skill in legitimizing their organizations with a wide range of civic, political, and educational players in their communities. As Madeline Talbott in Chicago observes, such interactions require staff who are "more program and professional-oriented to handle the challenging interplay of educators and community, unions and whatnot" than is typical of most organizers.

At the same time, these very strengths raise additional dilemmas for the practice of organizing. Staff continuity can undermine leaders' roles in strategy development, for example, when the political relationships formed through organizing rest with staff organizers, rather than with grassroots leaders. The extent to which community organizing for school reform pro-duces the community capacity gains that we describe in chapter 6 depends on the strength of leadership development among members, the commit-ment to a vision that grassroots leaders must drive the work, and the atten-tion to defining larger and more transformative visions of societal change around which to construct campaigns.

We have argued that community and school capacity generated through school-reform organizing interact to produce greater schooling account-ability, more powerful community engagement, and higher educational outcomes in communities. As this work grows, organizing groups, as well as the research and philanthropic organizations that support them, have the opportunity to explore in more detail the impacts of participation in organizing. To what extent are the emergent forms of community capacity we observed sustained beyond individuals' direct participation in organiz-ing? What are the effects of involvement in youth organizing on high school performance and college entry and completion? Under what circumstances do these individual-level gains shift the norms of political engagement and democratic control in communities that organizing strives for? All of these questions warrant further study.

In the introduction, we observed that the world is not particularly be-wildered by the question of what children need and deserve. Though there may be differences in how schools organize and deliver instruction, at core is a basic agreement that high expectations, enriching learning experiences, administrator and teacher capacity, and community involvement matter to educational success. Thus the challenge we face in this new political mo-ment is to set right the differential distribution of power so that all children get what they deserve. Reflecting on the work of the Community Coali-tion and its allies, educator and community advocate Maria Casillas in Los

Angeles observes, "What we've been able to do is to create a third power to keep things in balance—to force the district and to force the schools to create the desired and [just] policies [needed] to promote high school graduation and college-going rates that are satisfactory to our community." Casillas' observation cuts to the heart of the narratives shared in this volume—that community organizing serves as a vital and necessary force for deep and lasting reform in our nation's urban public school systems.

Resources and Study Sites

Additional research products from the study are available at www.annenberginstitute.org and include the
following reports and case studies:

Kavitha Mediratta. *Constituents of Change: Community Organizations and Public Education Reform*. New York: Institute for Education and Social Policy of New York University, 2004.

    An overview of the theory of action and school reform strategies guiding the organizing groups in our study.

Kavitha Mediratta, Seema Shah, Sara McAlister, Norm Fruchter, Christina Mokhtar, and Dana Lockwood. *Organized Communities, Stronger Schools: A Preview of Research Findings*. Providence, RI: Annenberg Institute for School Reform at Brown University, 2008.

    A summary of research findings from the six-year study.

Case Studies

Kavitha Mediratta, Seema Shah, and Sara McAlister. *Building Partnerships to Reinvent School Culture:*
Austin Interfaith. Providence, RI: Annenberg Institute for School Reform at Brown University, 2009.

    Through the Alliance Schools network, the group created new parent and school leadership, brought new resources to the district, and improved student performance.

Sara McAlister, Kavitha Mediratta, and Seema Shah. *Rethinking the Teacher Pipeline for Urban Public Schools: Chicago ACORN*. Providence, RI: Annenberg Institute for School Reform at Brown University, 2009.

    Organizing led to a new statewide, cross-sector program to train community residents as teachers for hard-to-staff schools.

Seema Shah, Kavitha Mediratta, and Sara McAlister. *Securing a College Prep Curriculum for All Students: Community Coalition (Los Angeles)*. Providence, RI: Annenberg Institute for School Reform at Brown University, 2009.

    Youth-led organizing and a citywide coalition resulted in a new district resolution mandating a college preparatory curriculum for all high schools.

Kavitha Mediratta, Sara McAlister, and Seema Shah. *Building a Campaign for Reading Reform in Miami: People Acting for Community Together.* Providence, RI: Annenberg Institute for School Reform at Brown University, 2009.

A new literacy program and extensive community engagement improved community–school relationships and helped raise low reading achievement in twenty-seven elementary schools.

Kavitha Mediratta, Sara McAlister, and Seema Shah. *Improving Schools through Youth Leadership and Community Action: Northwest Bronx Community and Clergy Coalition and Sistas and Brothas United.* Providence, RI: Annenberg Institute for School Reform at Brown University, 2009.

New school facilities and repairs relieved overcrowding and youth leaders collaborated with educators to open a new small high school with a youth leadership and community action model.

Seema Shah, Kavitha Mediratta, and Sara McAlister. *Building a Districtwide Small Schools Movement: Oakland Community Organizations.* Providence, RI: Annenberg Institute for School Reform at Brown University, 2009.

The creation of forty-eight new small schools fundamentally transformed the district landscape.

Sara McAlister, Kavitha Mediratta, and Seema Shah. *Keeping Parent and Student Voices at the Forefront of Reform: Eastern Pennsylvania Organizing Project and Youth United for Change (Philadelphia).* Providence, RI: Annenberg Institute for School Reform at Brown University, 2009.

Organizing won greater parental access to school information, and new small high schools showed gains in attendance and student college-going plans.

Contact Information for the Study Sites

Action Now
209 W. Jackson Blvd.
2nd Floor
Chicago, IL 60606
(312) 676-4280
http://www.actionnow.org

Austin Interfaith
1301 South IH 35, Ste 313
Austin Texas 78741
(512) 916-0100
http://www.austininterfaith.org

Community Coalition
8101 S. Vermont Ave
Los Angeles, CA 90044
(323) 750-9087
http://cocosouthla.org

Eastern Pennsylvania Organizing Project (EPOP)
2625 "B" Street
Philadelphia PA 19125
(215) 634.8922
http://epop-leaders.info

Northwest Bronx Community and Clergy Coalition (NWBCCC) and
Sistas and Brothas United (SBU)
103 East 196th St.
Bronx, NY 10468
(718) 584-0515
http://www.northwestbronx.org

Oakland Community Organizations (OCO)
7200 Bancroft Ave.
#2 Eastmont Town Ctr.
Oakland CA 94605
(510) 639-1444
http://www.oaklandcommunity.org

People Acting for Community Together (PACT)
316 NE 26th Terrace
Miami, FL 33137
(305) 572-0602
http://www.miamipact.org/

Youth United for Change (YUC)
1910 North Front Street,
Philadelphia, PA 19122
(215) 423-9588
http://yuc.home.mindspring.com

Notes

Introduction

1. Norm Fruchter, "American Public Education: Crisis and Possibility," *New Labor Forum* (Fall/Winter1998): 11.
2. Pierre Bourdieu, *Outline to a Theory of Practice* (London: Cambridge University Press, 1977); and Pierre Bourdieu, "The Forms of Capital," in *Handbook of Theory and Research for the Sociology of Education*, ed. John Richardson (New York: Greenwood, 1985), 241–258.
3. Glenn C. Loury, "A Dynamic Theory of Racial Income Differences," in *Women, Minorities and Employment Discrimination*, ed. Phyllis A. Wallace and Annette M. LaMond (Lexington, MA: Lexington Books, 1977), 153–188; and James S. Coleman, "Social Capital in the Creation of Human Capital," *American Journal of Sociology* 94 (Supplement: "Organizations and Institutions: Sociological and Economic Approaches to the Analysis of Structure," 1988): S95–S120.
4. Robert Putnam, "The Strange Disappearance of Civic America," *American Prospect* 24 (Winter 1996): 34–48; Bowling Alone: America's Declining Social Capital," *Journal of Democracy* 6 (1995): 65–78; and "The Prosperous Community: Social Capital and Public Life," *American Prospect* 13 (Spring 1993): 35–42.
5. James DeFilippis, "The Myth of Social Capital in Community Development," *Housing Policy Debate* 12, no.4 (2001): 781–806; and Alejandro Portes, "Social Capital: Its Origins and Applications in Modern Sociology," *Annual Review of Sociology* 24 (1998): 1–24.
6. Ross Gittel and Avis Vidal, *Community Organizing: Building Social Capital as a Development Strategy* (Thousand Oaks, CA: Sage Publications, 1998); Allan Wallis, Jarle P. Crocker, and Bill Schechter, "Social Capital and Community Building: Part One," *National Civic Review* 87, no. 3 (1998): 253–271; Susan Saegert, J. Philip Thompson, and Mark R. Warren, eds., *Social Capital and Poor Communities* (New York: Russell Sage Foundation, 2001).
7. *Reports:* See Eva Gold, Elaine Simon, and Chris Brown, *Strong Neighborhoods, Strong Schools: Successful Community Organizing for School Reform* (Chicago/Philadelphia: Cross City Campaign for Urban School Reform/Research for Action, Inc., 2002); Daniel HoSang and Barbara Bowes, "Youth and Community Organizing Today," *Social Policy* 34, no. 2 (2004): 66–70; Kavitha Mediratta and Jessica Karp, *Parent Power and Urban School Reform: The Story of Mothers on the Move* (New York: Institute for Education and Social Policy, 2003). *Book-length analyses:* See Jeannie Oakes, John Rogers, and Martin Lipton, *Learning Power: Organizing*

for Education and Justice (New York: Teachers College Press, 2006); Mark R. Warren, *Dry Bones Rattling: Community Building to Revitalize American Democracy* (Princeton, NJ: Princeton University Press, 2001); Dennis Shirley, *Community Organizing for Urban School Reform* (Austin, TX: University of Texas Press, 1997).

8. Interviews, surveys, and observational data with community organizers and adult and youth members were used to clarify the theories of action and resultant educational change strategies guiding organizing groups' work, as well as members' knowledge about education policy and their sense of efficacy in generating change within their schools and communities. Unless otherwise noted, quotations used throughout this book are from interviews conducted by the research team over the period 2002–2006.

Publicly available school-level administrative data, interviews with district and school leaders, and teacher surveys were used to analyze district-, school-, and student-level outcomes.

9. James P. Connell, Anne C. Kubisch, Lisbeth Schorr, and Carol H. Weiss, *New Approaches to Evaluating Community Initiatives: Contexts, Methods and Contexts* (New York: The Aspen Institute Roundtable on Comprehensive Community Initiatives for Children and Families, 1995); David C. Berliner, "Educational Research: The Hardest Science of Them All," *Educational Researcher* 31, no. 8 (2002): 18–20; Patti Lathe, "Scientific Research in Education," *Journal of Curriculum and Supervision, 20, no. 1(2004): 14–30 (joint publication with British Educational Research Journal 30, no. 6 [2004], 759–772),*

Chapter 1

1. Richard F. Elmore, "Getting to Scale with Good Educational Practice," *Harvard Educational Review* 66, no. 1(1996): 1; Joseph Murphy and Philip Hallinger, eds., *Restructuring Schooling: Learning from Ongoing Efforts* (Newbury Park, CA: Corwin Press, Inc., 1993), 280; Ann Lieberman, ed., *Building a Professional Culture in Schools* (New York: Teachers College Press, 1988), 251; David Tyack and Larry Cuban, *Tinkering Toward Utopia: A Century of Public School Reform* (Cambridge, MA: Harvard University Press, 1995).

2. See Christopher T. Cross, ed., *Putting the Pieces Together: Lessons from Comprehensive School Reform Research* (Washington, DC: The National Clearinghouse for Comprehensive School Reform, 2004); Mark Berends, Susan J. Bodilly, and Susan Natraj Kirby, *Facing the Challenges of Whole School Reform: New American Schools After a Decade* (Santa Monica, CA: Rand Corporation, 2002); and Michael Fullan, *Whole School Reform: Problems and Promises* (Chicago: Chicago Community Trust, 2001). For an articulation of the argument for school privatization, see Milton Friedman, *Public Schools: Make Them Private* (Washington, DC: Cato Institute, 1995); John E. Chubb and Terry M. Moe, *Politics, Markets, and America's Schools* (Washington, DC: Brookings Institution, 1990).

3. For a historical view of high-stakes testing, see Audrey L. Amrein, and David C. Berliner, "High-stakes Testing, Uncertainty, and Student Learning," *Education Policy Analysis Archives* 10, no. 18 (2002); see also Paul E. Peterson and Martin

R. West, eds., *No Child Left Behind? The Politics and Practices of School Account-ability* (Washington, DC: Brookings Institution, 2003).

4. A 2009 analysis by McKinsey & Company's Social Sector Office, reports: "On average, black and Latino students are roughly two to three years of learning behind white students of the same age. This racial gap exists regardless of how it is measured, including both achievement (e.g., test score) and attainment (e.g., graduation rate) measures. Taking the average National Assessment of Educational Progress (NAEP) scores for math and reading across the fourth and eighth grades, for example, 48 percent of blacks and 43 percent of Latinos are "below basic," while only 17 percent of whites are, and this gap exists in every state. A more pronounced racial achievement gap exists in most large urban school districts." (*The Economic Impact of the Achievement Gap in America's Schools* [April 2009], 7, www.mckinsey .com/clientservice/socialsector/).

5. Daniel de Vise, "Area Schools' Success Obscures Lingering Racial SAT Gap," *Washington Post*, September 10, 2007.

6. Dennis Shirley, *Community Organizing for Urban School Reform* (Austin, TX: University of Texas Press, 1997); Eric Zachary and oyeshola olatoye, *A Case Study: Community Organizing for School Improvement in the South Bronx* (New York: Institute for Education and Social Policy, 2001); Mark R. Warren, *Dry Bones Rattling: Community Building to Revitalize American Democracy* (Princeton, NJ: Princeton University Press, 2001); Eva Gold, Elaine Simon, and Chris Brown, *Strong Neighborhoods, Strong Schools: Successful Community Organizing for School Reform* (Chicago/Philadelphia: Cross City Campaign for Urban School Reform/Research for Action, Inc., 2002); Kavitha Mediratta and Jessica Karp, *Parent Power and Urban School Reform: The Story of Mothers on the Move* (New York: Institute for Education and Social Policy, 2003); Daniel HoSang and Barbara Bowes, "Youth and Community Organizing Today," *Social Policy* 34, no. 2 (2004): 66–70.

7. Kavitha Mediratta, Norm Fruchter, and Anne C. Lewis, *Organizing for School Reform: How Communities Are Finding Their Voices and Reclaiming Their Public Schools* (New York: Institute for Education and Social Policy, 2002); Thomas Kamber, *From Schoolhouse to Statehouse: Community Organizing for Public School Reform* (New York: National Center for Schools and Communities at Fordham University, 2002), 1–33; John M. Beam and Sharmeen Irani, *ACORN Education Reform Organizing: Evolution of a Model* (New York: National Center for Schools and Communities at Fordham University, 2003).

8. Saul D. Alinsky, *Rules For Radicals. A Pragmatic Primer for Realistic Radicals* (New York: Vintage Books, 1971).

9. Robert Fisher, *Let the People Decide: Neighborhood Organizing in America* (New York: Twayne Publishers, 1994).

10. Harry C. Boyte, *The Backyard Revolution: Understanding the New Citizen Movement* (Philadelphia: Temple University Press, 1980); Lawrence Goodwyn, *The Populist Moment: A Short History of the Agrarian Revolt in America* (New York: Oxford University Press, 1978).

11. Fisher, *Let the People Decide*.

12. Warren, *Dry Bones Rattling*.

13. Fisher, *Let the People Decide*.

14. Warren, *Dry Bones Rattling*.
15. The work described in this book was carried out by Chicago ACORN until January 2008, when the director, staff, and board left ACORN to start a new group called Action Now, which is continuing the education and other organizing campaigns it initiated while affiliated with ACORN.
16. Fisher, *Let the People Decide*.
17. Shirley, *Community Organizing for Urban School Reform*; Dennis Shirley, *Valley Interfaith and School Reform: Organizing for Power in South Texas* (Austin, TX: University of Texas Press, 2002); and Warren, *Dry Bones Rattling*.
18. Erika Hayasaki, "College Prep Idea Approved in L.A," Los Angeles Times, June 15, 2005, 2005, section B.
19. Erving Goffman, *Frame Analysis: An Essay on the Organization of Experience* (London: Harper & Row, 1974); and David A. Snow and Robert D. Benford, "Ideology, Frame Resonance, and Participant Mobilization," *International Social Movement Research* 1 (1988): 197–221.
20. "Focusing Attention Within a Field of Meaning Using Frames," Value Based Management. net, http://www.valuebasedmanagement.net/methods_tversky_framing .html.
21. Jeannie Oakes and John Rogers with Martin Lipton, *Learning Power: Organizing for Education and Justice* (New York: Teachers College Press, 2006), 158–159.

Chapter 2

1. See Geoffrey Borman, Gina M. Hewes, Laura T. Overman, and Shelly Brown *Comprehensive School Reform and Achievement: A Meta Analysis*. Researchers found that schools implementing reform for one year or more were more likely to show strong effects on student achievement.
2. Michael G. Fullan, *The New Meaning of Educational Change*, 4th edition (New York: Teachers College Press, 2007).
3. Penny Bender Sebring, Elaine Allensworth, Anthony S. Bryk, John Q. Easton, and Stuart Luppescu, *The Essential Supports for School Improvement* (Chicago: University of Chicago Consortium on Chicago School Research, 2006).
4. Anthony S. Bryk and Barbara L. Schneider, *Trust in Schools: A Core Resource for Improvement* (New York, NY: Russell Sage Foundation Publications, 2002); Richard F. Elmore, Penelope L. Peterson, and Sarah J. McCarthey, *Restructuring in the Classroom: Teaching, Learning, and School Organization* (San Francisco: Jossey-Bass, Inc., 1996); Richard F. Elmore, *Bridging the Gap Between Standards and Achievement: The Imperative for Professional Development in Education* (Washington, DC: Albert Shanker Institute, 2002); Daniel P. Mayer, John E. Mullens, Mary T. Moore, and John Ralph, *Monitoring School Quality: An Indicators Report* (Washington, DC: U.S. Department of Education; National Center for Education Statistics, NCES 2001–030, 2000); and Eva Gold, Elaine Simon, and Chris Brown, *Strong Neighborhoods, Strong Schools: Successful Community Organizing for School Reform* (Chicago/Philadelphia: Cross City Campaign for Urban School Reform/Research for Action, Inc., 2002).
5. Sebring et al., *The Essential Supports for School Improvement*.

6. Bryk and Schneider, *Trust in Schools*.

7. Ibid., 144.

8. Fullan, *The New Meaning of Educational Change*, 4th edition,; Sebring et al., *The Essential Supports for School Improvement*; Richard F. Elmore, "Hard Questions About Practice," *Education Leadership* 59, no. 8 (2002): 22–25; M. Cohen, M. 1987. "Improving School Effectiveness, Lessons from Research," in *Educator's Handbook: A Research Perspective*, ed. Virginia Richardson-Koehler, 474–490 (New York: Longman); Susan J. Rosenholtz, *Teachers' Workplace: The Social Organization of Schools* (New York: Longman, 1989).

9. The Chicago Consortium for School Research defines *professional capacity* as teacher quality, teachers' commitment to the school and beliefs about their responsibility for change, collaboration among teachers, and quality professional development. See Sebring et al., *The Essential Supports of School Improvement*.

10. Michael G. Fullan, *The New Meaning of Educational Change*, 2nd edition (New York: Teachers College Press, 1991).

11. Elmore, "Hard Questions About Practice"; and Richard F. Elmore, "Getting to Scale with Good Educational Practice," *Harvard Educational Review* 66, no. 1 (1996): 1.

12. Fullan, *The New Meaning of Educational Change*, 4th edition.

13. Richard F. Elmore, "Beyond Instructional Leadership: Hard Questions About Practice," *Educational Leadership* 59, no. 8 (May 2002): 22–25; James P. Spillane, Richard Halverson, and John. B. Diamond, "Towards A Theory of School Leadership Practice: Implications of a Distributed Perspective," *Journal of Curriculum Studies* 36, no. 1 (2004): 3–34; Larry Lashway. Distributed Leadership. *Research Roundup* 19 no. 4 (Summer 2003), http://www.eric.ed.gov/ERICDocs/data/ericdocs2sql/content_storage_01/0000019b/80/1b/1f/dd.pdf.

14. Sebring et al., *The Essential Supports for School Improvement*; and Elmore, "Hard Questions About Practice."

15. Walt Haney, "The Myth of the Texas Miracle in Education," *Education Policy Analysis Archives* 8, no. 41 (2000); and Daniel Koretz, *Measuring Up: What Educational Testing Really Tells Us* (Cambridge, MA: Harvard University Press, 2008).

16. *An Evaluation of the Oakland New Small School Initiative: A Report for the Oakland Unified School District* (Oakland, CA: Strategic Measurement and Evaluation, Inc., 2007).

17. See the 2006 "CSRQ Center Report on Elementary School Comprehensive School Reform Models" for a review of studies on the positive effects of Direct Instruction (full-immersion model) on reading. The report identified Direct Instruction as one of only two programs (out of twenty-two reform models) for which there was convincing data of a moderately strong effect on student achievement; see (Washington, DC: The Comprehensive School Reform Quality Center, 2006), 1–355).

18. Fullan, *The New Meaning of Educational Change*, 4th edition.

19. Michelle Renée, Kevin G.Welner, and JeannieOakes, "Social Movement Organizing and Equity-Focused Educational Change: Shifting the 'Zone of Mediation,'" in *International Handbook of Educational Change, Second Edition*, eds. Andy Hargreaves, Michael Fullan, David Hopkins, and Ann Lieberman (New York: Springer International Handbooks, in press).

20. Reneé, Welner, and Oakes, "Social Movement Organizing and Equity-Focused Educational Change"; Kevin G. Welner, *Legal Rights, Local Wrongs: When Community Control Collides with Educational Equity* (Albany, NY: SUNY Press, 2001); Jeannie Oakes and John Rogers, with Martin Lipton, *Learning Power: Organizing for Education and Justice* (New York: Teachers College Press, 2006).

21. Renée, Welner, and Oakes, "Social Movement Organizing and Equity-Focused Educational Change.

22. Seymour Sarason, *Revisiting "The Culture of the School and the Problem of Change"* (New York: Teachers College Press, 1996) 338.

Chapter 3

1. Jonathan Schorr, *Hard Lessons: The Promise of an Inner City Charter School* (New York: Ballantine Books, 2002.)

2. Quoted from Jill Davidson, "Oakland's Community Propels Change for Equity: The Small Schools Initiative," *Horace* 18, no. 4 (Summer 2002), http://www.essentialschools.org/cs/cespr/view/ces_res/267.

3. Deborah Meier, *The Power of Their Ideas: Lessons for America from a Small School in Harlem* (Boston: Beacon Press, 1995)

4. Jonathan Schorr chronicles the struggles and successes of these new charter schools in *Hard Lessons.*

5. Kathleen Cotton, "School Size, School Climate, and Student Performance," *School Improvement Research Series* (May1996), http://www.nwrel.org/scpd/sirs/10/c020.html; Diana Oxley, "Organizing Schools into Smaller Units: The Case for Educational Equity," in *Practical Approaches to Achieving Student Success in Urban Schools*, no. 96-2, eds. Don E. Gordon and Jesse R. Shafer (Philadelphia: Mid-Atlantic Laboratory for Student Success; National Research Center on Education in the Inner Cities, 1996); Michelle Fine and Janis I. Somerville "Essential Elements of Small Schools," in *Small Schools, Big Imaginations: A Creative Look at Urban Public Schools*, eds. Michelle Fine and Janis I. Somerville, 104–112. (Chicago: Cross City Campaign for Urban School Reform, 1998); Robert Gladden. "The Small School Movement: A Review of the Literature," *Small Schools, Big Imaginations*, 113–133.

6. "New Small Autonomous Schools: District Policy," revised draft, Oakland Unified School District, April 24, 2000.

7. OCO press release, April 2, 2009.

8. Richard J. Murnane and Frank Levy, *Teaching the New Basic Skills: Principles for Educating Children to Thrive in a Changing Economy* (New York: Free Press, 1996). Austin Interfaith's work to improve Zavala is well documented in a book by economists Richard Murnane of Harvard University and Frank Levy of the Massachusetts Institute of Technology, 1997, who describe the process that IAF used to engage parents and build trust among teachers so that the school community could work as a cohesive unit to improve student learning. See also Dennis Shirley, *Community Organizing for Urban School Reform* (Austin, TX: University of Texas Press, 1997; Dennis Shirley, *Valley Interfaith and School Reform: Organizing for*

Power in South Texas (Austin: University of Texas Press 2002); Mark R. War-
ren, *Dry Bones Rattling: Community Building to Revitalize American Democracy*
(Princeton, NJ: Princeton University Press, 2001); Mark R. Warren and Richard L.
Wood, "Faith-Based Community Organizing: The State of the Field", 2001, http://
comm-org.wisc.edu/papers.htm; and Eva Gold, Elaine Simon, and Chris Brown,
*Strong Neighborhoods, Strong Schools: Successful Community Organizing for
School Reform* (Chicago/Philadelphia: Cross City Campaign for Urban School
Reform/Research for Action, Inc., 2002).

9. Murnane and Levy, *Teaching the New Basic Skills.*

10. U.S. Department of Education, *Characteristics of the 100 Largest Public Elementary and Secondary School Districts* (Washington, DC: National Center for Education Statistics, 1995), 1–75, NCES 98-214. http://nces.ed.gov/pubs98/98214.pdf.

11. Data provided by the Texas Education Agency.

12. Linda Darling-Hammond and Carol Ascher, *Creating Accountability in Big City
School Systems*, National Center for Restructuring Education, Schools and Teaching,
Urban Diversity Series, no. 102 (New York: Columbia Teachers' College, 1991). See
also David Rogers, *110 Livingston Street: Politics and Bureaucracy in the New York
City School System* (New York: Vintage Books, 1969)

13. Florida Department of Education, *NRT: 1995 Grade 4 Report*, http://fcat.fldoe.
org/nrt/nrtrd495.asp.

14. See the 2006 CSRQ Center Report on Elementary School Comprehensive School
Reform Models for a review of studies dating to the mid 1980s showing evidence
on the positive effects of Direct Instruction (full-immersion model) on reading.
The CSRQ report identified Direct Instruction as one of only two (out of a total of
twenty-two) reform models for which there was convincing data of a moderately
strong effect on student achievement.

15. In 2001, the federal government passed the No Child Left Behind Act and required
that school-reform models paid for by federal funds show empirical evidence of
their effectiveness. PACT used this mandate to push the district to use NCLB's
"Reading First" funds to support Direct Instruction. (*Reading First* refers to federal
funds specifically targeted for reading instruction in Title I schools.)

16. Michelle Renée, Kevin G.Welner, and JeannieOakes, "Social Movement Organizing and Equity-Focused Educational Change: Shifting the 'Zone of Mediation,'" in
International Handbook of Educational Change, Second Edition, eds. Andy Hargreaves, Michael Fullan, David Hopkins, and Ann Lieberman (New York: Springer
International Handbooks, in press).

17. Charles Payne and Mariame Kaba, "So Much Reform, So Little Change: Building-
level Obstacles to Urban School Reform," *Journal of Negro Education* 2 (February
2001); Larry Cuban, and Michael Usdan, eds., *Powerful Reforms with Shallow Roots:
Improving America's Public Schools* (New York: Teachers College Press, 2003).

18. Michael G. Fullan, *The New Meaning of Educational Change*, 4th edition (New
York: Teachers College Press, 2007); Seymour B. Sarason, *The Culture of the School
and the Problem of Change*, 2nd edition (Boston: Allyn and Bacon, Inc., 1982);
Charles Payne, *So Much Reform So Little Change* (Cambridge, MA: Harvard Education Press, 2008).

Chapter 4

1. James Taylor, *Sustainability: Examining the Survival of Schools' Comprehensive School Reform Efforts* (Washington, DC: American Institutes of Research, 2005).
2. Jeffrey R. Henig, Richard C. Hula, Marion Orr, and Desiree S. Pedescleaux, *The Color of School Reform: Race, Politics, and the Challenge of Urban Education* (Princeton, NJ: Princeton University Press, 1999), 14.
3. Ibid.; and Clarence Stone, "Linking Civic Capacity and Human Capital Formation," in *Strategies for School Equity: Creating Productive Schools in a Just Society*, ed. M. J. Gittell (New Haven, CT: Yale University Press), 163–176.
4. Clarence N. Stone, "The Politics of Urban School Reform: Civic Capacity, Social Context, and the Intergroup Context," paper presented at the annual meetings of the American Political Science Association, San Francisco, August 1996.
5. Kavitha Mediratta, *Mapping the Field of School Reform Organizing. A Report on Education Organizing in Baltimore, Chicago, Los Angeles, New York, Philadelphia, Washington, .D.C, the Mississippi Delta, and the San Francisco Bay Area* (New York: Institute for Education and Social Policy, 2001)
6. Amanda Tattersall, *There Is Power in Coalitions: A Framework for Analyzing the Practice of Union-Community Coalitions* (Sydney, Australia: University of Sydney, 2006), http://comm-org.wisc.edu/papers2006/tattersall.htm.
7. Gretchen E. L. Suess and Kristine S. Lewis, "Youth Leaders Carry On Campaign for Small Schools: Two Student Organizations Imagine a Different Kind of High School," *Philadelphia Public School Notebook*, Spring 2005.
8. "YUC on the March: The Battle for a New Kensington," *Youth United for Change Newsletter*, Spring 2005.
9. Concordia, LLC. 2006. *Kensington High Schools Community Plan*. Philadelphia, PA: Philadelphia Education Fund, http://www.philaedfund.org/kensingtonhs/pdf/kfinalreport.pdf.
10. "A Policy for Community-Centered Small High Schools," position paper by the Small Schools Policy Subcommittee, 2005, http://www.philaedfund.org/kensingtonhs/files/Small%20Schools%20Policy%20Paper-KHS.doc. The S Subcommittee is a working group of the Education First Compact and the Philadelphia Chapter of Cross Cities for Urban School Reform.
11. Gretchen E. L. Suess and Kristine S. Lewis, "The Time Is Now: Youth Organize to Transform Philadelphia Schools," *Children, Youth and Environments* 17, (2) (June 2007): 364–379.
12. Gregory Thornton, public remarks, American Friends Service Committee, Philadelphia, June 6, 2005.
13. Concordia, LLC, *Kensington High Schools Community Plan*.
14. Maria Newman, "After Three Years, New Delays for School in the Bronx," *New York Times*, August 1, 1996, section B.
15. Ibid.
16. Andrea K. Walker, "Neighborhood Report: Bronx Up Close; Irate Parents Get Promise On Repairs," *New York Times*, November 3 1996, section 13.
17. Joan Byron,, Hillary Exter, and Kavitha Mediratta, "Places to Learn: School Facilities Provide an Entry Point for Community Organizers," *Shelterforce* July/August 2001.

18. Kavitha Mediratta, Dana Lockwood, and Norm Fruchter, *Planning for Failure*, report prepared for the Northwest Bronx Community and Clergy Coalition by the Annenberg Institute for School Reform, 2007.

19. Jeannie Oakes, Julie Mendoza, and D. Silver, "College Opportunity Indicators: Informing and Monitoring California's Progress Toward Equitable College Access," http://ucaccord.gseis.ucla.edu/publications/pubs/Indicators2004.pdf (accessed September 23, 2008).

20. Ibid,

21. Walker, "Neighborhood Report."

22. United Way of Greater Los Angeles, *The A-G Story: Lesson from a Grassroots Movement for Educational Equity in Los Angeles*, 2007, p. 1, http://www.united-wayla.org/getinformed/rr/socialreports/Pages/TheA-GStory.aspx.

23. Inner City Struggle, an organizing group based in East Los Angeles, also played a leading role in the coalition. See *The A-G Story*, 1.

24. Originally known as the High School for High Achievement Task Force, the coalition adopted the name Communities for Educational Equity in February 2005.

25. A *power analysis* is an organizing tool that maps out key stakeholders, their respective power in the political landscape, and their positions on the issue that the organizing group is trying to influence. A power analysis can help groups develop their strategy.

26. Communities for Educational Equity. *The Schools We Deserve* (Los Angeles: Families in Schools, 2005), 1–10.

27. The resolution was slated for a vote during the May 2005 school board meeting, but board members decided to postpone a vote until the June 14, 2005, school board meeting in order to have more time to consider the merits of the resolution.

28. Joel Rubin, "School Board Delays Vote to Put All Students on College Prep Track," *Los Angeles Times*, May 25, 2005, section B.

29. Ibid.

30. Erika Hayasaki, "College Prep Idea Approved in L.A.," *Los Angeles Times*, June 15, 2005, section B.

31. Ibid.

32. Doug Timmer, "Instructional Inequality and its Impact on ACORN Neighborhood High Schools" (March 2001), http://www.teachingquality.org/; "Preliminary Findings from the Second Report: Instructional Inequality in Seventy-one Chicago Public Schools" (October 2001), http://www.teachingquality.org/; "Instructional Inequality in Seventy-one Chicago Public Schools, Teaching Experience and Turnover: How Do They Impact on Student Learning?" (March 2002), http://www.teachingquality.org/.

33. Rosalind Rossi, "End Teacher Shortage Now, Parents Urge," *Chicago Sun-Times* (February 22, 2001).

34. Rosalind Rossi, "Teacher Woes Worst in Poor Schools," *Chicago Sun-Times*, October 10. 2001, News Special Edition; Rosalind Rossi, Becky Beaupre, and Kate N. Grossman, "Other States Do It Better," *Chicago Sun-Times*, September 9, 2001, News Special Edition; Rosalind Rossi, Becky Beaupre, and Kate N. Grossman, "Poor Kids Often Wind Up with the Weakest Teachers," *Chicago Sun-Times*, September 7. 2001; Rosalind Rossi and Kate N. Grossman, "Substandard Teachers Under the Microscope," *Chicago Sun-Times*, September 24, 2001, News Special

Edition section; and Janet Rausa Fuller, "Parents Interest a Key to Success; Volunteer, Keep Tabs on Children," *Chicago Sun-Times*, September 10, 2001, News Special Edition section.

35. Debra. Williams, "More New Teachers Leaving CPS," *Catalyst Chicago*, November 2003, www.catalyst-chicago.org/news/index.php?item=1187&cat=23; and Kate N. Grossman, "Teacher Turnover High in Poor Areas, Study Says," *Chicago Sun-Times* June 26, 2004, News Special Edition section.

36. GYO Teachers/Grow Your Own Illinois, *Grow Your Own Teachers: An Illinois Initiative*, February 14, 2008, www.growyourownteachers.org/BeAnAdvocate/Resources.htm, is an overview of the Grow Your Own Program.

37. David M. Chavis, "The Paradoxes and Promise of Community Coalitions," *American Journal of Community Psychology* 29, no. 2, (2001): 309–320; Arthur T. Himmelman, On Coalitions and the Transformation of Power Relations: Collaborative Betterment and Collaborative Empowerment," *American Journal of Community Psychology* 29, no. 2 (2001): 277–284; and Charles Kadushin, Matthew Lindholm, Dan Ryan, Archie Bordsky, and Leonard Saxe, "Why It Is So Difficult to form Effective Community Coalitions," *City & Community* 4, no. 3 (2005): 255–275.

38. Kadushin et al., "Why It Is So Difficult to Form Effective Community Coalitions."

39. John Gaventa, *Power and Powerlessness: Quiescence and Rebellion in an Appalachian Valley* (Urbana, IL: University of Illinois Press, 1980); Heidi J. Swarts, "Shut Out from the Economic Boom: Comparing Community Organizations' Success in the Neighborhoods Left Behind," working paper, Aspen Institute Nonprofit Sector Research Fund, 2002.

40. Michelle Renée, Kevin G.Welner, and Jeannie Oakes, "Social Movement Organizing and Equity-Focused Educational Change: Shifting the 'Zone of Mediation,'" in *International Handbook of Educational Change, Second Edition*, eds. Andy Hargreaves, Michael Fullan, David Hopkins, and Ann Lieberman (New York: Springer International Handbooks, in press).

41. Kadushin et al., "Why It Is So Difficult to Form Effective Community Coalitions."

42. Renée, Welner, and Oakes, "Social Movement Organizing and Equity-Focused Educational Change."

Chapter 5

1. Sarah-Kathryn McDonald, Venessa Ann Keesler, Nils J. Kauffman, and Barbara Schneider, "Scaling-Up Exemplary Interventions," *Educational Researcher* 35, no. 15 (2006): 15–24.

2. Cynthia E. Coburn, "Rethinking Scale: Moving Beyond Numbers to Deep and Lasting Change," *Educational Researcher* 32, no. 6 (2003): 3–12.

3. Seymour B. Sarason, *Revisiting the Culture of the School and the Problem of Change*, (New York: Teachers College Press, 1996); Michael G. Fullan, *The New Meaning of Educational Change*, 4th edition (New York: Teachers College Press, 2007); P. Berman and M. W. McLaughlin, Rand Change Agent Study: Federal Programs Supporting Educational Change, vol. VII, *Factors Affecting Implementation and Continuation*. (Washington, DC: Department of Health, Education, and

Welfare, 1977); Matthew B. Miles and Michael Huberman, *Qualitative Data Analysis: A Sourcebook of New Methods* (Newbury Park, CA: Sage, 1984).

4. Oakland Unified School District, *New Small Autonomous Schools Policy*, 2000 http://www.smallschoolsproject.org/PDFS/oaklandpolicy.pdf.

5. See, for example, Charles M. Payne, *So Much Reform So Little Change: The Persistence of Failure in Urban Schools.* (Cambridge, MA: Harvard Education Press, 2008).

6. *A Recent History of OUSD*, 2008, http://perimeterprimate.blogspot.com/2008/02/recent-history-of-ousd_20.html.

7. Coburn, "Rethinking Scale."

8. Gamaliel Foundation. 2006. *Metro Equity Campaigns*, www.gamaliel.org/NewsRoom/NewsMetroEquity.htm.

9. Karen Royster, Institute for Wisconsin's Future.

10. http://www.senate.state.tx.us/75r/senate/commit/c835/handouts08/0804-Kathleen-Staudt.pdf.

11. Gary Scharrer, "Legislators May Make TAKS a Thing of the Past," *Houston Chronicle*, March 5, 2009, section B.

12. Kate Alexander, "House, Senate Ease School Accountability Standards," *Austin-American Statesman*, April 30, 2009.

13. Robert Fisher, *Let the People Decide: Neighborhood Organizing in America* (New York: Twayne Publishers, 1994).

14. Direct Action and Research Training Center, *Accomplishments*, 2009, http://www.thedartcenter.org/accomplishments.html.

15. Robert Kleidman, "Community Organizing and Regionalism," *City & Community* 3 , no. 4 (2004), 403–421.

Chapter 6

1. Mark R. Warren, "Communities and Schools: A New View of Urban Education Reform," *Harvard Educational Review* 75, no. 2 (Summer 2005): 133; Pedro A. Noguera, *City Schools and the American Dream: Reclaiming the Promise of Public Education* (New York: Teachers College Press, 2003); Jean Anyon, *Radical Possibilities: Public Policy, Urban Education, and A New Social Movement* (New York: Routledge, 2005); Dennis Shirley, *Community Organizing for Urban School Reform* (Austin: University of Texas Press, 1997).

2. We collected 241 adult member surveys and 124 youth member surveys to understand how involvement in community organizing influenced leadership skills and attitudes and behaviors related to community and political engagement among the core leadership of the community organizations in our study. Adult survey data were collected through paper-and-pencil administration of the survey at organizational events across a four-week period in October 2003. Youth survey data were collected through both paper-and-pencil and online administration of the survey in July and August 2005. Four-week periods were selected based on high levels of activity in prior years, which suggested that this timeframe would yield a larger sampling frame. The survey asked about demographic information, involvement in

the organization and changes in organizing skills, involvement in the community and in the school system, and behavioral changes relating to the community, the school system, and the home. Survey scales and items measuring school and community engagement were drawn from the *Sense of Community Index* developed by David Chavis, Association for the Study and Development of Community; and the *Neighborhood and Family Initiative Survey* by Robert Chaskin, University of Chicago Chapin Hall Center for Children. Survey scales and items related to participation in organizing were developed by the study team based on analyses of qualitative data collected during the first year of the study.

3. National data were collected in spring 2002 by the Center for Information and Research on Civic Learning and Engagement. Circle conducted a national telephone survey of 3246 individuals, aged fifteen and older, to assess a range of behaviors related to civic and political engagement.

4. Alejandro Portes, "Social Capital: Its Origins and Applications in Modern Sociology," *Annual Review of Sociology* 24 (1998): 1–24.

5. Ibid.

Chapter 7

1. Joyce Epstein, *School, Family and Community Partnerships: Your Handbook for Action, Third Edition* (Thousand Oaks, CA: Corwin Press, 2009).

2. Michael G. Fullan, *The New Meaning of Educational Change*, 2nd edition (New York: Teachers College Press, 1991).

3. Anne T. Henderson and Karen Mapp, A New Wave of Evidence: The Impact of School, Family and Community Connections on Student Achievement (Austin, TX: Southwest Educational Development Laboratory, 2002); Chad Nye, Herb Turner, Jamie Schwartz "Approaches to Parental Involvement for Improving the Academic Performance of Elementary School Children in Grades K–6," report by the Family Involvement Network of Educators, Harvard Family Research Project, Harvard Graduate School of Education, November 2006. This report summarizes the most dependable evidence on the effect of parental involvement intervention programs for improving the academic performance of elementary school-age children. The authors show that parent involvement has a positive and significant effect on children's overall academic performance; Sam Redding, Janis Langdon, Joseph Meyer, Pamela Sheley "The Effects of Comprehensive Parent Engagement on Student Learning Outcomes,"research report presented at the annual convention of the American Educational Research Association, San Diego, April 14, 2004. This study examined the school-level effects on tested student achievement in 129 high poverty elementary schools that implemented a common set of comprehensive parent-engagement strategies over a two-year period.

4. Kavitha Mediratta and Norm Fruchter, *From Governance to Accountability: Building Relationships That Make Schools Work* (New York: Drum Major Institute for Public Policy, 2003).

5. Marisol Bello, "Amid Struggle, Parents, Teachers at Odds," *Philadelphia Daily News*, May 30, 1995, Local section.

6. David Tyack and Larry Cuban, *Tinkering Toward Utopia* (Cambridge, MA: Harvard University Press, 1995); Seymour B. Sarason, *The Culture of the School and the Problem of Change* (Boston: Allyn and Bacon, 1982): Sara Lawrence Lightfoot and Jean V. Carew, *Beyond Bias: Perspectives on Classrooms* (Cambridge, MA: Harvard University Press, 1979)

7. Larry Cuban, "The Turnstile Superintendency? How Some School Leaders Have "Defied the Odds and Thrived," *Education Week* 28, no. 1(2008): 26–27, 29, http://www.austinisd.org/inside/superintendent/school_reform.phtml.

8. James Taylor, *Sustainability: Examining the Survival of Schools' Comprehensive School Reform Efforts* (Washington, DC: American Institutes of Research, 2005).; Fullan, *The New Meaning of Educational Change.*

9. Gary Scharrer, "Legislators May Make TAKS a Thing of the Past," *Houston Chronicle*, March 5, 2009, section B.

Acknowledgments

We are deeply indebted to the organizers and leaders of the community organizations in our study for generously sharing their time and work with us. We are also grateful to the district officials, principals, teachers, and school-reform advocates in each site for sharing their insights with us.

We also wish to thank our colleagues at the Annenberg Institute for School Reform of Brown University and at the Institute for Education and Social Policy of New York University for their thoughtful contributions to this research. Edwina Branch-Smith, Mary Ann Flaherty, Norm Fruchter, Barbara Gross, Janice Hirota, Nina Johnson, Dana Lockwood, Yolanda McBride, Christina Mokhtar, Deinya Phenix, Beth Rosenthal, Tom Saunders, and Meryle Weinstein provided invaluable assistance in data collection and analysis. Additional research assistance was provided by Tara Bahl, Evelyn Brosi, Allison Cohen, Angelica Crane, Nadine Dechausay, Lamson Lam, Jim Laukhardt, Hannah Miller, Natalie Price, Anna Reeve, Kate Sedey, Kat Stergiopolous, Cate Swinburn, and Kelly Whitaker.

We extend a special thank you to Anne Henderson for her role as a thoughtful partner on this project, and to Robert Tobias of New York University for his guidance on the administrative data analyses in our study. We also would like to express our appreciation to Jeannie Oakes of the Ford Foundation, Karen Mapp and Mark Warren of Harvard University; Robert Rothman of the Annenberg Institute; and Caroline Chauncey and her colleagues at Harvard Education Press for their support and guidance on this project.

Finally, we wish to acknowledge Christine Doby of the Charles Stewart Mott Foundation for her vision, leadership, and ability to ask prescient questions about the impact of community organizing—all of which made this research possible.

About the Authors

Kavitha Mediratta, was principal investigator for Brown University's Annenberg Institute for School Reform's six-year study of the impact of community organizing on public school reform. She has worked extensively with youth and community organizing groups in New York City and has taught in public and private schools. She was the primary author of several studies by New York University's Institute for Education and Social Policy, including *Constituents of Change*, the initial report from this study. She holds an MEd from Teachers College, Columbia University, and is currently a program officer at the New York Community Trust.

Seema Shah, director of the community organizing study, has worked extensively with public schools and nonprofit organizations as an evaluator and researcher. She has a PhD in clinical-community psychology from DePaul University and completed a post-doctoral fellowship at Yale University.

Sara McAlister is a research associate at the Annenberg Institute. She taught for four years at a dual-language elementary school in the Bronx and holds an MA in public administration from New York University's Wagner School.

Index